THE PARTHENON

Illustrations · Introductory Essay · History · Archeological Analysis · Criticism

NORTON CRITICAL STUDIES IN ART HISTORY

CHARTRES CATHEDRAL *edited by* Robert Branner

GIOTTO: THE ARENA CHAPEL FRESCOES *edited by* James H. Stubblebine

MICHELANGELO: THE SISTINE CHAPEL CEILING *edited by* Charles Seymour, Jr.

THE PARTHENON *edited by* Vincent J. Bruno

RUBENS: THE ANTWERP ALTARPIECES: The Raising of the Cross and the Descent from the Cross *edited by* John Rupert Martin

A NORTON CRITICAL STUDY IN ART HISTORY

THE PARTHENON

Illustrations · Introductory Essay · History · Archeological Analysis · Criticism

EDITED BY

VINCENT J. BRUNO

THE STATE UNIVERSITY OF NEW YORK AT BINGHAMTON

W · W · NORTON & COMPANY · INC.

NEW YORK

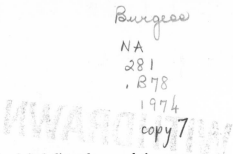
This book is dedicated to my father.

Copyright © 1974 by W. W. NORTON & COMPANY, INC.

FIRST EDITION

Library of Congress Cataloging in Publication Data

Bruno, Vincent J   comp.
    The Parthenon.
    (A Norton critical study in art history)
    Bibliography: p.
    1. Athens. Parthenon. I. Title.
NA281.B78   1974   726'.1'20809385   73–18388
ISBN 0–393–04373–8
ISBN 0–393–09354–9 (pbk.)

1 2 3 4 5 6 7 8 9 0

CONTENTS

v

LIST OF ILLUSTRATIONS

GENERAL VIEWS

THE FRIEZE SCULPTURES

ATHENA PARTHENOS

THE PEDIMENTAL SCULPTURES

The names of the gods follow the traditional attributions of the British Museum catalogue, with Evelyn B. Harrison's attributions for the east pedimental figures (*infra,* pp. 225–310) in parentheses where they differ.

THE METOPES

PREFACE

THE INTERPRETATION of ancient monuments often requires the collaboration of specialists in many different fields: classics, epigraphy, numismatics, the techniques of architecture, painting, and sculpture, among others. From the moment of discovery, long periods of time may elapse before any kind of general agreement can be reached concerning the proper identity and classification of an ancient work. The dating and attribution, the basic catalogue description of even well-known masterpieces, may time and again be called into question as new information becomes available through excavation and research. The result is that the art-historical and aesthetic evaluation of ancient works is often likely to be beset by many difficulties and uncertainties.

Such has been the case for the Parthenon and its extraordinary sculptures until very recently. Fortunately, new discoveries by modern archeologists seem to have clarified many of the major problems of the Parthenon, although even now controversies continue on a number of basic issues: on the function of certain rooms and spaces in the cella building of the temple as well as their purpose in ancient ritual; on the interpretation of themes and individual figures in the sculptures, especially in the metopes and frieze; on the probable role of the artist, Pheidias, in the design of the temple and its sculptural decorations. Indeed, the character of the ancient goddess who once resided beneath the marble roof of this great temple is still very much a matter of speculation. In part a fierce protectress, in part a symbol of perfect wisdom and beauty, Athena's role as the virgin goddess of the Parthenon seems entirely unexpected, and her intangible spirit is only dimly suggested by the silent, weathered surfaces of carved marble which the accidents of history and the efforts of men have preserved for us. A number of these age-old problems of the Parthenon are analyzed in the Introductory Essay (pp. 57–97).

xiii

Because new evidence is constantly appearing (e.g., the finding last year at Athens of the hand of Zeus of the east pediment) the publications of contemporary field archeologists are of overwhelming importance in the study of the Parthenon, leaving little room for the literature of earlier periods. Accordingly, the reader will discover that, with a single exception, this anthology consists exclusively of works by contemporary writers, including some first publications. The exception is an account of the explosion of the Parthenon in 1687 (until then, the building had remained in almost perfect condition). This account, aside from its antiquarian interest, has a certain sad relevance to the present, underlining as it does the futility of those military battles that destroy much that is of value yet prove to have no significant results, either for the victors or the vanquished.

The lack of material drawn from earlier periods and the concentration on recent analysis make the present anthology something of a departure in both form and content from other volumes in the Norton Critical Studies in Art History. For the Parthenon, the speculations of the eighteenth and nineteenth centuries are already mostly out of date, and original source materials are rare. Apart from the factual information on the Parthenon preserved in Plutarch and in one or two other ancient descriptions, there are extant a few anecdotes that are of interest, like the story of the mule who worked and grew old in the service of the Parthenon workshops, hauling heavy wagons up the Acropolis hill. This mule, having at last been set at liberty in its old age, with nothing more to do than to enjoy life, returned of its own accord to the Acropolis works, trotting along besides the younger mules, exhorting them to greater and greater efforts. In their astonishment and gratitude, the citizens of Athens voted to provide the aged mule with a more honorable retirement, a lifelong pension set up at public expense.[1]

Anecdotes like this seem to reflect the spirit that undoubtedly prevailed at Athens as a plan took shape to reconstruct the sanctuary which had been left in ruins by the Persians. As the gleaming walls and colonnades of the Parthenon began to rise above the city on the cliffs of the Acropolis, the interest and enthusiasm of the citizens of Athens must have been very great. Since we have so little information by which we can judge the attitudes of the Athenian populace toward the costly building projects that, under Pericles, brought forth the glorious monuments of classical art as we know

---

1. The story of the mule is told by Aristotle, Plutarch, and Aelian. References have been collected and are discussed by Jane E. Harrison, *Primitive Athens as Described by Thucydides* (Cambridge, 1906), pp. 155 f. and notes.

them today, the hints that may be drawn from classical writings take on exceptional value. Russell Meiggs, in the essay with which this anthology begins, explores the possibilities for research in this direction.

In "The Political Implications of the Parthenon," Meiggs searches the ancient literary sources for whatever light they can shed upon the background of social and political events during the period after Pericles came to power in 450 B.C., when the construction of the Parthenon was carried to completion despite grave difficulties. Meiggs constructs a vivid picture of the internal political situation in mid-fifth-century Athens and re-evaluates the facts recorded by Plutarch and other ancient writers.

The second selection was generously written and contributed to this volume by the noted Renaissance scholar Charles Mitchell in response to my plea for an explanation of the many idiosyncrasies of the drawings and writings on the Parthenon by the Renaissance traveler Ciriaco d'Ancona. The drawings and descriptions that are treated by Mitchell constitute the earliest existing documentary record of the Parthenon after the close of antiquity.

An eyewitness account of the siege of Athens by a Venetian force under Count Morosini, written by a Yugoslavian member of Morosini's staff, Cristoforo Ivanovich, describes the bombardment of Athens and the events leading up to the explosion that destroyed the Parthenon after it had been miraculously preserved for so many centuries. Our version is an abridgment of this revealing document, here translated into English for the first time.

Following this is an article by Jacob Rothenberg on the Elgin controversy. Lord Elgin's activities and motives in bringing the sculptures of the Parthenon to England are carefully set forth so that the reader may judge for himself the rights and wrongs of Elgin's actions.

Among the earliest publications on the Parthenon by an American scholar were the studies of W. B. Dinsmoor on the stone inscriptions discovered on the Acropolis in which we find a record of expenses for materials and services paid out by the Athenian treasury in the course of the construction of the temple.[2] From this starting point, Dinsmoor over the years developed his knowledge of the building, taking new measurements and checking his findings against those recorded by his predecessors. The results of all these studies are embodied in the description of the Parthenon in Chapter 5 of his book *The Architecture of Ancient Greece*, excerpts from which

2. William Bell Dinsmoor, "Attic Building Accounts I, the Parthenon." *AJA*, XVII (1913), pp. 53–80.

appear in this anthology. The article by A. Mavrikios, a study of the horizontal curvature of the Parthenon, constitutes in effect a complete and somewhat iconoclastic reinterpretation of the so-called classical "refinements." Mavrikios rightly believes that we have come to rely too heavily on old interpretations of the refinements. He shows how the curvature of the stylobate, taken together with other aspects of the design, while resulting in a feeling of grace and beauty, creates not lightness, but its opposite, a precise impression of weight, an expression of downward thrust. This sense of weight, according to Mavrikios, suggests the repose and stability that in fact characterizes the art of the high classical period. In attempting to extend the aesthetic laws of fifth-century sculpture to an architectural composition, the architects of the Parthenon created a unique masterpiece. This is Mavrikios' theme, and whether we accept it or not, his statement must at any rate force us to reconsider our critical terminology as it pertains to the architecture of the Parthenon.

Professor Evelyn B. Harrison's recent reconstruction of the east pediment of the Parthenon, the design for which has been lost, is reprinted in its entirety. This essay is easily the most significant contribution to the literature of the Parthenon made in the last decade or more. The work is a model of archeological method, sifting through older interpretations of the pediment, introducing a series of interesting new ideas derived in part from a review of literary sources and in part from a re-examination of the sculptures and stones of the Parthenon itself.

Although Philipp Fehl presents a review of the various interpretations of the Parthenon frieze suggested by modern scholars he is mainly concerned not so much with a thematic as with a stylistic problem—the interpretation of space by classical artists. Especially in the east frieze, where we see the Olympian gods and goddesses witnessing the sacrifices that are about to begin, his analysis of pictoral relationships raises some interesting questions about the treatment of space in ancient Greek reliefs.

Although some of the selections in this book have the character of polished and final statements, my main concern has been not to present final results as much as to involve the reader in a series of continuing dialogues about the Parthenon and its art. From that point of view, each of the selections may be considered as an introduction to a topic that the reader may pursue as individual interest dictates.

The translation of Greek words and names into English is largely a matter of taste and custom, depending upon individual preference and training. In an anthology made up of the works of a number of authors of widely different backgrounds, there is little possibility of achieving absolute consistency in the English spellings of foreign and ancient names and terms. In the process of copy editing, the Latin form has been used wherever possible, but there are exceptions. If, for example, an author prefers to write *tympanon*, the Greek form, rather than *tympanum*, the Latin, I have not felt it necessary to change the spelling. However, for the reader's convenience, all the architectural and mythological terms, including variant spellings, have been collected and defined in the Glossary.

A similar problem arose in connection with the footnotes. Different scholarly publications require different forms for the listing of bibliographic references. An attempt to make the footnotes uniform in style has been made, but certain inconsistencies were allowed to remain. A list of abbreviations covering all those employed in bibliographical references throughout the volume is provided on page 53.

I wish here to acknowledge my gratitude first to Alison Frantz for her great generosity in permitting us to include a number of previously unpublished photographs. It was my plan originally that all the Alison Frantz photographs be kept together at the beginning of the section of illustrations to form a kind of "gallery"; but some exceptions had to be made so that in addition to the first group of plates, which are largely the work of this photographer, other pictures by Miss Frantz will be found scattered throughout.

I also offer special thanks to Charles Mitchell and Jacob Rothenberg, who have contributed previously unpublished writings to this anthology thereby covering difficult topics not appropriately analyzed in the available literature. In addition, I owe thanks to Evelyn B. Harrison, Otto J. Brendel, and Frank E. Brown for many corrections and helpful ideas, and to H. Stafford Bryant, Jr., my editor on the Norton staff, for his guidance and assistance in the preparation and design of this volume. Thanks are also due to Harry and Elizabeth Dixon, Melanie Schwarzer, and Eileen Corrigan for technical assistance, and to my Norton copy editor, Carol Flechner, for her infinite patience and hard work.

VINCENT J. BRUNO
State University of New York at Binghamton

THE ILLUSTRATIONS

PHOTO CREDITS: Both the editor and publisher are grateful to all who have provided photographs, in particular the following: Alison Frantz, 1–5, 10–27, 30, 33–36, 39–41, 43–45, 62; London, British Museum, 28, 29, 31, 32, 37, 38, 42, 46–53, 55–61, 63; Foto Stampa Angela-Terni, 6; American School of Classical Studies in Athens, John Travlos drawings, 7, 8; American School of Classical Studies at Athens, G. P. Stevens model, 9; and Giraudon, 54.

1. The Parthenon from the northwest

2. View of the Acropolis from the southwest

3. Parthenon, colonnade of the west façade

4. View of the Acropolis from the northwest

5. Parthenon, west façade

6. The Temple of Poseidon at Paestum, showing the heavier proportions of the Doric order in the period preceding the Periclean Age (*ca.* 460 B.C.)

7. An archeological reconstruction of the west façade of the Parthenon, with sculptures and other dedications as they appeared in antiquity. Drawing by John Travlos. (From G. P. Stevens, *The Setting of the Periclean Parthenon, Hesperia*, Supplement III [Princeton, 1940], courtesy of the American School of Classical Studies at Athens)

8. Artist's view of the Acropolis from the Propylaea, or entrance hall, as it appeared to an ancient visitor. Drawing by John Travlos. (From G. P. Stevens, *The Setting of the Periclean Parthenon, Hesperia*, Supplement III [Princeton, 1940], courtesy of the American School of Classical Studies at Athens)

9. Model of the Acropolis by Gorham Phillips Stevens. (Photograph courtesy of the American School of Classical Studies at Athens)

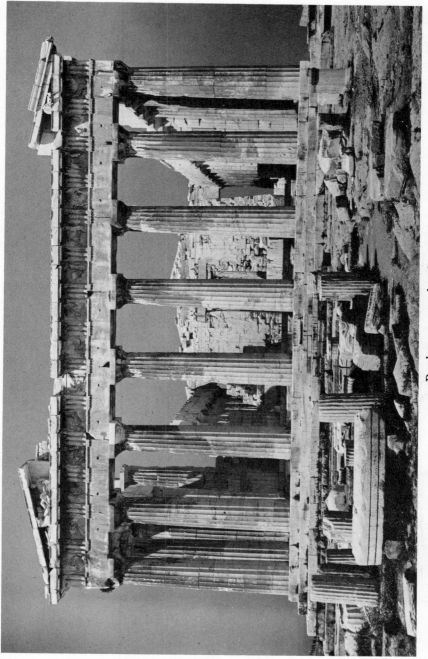

10. Parthenon, east façade

11. Parthenon, detail of the west façade, showing the capitals of the columns, the architrave, the triglyph and metope frieze, and the pediment with a fragment of the original sculptures still *in situ*

12. Parthenon, interior, looking east

13. Parthenon, interior, looking west through the doorway of the opisthodome

14. Parthenon, the southwest corner: detail of the entablature

15. Parthenon, the northeast corner: detail of the entablature

16. Parthenon, the west façade, looking upward into the peripteron, where the west frieze is visible *in situ* above the architrave of the opisthodome porch colonnade. From here the frieze traveled along the top of the walls of the cella on the north and south and around to the front on the east

17. West frieze at the south end, usually taken to be the starting point of the frieze showing the horsemen getting ready at the gathering place of the Panathenaic procession, outside the walls of the city (*in situ*)

18. West frieze: as the procession gets under way, a cavalryman tries to calm his excited horse before mounting (*in situ*)

19. West frieze: detail of the horsemen (*in situ*)

20. West frieze: detail of the horsemen (*in situ*)

21. West frieze: detail of one of the riders with flying cloak (*in situ*)

22. West frieze: detail of the horsemen slowing down (*in situ*)

23. West frieze: closer view of the horseman on the right in fig. 22
(*in situ*)

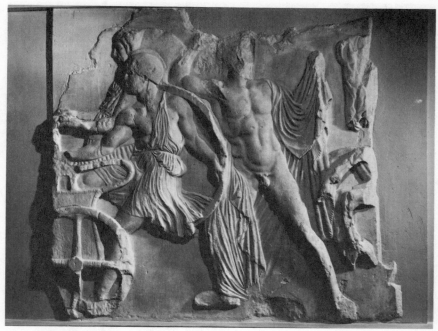

24. North frieze: detail of a chariot scene. (Acropolis Museum, Athens)

25. North frieze: detail of youths carrying water jugs. (Acropolis Museum, Athens)

26. North frieze: sacrificial beasts with attendants. (Acropolis Museum, Athens)

27. North frieze: head of a sacrificial bull. (Acropolis Museum, Athens)

28. North frieze: detail of attendants accompanying sacrificial beasts. (British Museum, London)

29. North frieze: detail of horsemen. (British Museum, London)

30. North frieze: detail of horsemen. (Acropolis Museum, Athens)

31. South frieze: sacrificial beasts with attendants. (British Museum, London)

32. South frieze: sacrificial beasts with attendants. (British Museum, London)

33. South frieze: scene with a four-horse chariot. (British Museum, London)

34. East frieze: detail of an official conducting the ceremonies in front of the Parthenon as the procession arrives. (Acropolis Museum, Athens)

35. East frieze: fragment in Acropolis Museum supplemented by cast of a fragment in the British Museum. Figures of maidens at the head of the Panathenaic procession as it arrives in front of the Parthenon

36. East frieze: Hermes, Dionysus, Demeter, and Ares. (British Museum, London)

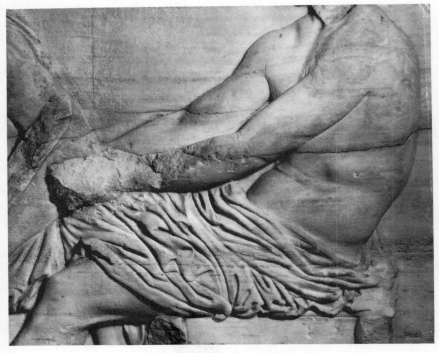

37. East frieze: detail of Ares from fig. 36

38. East frieze: detail of the drapery of Demeter from fig. 36

39. East frieze: Poseidon, Apollo, and Artemis. (Acropolis Museum, Athens)

40. East frieze: head of Poseidon (detail from fig. 39)

41. East frieze: Artemis (detail from fig. 39)

42. East frieze: the "cult scene" from the center of the frieze where we see the folding of Athena's peplos as it is placed in the Parthenon after being brought there as part of the Panathenaic procession. (British Museum, London)

43. The Lenormant statuette, an ancient copy of the *Athena Parthenos* by Pheidias (found in Athens in 1859). (National Museum, Athens)

44. The Lenormant statuette: side view, showing the design on the shield—a battle of Greeks and Amazons

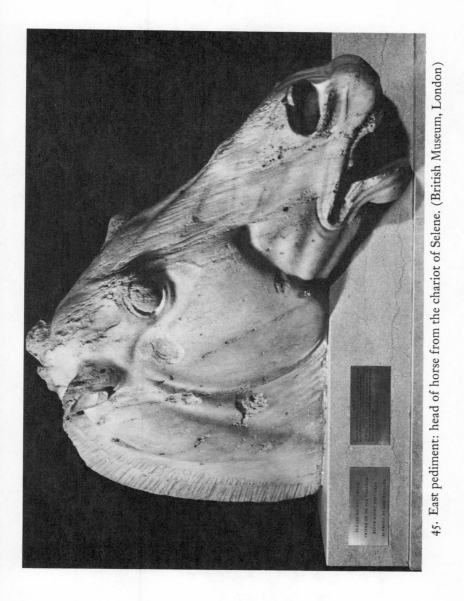

45. East pediment: head of horse from the chariot of Selene. (British Museum, London)

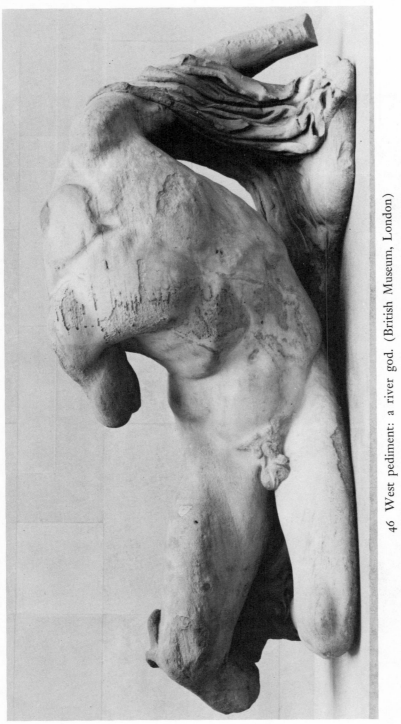

46 West pediment: a river god. (British Museum, London)

47. East pediment: Dionysus (Heracles?). (British Museum, London)

48. West pediment: Iris. (British Museum, London)

49. East pediment: Hebe (Artemis?). (British Museum, London)

50. East pediment: Hestia, Dione, and Aphrodite. (British Museum, London)

51. East pediment: Persephone (Kore?) and Demeter. (British Museum, London)

52. West pediment: Amphitrite. (British Museum, London)

53. West pediment: fragment of the lower torso and legs of Orithyia.
(British Museum, London)

54. East pediment: the Laborde head. Previously believed to belong to a figure on the west pediment, this head is now assigned to a figure of Amphitrite riding a sea horse in the east pediment by Evelyn B. Harrison (see *infra*, pp. 263 ff.). (Louvre, Paris)

55. West pediment: torso of Hermes. (British Museum, London)

56. South metope, no. 28: centaur rearing over fallen Lapith warrior. (British Museum, London)

57. South metope, no. 27: centaur and Lapith in combat. (British Museum, London)

58. South metope, no. 7: centaur and Lapith in combat. (British Museum, London)

59. South metope, no. 31: centaur and Lapith in combat. (British Museum, London)

60. South metope, no. 29: centaur carrying off Lapith woman. (British Museum, London)

61. South metope, no. 30: centaur and Lapith in combat. (British Museum, London)

62. South metope, no. 12: centaur attacking Lapith woman. (Acropolis Museum, Athens)

63. Fragments of one of the north metopes, now *in situ* on the Parthenon in Athens, showing a goddess, perhaps Athena, sitting on a rock as she receives a messenger. Photograph from a cast in the British Museum, London

ABBREVIATIONS OF PERIODICALS CITED

AA Archäologischer Anzeiger
ActaA Acta Archaeologica
AJA American Journal of Archaeology
AM Mitteilungen des deutschen Archäologischen Institut: Athenische
    Abteilung
AnnArch Annales archéologiques
Annuario Annuario della scuola archeologica di Atene e delle Mis-
    sioni Italiani in Oriente
AntDenk Antike Denkmäler
ArchAnz Archäologischer Anzeiger (same as *AA*)
ArchEph Archaiologike Ephemeris
AthMitt see *AM*
BCH Bulletin de la correspondance héllenique
Bolld'Arte Bolletino d'arte del Ministero della Pubblica Istruzione
BSA Annual of the British School at Athens
BullComm Bulletino della Commissione Archaeologica Communale
    di Roma
CRAI Comptes rendus de l'Académie des inscriptions et belles lettres
CVA Corpus Vasorum Antiquorum
DLZ Deutsche Literatur-Zeitung
EphArch see *ArchEph*
FR Furtwängler und Reichhold, Griechische Vasenmalerei
GBA Gazette des beaux-arts
GGA Gottingische gelehrte Anzeiger
IG Inscriptiones graecae
JDAI or *Jdl* Jahrbuch des deutschen archäologischen Instituts
JHS Journal of Hellenic Studies
JOAI Jahreshefte des oesterreichischen archäologischen Instituts
JRS Journal of Roman Studies
JWC Journal of the Warburg and Courtauld Institutes

Meded Mededeelingen van het Nederl. Historisch Instituut te Rome

MonPiot Monuments et Mémoires publiés par l'Académie des Inscriptions et Belles Lettres (Fondation Eugène Piot)

NJbb Neue Jahrbücher für das klassische Altertum

RA Revue archéologique

RE Pauly-Wissowa, Real-encyclopädie der klassischen Altertumwissenschaft

RevArch see *RA*

RGZM Römisch-germanische Zentralmuseum, Mainz, Jb.

RM or *Röm. Mitt.* Mitteilungen des deutschen archäologischen Instituts: Römische Abteilung

THE PARTHENON AND THE
THEORY OF CLASSICAL FORM

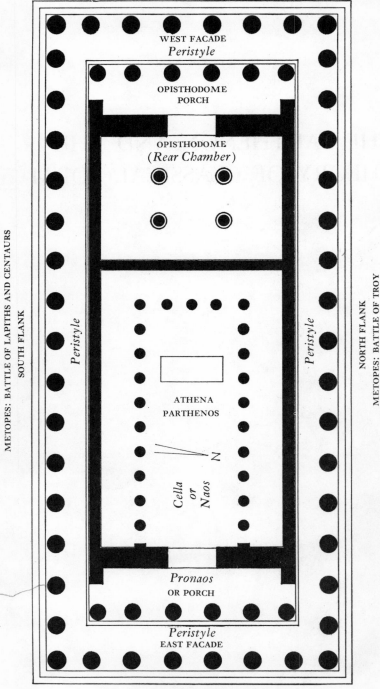

METOPES: BATTLES OF GREEKS AND AMAZONS
PEDIMENT: DISPUTE OF ATHENA AND POSEIDON

WEST FACADE
Peristyle

OPISTHODOME
PORCH

OPISTHODOME
(*Rear Chamber*)

Peristyle

METOPES: BATTLE OF LAPITHS AND CENTAURS
SOUTH FLANK

NORTH FLANK
METOPES: BATTLE OF TROY

1. Plan of the Parthenon.

Peristyle

ATHENA
PARTHENOS

N

*Cella
or
Naos*

Pronaos
OR PORCH

Peristyle
EAST FACADE

METOPES: BATTLE OF GODS AND GIANTS
PEDIMENT: BIRTH OF ATHENA

1

The plastic system of Doric work is so pure that it gives almost the feeling of a natural growth, but we must realize that Doric architecture did not grow in the fields with the asphodels. It is entirely man's creation, and affords us the complete sensation of a profound harmony. The forms used . . . are so deeply thought out in regard to light and materials that they seem, as it were, linked to earth and sky as if by nature. This creates a fact as reasonable to our understanding as the fact "sea" or the fact "mountain." How many works of man have attained this height?

—Le Corbusier

THESE LINES, by the modern architect Le Corbusier, accompany a series of sketches and drawings he made of the Parthenon during a visit to Athens,[1] for it was the Parthenon more than any other monument of antiquity that inspired his aesthetic philosophy. Le Corbusier understood better than most modern critics the manner in which the Doric system was calculated in the Parthenon to evoke that "sensation of a profound harmony" that philosophers have sometimes called the aesthetic emotion. The psychology of this emotion is still inexplicable in scientific terms, but there is nothing mysterious in what we feel. In the presence of an architectural masterpiece such as the Parthenon, our pleasure and satisfaction are indeed profound and real, and evidently this experience is universal to all mankind. Because the source of our pleasure, the man-made structure, is so unlike anything in nature, so different from the everyday sights and sensations that ordinarily give us satisfaction, we are at a loss to understand or describe the laws governing such experiences. Ancient Greek artists of the fifth century B.C. were the first to attempt to describe and interpret the human response to monumental art. They developed a special vocabulary for discussions on art, employing terms such as *harmony*, *rhythm*, and *proportion* to describe the qualities of three-dimensional designs. These discussions seem to have played an important role in

1. In the Praeger edition of Le Corbusier's book, *Towards a New Architecture* (New York, 1960), the commentary on the Parthenon from which the quotation is drawn appears in the form of captions to a series of photographs of the building and its details (pp. 192 ff.).

the development of the classical style. At a certain moment, a group of these same artists at Athens were called upon to collaborate on the construction of a great new temple on the Acropolis, and they seem to have been prepared to set aside older conventions in order to give concrete shape in the design of the temple to new principles of art, principles that were then in the process of formulation. What they produced was the Parthenon—a plastic system so pure, so perfect an expression of the ideal in formal design, that it has continued to be an inspiration and model down to the present day.

The dramatic nature of the achievement of Greek art as it is expressed in the Parthenon is made clear the moment we try to answer the question Le Corbusier puts before us: how many works of man have attained this height? If we make a list of monuments that we may judge to be of comparable beauty, it will doubtless prove to be a very short one. It might include the cathedral of Chartres, and Saint Peter's in Rome. It might also include a less famous church, perhaps an example of the Romanesque style. In addition, we might be tempted to place on such a list a favorite country mansion in England, or the gate building to a Japanese shrine, or a primitive clubhouse in New Guinea, or even one of those magnificent barns in Shaker country north of New York City. At the end of the list, we might add a modern skyscraper. There are a number of things about a list of this kind that seem of interest. First of all, it is obvious that each of the structures named belongs to a larger class, yet each is in some sense unique. There are many Gothic cathedrals, but only one Chartres; there are many primitive clubhouses in New Guinea, but few in which an instinct for architectural sculpture and an eye for proportion have transformed a modest shelter into something exciting and full of interest. In each case, we select a certain monument because it seems to be the most perfect example of a given form or composition. The basic design has in every instance been dictated by traditions that evolved gradually in accordance with the needs of some closely knit social or religious community. In each case, an artist or a group of collaborating artists, working with the traditional form, has given it a quality of timeless and eternal beauty, transforming and lifting it above the ordinary by some mysterious adjustment of the proportions and outlines of its volumes or by some inspired refinement of its coloring and decoration. In this way one example of a series of similar structures is made to seem ideal or perfect, a pinnacle of achievement within its class. In the history of the Western world, there are relatively few monuments in which men have achieved this kind of perfection as a conscious and deliberate act of the creative imagination. The Parthenon was one of the first. The masters of the Parthenon were among the earliest artists to achieve a formal beauty essentially abstract and philosophical in character, a beauty independent of narrative theme or practical functionalism. To later generations of all periods this beauty seems to have had the impact of a basic human law, a kind of definition of the activity of art. When we come to the writings of a great modern architect like Le Corbusier, we find that we do not see the Parthenon as an archeologist might—i.e., as a sacred building belonging to a Greek city of a certain period. To follow the development of Le Corbusier's thought, it is hardly necessary that we know the date of the building or even the name of the goddess it once honored. In Le Corbusier's aesthetic system, the Parthenon simply represents the definition of beauty in architecture; in his moral philosophy, it exemplifies the highest ideals of the architect with respect to his responsibilities toward society.

In the history of ancient art the Parthenon comes during a period of artistic revolution—a turning point between an essentially traditional approach to form and an approach that, for an ancient culture, allowed for a high degree of artistic freedom and a new awareness of the creative process. Two great men, each noted as an innovator in his own right, collaborated on the design of the Parthenon Pheidias, one of the most original sculptors of his age, was overseer of all the works on the Acropolis under Pericles; he was the creator of the cult image, the *Athena Parthenos*, that would take shape within the cella of the temple (figs. 43, 44) and the designer of the architectural sculptures. Ictinus, whose career as an architect was also characterized by inventiveness and originality, was responsible for the construction of the temple.[2] Whatever else we may say about the creators of the Parthenon, it is clear from the outset that it was their goal as collaborators to reconsider the entire relationship between architecture and sculpture in the peripteral Doric temple (text fig. 1). First of all, they radically altered the character of the

2. To these two names a third is usually added, that of the architect Callicrates: Plutarch, *Life of Pericles*, XIII, 4. Cf. *RE*, X, 2, 1634 ff. According to Rhys Carpenter's recent reinterpretation of the building history of the Parthenon, a pre-Periclean project for the Parthenon under Cimon was supervised by Callicrates, while Ictinus continued the project under Pericles: Rhys Carpenter, *The Architects of the Parthenon* (Baltimore, 1970). Cf. Alison Burford, "The Builders of the Parthenon," in *Parthenos and Parthenon*, ed. G. T. W. Hooker, supplement to vol. X of *Greece and Rome* (Oxford, 1963), pp. 25 ff. The Parthenon building inscription, fragments of which were found on the Acropolis, names both Ictinus and Callicrates as architects for the Periclean project: William Bell Dinsmoor, "Attic Building Accounts I, the Parthenon," *AJA*, XVII (1913), pp. 53–80.

interior of the cella as an architectural setting for the cult image. Second, they drastically revised the role of sculpture on the exterior façades and in the peripteron, increasing the architectonic power of pedimental compositions and introducing a secondary sculptural rhythm in the form of a continuous frieze along the walls and entablatures of the cella and the opisthodome (fig. 16). The result of the collaboration between Pheidias and Ictinus was an unprecedented unity of the architecture and the sculptural program in the Parthenon, with the sculptural enrichment receiving new emphasis. The continuous frieze, until then traditionally a feature of the Ionic order, was introduced into Doric composition, not in place of Doric decoration, but in addition to Doric sculptural elements. Thus the collaboration between sculptor and architect had certain unexpected consequences that were to have far-reaching effects for the future of classical building. For the architecture, the collaboration meant that the shape of each block of stone making up the traditional composition of the Doric order had to be redrawn. Traditionally, each individual component of the Doric design was considered as a separate motif, its contours studied and perfected with respect to its particular function. Now, in the Parthenon, each was reproportioned to bring the design into accord with a revised aesthetic system (fig. 11). The whole process of cutting the stones for the architectural members seems to have duplicated the artistic method of the sculptor. For the sculptures of the Parthenon, the collaboration meant that traditionally narrative, representational motifs were given a greater sense of scale and formal continuity. Geometric masses and volumes in each figure were emphasized and rhythmically unified so that the figurative designs could be brought into rapport with the abstract, rhythmic power of the architectural composition. Thus form, in the rendering of the sculptured figures, approached an ideal of monumental clarity and simplicity, just as in the architectural elements of the Doric order, the forms took on a finesse that approached sculptural perfection.

The great contrast between the Parthenon and earlier sanctuary architecture in Greece (compare figs. 5 and 6) is revealed when we study the archeological remains of the preceding periods on the Acropolis. When the Persians captured the city of Athens in 480 B.C., the Acropolis consisted of a conglomeration of buildings huddled together behind a complex defensive system of circuit walls and towers. Its function as a fortress was still very obvious, and there must have been little sense of a unified architectural plan within the sanctuary. Armories, temples, treasuries, and other official buildings preserved signs of an architectural history reaching as far back

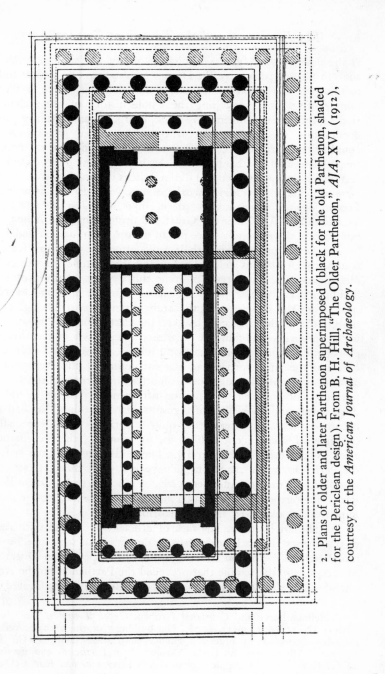

2. Plans of older and later Parthenon superimposed (black for the old Parthenon, shaded for the Periclean design). From B. H. Hill, "The Older Parthenon," *AJA*, XVI (1912), courtesy of the *American Journal of Archaeology*.

as the days of the Mycenaean citadel—one of the few important citadels in Greece to survive the Dorian migrations. The statues and the dedications that crowded around these buildings were a pleasant jumble of styles, representing the whole history of the archaic period.[3] Everywhere enlivened by vivid, energetic, and brightly painted decorations, the archaic sanctuary had a special atmosphere that could never be recreated. When it vanished overnight at the hands of the Persians along with a good deal of the city lying unprotected at its feet, much that was sacred and old in Athens vanished with it. Precious materials, including famous works of art, were carried away to the Persian capital, where some (for example, the *Tyrannicides*) were later found by Alexander the Great and brought back to Athens. The buildings of the Acropolis were put to the torch and demolished.

As they returned from their exile after the Persians were defeated, the Athenians delayed rebuilding the temples of the Acropolis. Then, after an interval of some thirty years, a group of sacred buildings began to rise on the Acropolis different in almost every respect from the structures of the archaic sanctuary (text fig. 3). To the Greeks of the fifth century B.C., the Parthenon and its surrounding monuments undoubtedly expressed their own conception of a thoroughly "modern" artistic idiom. Indeed, the past had been wiped out, and the entire process of reconstruction of the Acropolis was carried on against a background of utter confidence in the fact that the new, contemporary art of mid-fifth-century Athens would produce better and more beautiful results than anything that had gone before—a fact which may seem quite surprising to us, especially in the light of such recent failures as, for example, the reconstruction after World War II of central Le Havre. By contrast, the artists of the Periclean Age managed to achieve just what they set out to accomplish. To the ancients themselves, as much as to Le Corbusier, the Periclean Parthenon represented not only a change, but a definite improvement over past artistic performances.

For the art historian, the task of crucial importance with respect to the history of the Parthenon is to determine in what precise ways the Periclean Parthenon differed from earlier peripteral Doric temples, especially the temple that preceded the Parthenon on the Acropolis of Athens itself. This question is unexpectedly complicated. The

3. Helmut Berve and Gottfried Gruben, *Greek Temples, Theaters and Shrines* (New York, 1963), p. 78. The buildings of the archaic Acropolis probably included an official residence and guest facilities. Cf. H. J. Hopper, "Athens and the Early Akropolis," in *Parthenos and Parthenon*, ed. G. T. W. Hooker, supplement to vol. X of *Greece and Rome* (Oxford, 1963), pp. 13 ff.

earliest predecessor of the Parthenon on the actual site of the present building was probably an archaic temple constructed in the years immediately preceding or following 566 B.C., when the Panathenaic festivals were inaugurated.[4] The worship of Athena on the Acropolis was, of course, much older. The center of her worship was evidently not near the Parthenon, but farther to the north in the area of the Erechtheum. Important changes on the Acropolis took place in the late sixth century B.C., during the period of Pisistratidae, when an older geometric or archaic temple near the Erechtheum was replaced. The earliest marble temple actually occupying the site of the present Parthenon, however, the plan of which is known to us from the reconstruction by B. H. Hill (text fig. 2),[5] can be no earlier than the second decade of the fifth century B.C.[6] Dinsmoor argues that such a temple, together with other renovations of the Acropolis buildings, for instance in the propylon,[7] were undertaken by the Athenians in commemoration of their victory over the Persians at Marathon in 490 B.C., and that before these new works could be completed, they were destroyed during the second Persian invasion ten years later, when Athens was captured and left in ruins.[8]

For any art-historical treatment of the Periclean Parthenon, the most important point about the older Parthenon is that it was already considered old-fashioned when, in 448 B.C., the project received a fresh start. The new architects of the Parthenon followed a design so different in character from the old that it became necessary to reposition every block of stone from the foundations up; and not only the foundations, but elements of the steps, the stylobate, and the columns of the peristyle as well, all of which had already been

4. William Bell Dinsmoor, "The Hekatompedon on the Athenian Acropolis," *AJA*, LI (1947), pp. 109– The importance of this date was originally explained by Dinsmoor in his work on the Athenian calendar, *The Athenian Archon List in the Light of Recent Discoveries* (New York, 1939), p. 206.

5. B. H. Hill, "The Older Parthenon," *AJA*, XVI (1912), pp. 535 ff.

6. Various possibilities for the dating of the older Parthenon were discussed by William Bell Dinsmoor in "Peisistratos, Kleisthenes, Themistokles, Aristeides oder Kimon: Wer hat den alteren Parthenon begonnen?" *JDAI*, LII (1937), pp. 3 ff.; *id.*, "The Date of the Older Parthenon," *AJA*, XXXVIII (1934), pp. 408–448.

7. William Bell Dinsmoor, *The Architecture of Ancient Greece: An Account of Its Historic Development*, (London, 1950), p. 198, n. 2; Berve and Gruben, *op. cit.*, p. 80.

8. Rhys Carpenter reopened the controversy on this question in his recent book *The Architects of the Parthenon, op. cit.*, arguing in favor of an intermediary period of construction occurring between the post-Marathonian and the Periclean projects (*supra*, n. 2).

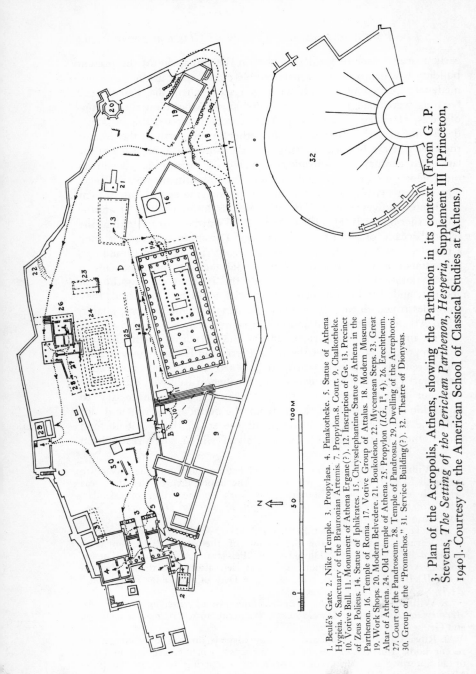

3. Plan of the Acropolis, Athens, showing the Parthenon in its context. (From G. P. Stevens, *The Setting of the Periclean Parthenon, Hesperia*, Supplement III [Princeton, 1940].·Courtesy of the American School of Classical Studies at Athens.)

1. Beulé's Gate. 2. Nike Temple. 3. Propylaea. 4. Pinakotheke. 5. Statue of Athena Hygieia. 6. Sanctuary of the Brauronian Artemis. 7. Propylon.8. Court. 9. Chalkotheke. 10. Votive Bull. 11. Monument of Athena Ergane(?). 12. Inscription of Ge. 13. Precinct of Zeus Polieus. 14. Statue of Iphikrates. 15. Chryselephantine Statue of Athena in the Parthenon. 16. Temple of Roma. 17. Votive Group of Attalus. 18. Modern Museum. 19. Work Shops. 20. Modern Belvedere. 21. Boukoleion. 22. Mycenaean Steps. 23. Great Altar of Athena. 24. Old Temple of Athena. 25. Propylon (*I.G.*, I². 4). 26. Erechtheum. 27. Court of the Pandroseum. 28. Temple of Pandrosus. 29. Dwelling of the Arrephoroi. 30. Group of the "Promachos." 31. Service Building(?). 32. Theatre of Dionysus.

put into place for the earlier structure. The scale of the new temple was only slightly larger than the old, and its material was the same—Pentelic marble. But the proportions of the building and certain features of its plan were different. Thus the decision to redesign the temple rather than to continue with the earlier, partially built structure takes on an extraordinary art-historical interest. Evidently this decision aimed at nothing less than a complete transformation of the earlier design, inside and out, regardless of cost. Whatever political or practical motives might have been involved in such a decision, it is perfectly clear that the plan for the Parthenon was expected to be an expression of the latest trends, for older ideas of proportion and harmony in the Doric system were now found unacceptable. The symbolic message that the Parthenon addressed to the ancient world was clearly not bound by either religious or political considerations. It was in part a message having to do with a sense of progress and change in intellectual achievement and in art.

In many ways, the Periclean reconstruction of the Acropolis (fig. 9 and text fig. 3) reflects the character of the events that had taken place in the lives of the Athenians in the period during and after the Persian wars. Functionally as well as stylistically the new Acropolis buildings represented a markedly changed society. The most spectacular of the Athenian successes against the Persian forces had been made possible by her diplomacy and navy, and the military importance of the fortifications on the Acropolis now seem greatly diminished. The navy and the defense of the port of Athens were the first priorities. As the leader of a newly formed league of Greek states, Athens gained steadily in power and prestige throughout this period, and the architectural and artistic embellishment of the city became a matter of political importance. Simultaneously, the religious ceremonies and the contests connected with the Panathenaic festivals, which took place at Athens every fourth year, assumed more and more the character of an international festival as time went on. Artists and poets from all over Greece gathered in Athens during these years. Under Pericles the Acropolis was redesigned, not primarily as a fortress, but rather as a setting for important state ceremonies, a place where representatives from all parts of the Greek world might come together in a spirit of pride in their accomplishments to celebrate and to do honor to their gods. The audiences at the festival were international, and they came in part to enjoy the theatrical contests and games. Thus in place of the Cyclopean fortifications that had once protected the western approach to the Acropolis, there now arose the open colonnades of the Propylaea, whose central passageways and wings provided a convenient shelter and resting place for visitors. The gates of the new Propylaea were not flanked by defensive towers from which an attacking enemy might be caught in a crossfire, as of old; on one side there was now a museum,[9] and on the other the highly decorative miniature temple of Athena Nike in the Ionic style, whose carved marble balustrade, overhanging the approach ramp to the Propylaea, is one of the greatest masterpieces of classical art.[10] In place of a defensive system there was now a display of art, and the entire mood of the entrance to the Acropolis was altered.

In contrast to the archaic sanctuary, the new temples of the Acropolis seemed to reach outward in every direction. Each building could be seen from a distance not only as an independent unit, but as part of an over-all design as well (fig. 2). The Parthenon, raised aloft on its terraces, dominated all by its size. The scale of the columns was related more to the gigantic ribs of rock that form the hill of the Acropolis itself than to other buildings. At the same time, its architectural sculptures provided a symbolic theme the variations of which would continue to be heard throughout Attica and Greece for centuries.

In all discussions of the Parthenon the name of Pheidias, by all accounts the most famous sculptor of the ancient world, looms large. Yet the question arises: what role did Pheidias play in the creation of the sculptures? Were the sculptures carved from Pheidian

9. The so-called pinakotheke, where Pausanias saw a collection of classical paintings (Pausanias, *Description of Greece*, trans. J. G. Frazer, 6 vols. 2nd ed. [London, 1897], I, p. 22, pl. 6). Dinsmoor states that the old propylon also contained pictures, but these were in the form of murals, set into the walls (Mary Swindler, *Ancient Painting* [New Haven, 1929], p. 424, n. 14a, written by William Bell Dinsmoor). The pictures in the pinakotheke were individually framed panels, or easel paintings, on a variety of themes, making it something like a museum collection in the modern sense. According to Dinsmoor's interesting theory (*loc. cit.*), some of these panels may have been fragments rescued from the murals of the old propylon, perhaps by Polygnotus.

10. Rhys Carpenter, *The Sculpture of the Nike Temple Parapet* (Cambridge, Mass., 1929; reprinted College Park, Md., 1971). In the Turkish period, when the Acropolis had regained its military importance, this temple was dismantled. Its stones, together with the sculptured balustrade, were found reused in the western Acropolis fortifications of the Turkish period. In 1835, after the Greeks gained control of Athens, the stones belonging to the temple of Athena Nike were reassembled and the temple was rebuilt. The battered remains of the balustrade reliefs may now be seen in the Acropolis Museum. It is interesting to note that already under the Frankish knights in the thirteenth century, the intercolumniations of the Periclean Propylaea were filled in with masonry to form a continuous wall, and there was a gateway greatly reduced in size, very much as in the Mycenaean and archaic citadels.

models by workshop craftsmen? Did Pheidias himself have a hand in the actual carving? [11] Pericles, when he came to power in 450 B.C., seems to have realized at the outset that, whatever he might undertake in the way of new construction on the Athenian Acropolis, account would have to be taken of the artistic ferment then in the air. In placing Pheidias in charge of the Acropolis projects, he chose one of the finest talents available. Although the artist's precise role in the execution of the sculptures has been a subject of controversy, few critics continue to have any serious doubts that the great power and originality of the Parthenon sculptures may be ascribed in some measure to his genius. There is the further question, however, of whether or not he made his influence felt on the architectural design as well.

It has often been suggested that the Parthenon was designed not so much as a cult temple in the ordinary sense, but rather as a great dedication to Athena—in other words, that it was conceived to some degree as a monument of art and sculpture rather than as a functioning building. Indeed, Karl Boettiker and Adolfe Michaelis,[12] among the earliest of the nineteenth-century archeologists to take up the study of the Parthenon, saw the temple in this light. Some later writers have disagreed with this early view, but it has nevertheless continued to color the thoughts of scholars in more recent decades. The extraordinary refinement and perfection of the structural elements of the Parthenon contribute strongly to the impression that the building may have been considered in antiquity as something on the order of a gigantic votive offering, something miniature blown up to monumental scale. Once we actually move among the columns of the Parthenon, however, or stand beneath the massive architraves, once we experience the sheer intelligence and strength of the architectonic system, we know that this is sacred architecture, and any argument to the contrary seems hollow and contrived.

While the older cult of Athena continued to be practiced on the altars of the Acropolis, the Parthenon gave expression to a new concept of the goddess—as the word *parthenon* itself implies.[13] This name was applied in Greek houses to the room set aside for the

11. These questions are discussed by many modern writers. The literature on the so-called "Pheidias problem" is summarized and re-evaluated by Bernhard Schweitzer, "Prolegomena zur Kunst des Parthenon-Meisters, I," *JdI*, LIII (1938), pp. 1–81, and by Giovanni Becatti, *Problemi Fidiaci* (Milan and Florence, 1951).

12. Karl Boettiker, "Über agonale Fest-tempel und Thesauren . . ." *Philologus*, XVII (1861), pp. 385 ff., 577 ff., especially, pp. 408 and 603; Adolfe Michaelis, *Der Parthenon* (Leipzig, 1871), p. 28.

13. C. J. Herington, *Athena Parthenos and Athena Polias: A Study in the Religion of Periclean Athens* (Manchester, 1955).

use of a virgin daughter before her marriage. The cella in the temple of a virgin goddess (such as Artemis) might also be called a *parthenon*, but at Athens there is no evidence for the use of the term to designate a temple of Athena before the classical period. The title, like the design of the building itself, expresses a new philosophy, a concept of the goddess that is in some ways in striking contrast to older ideas. Earlier an instructress in the practical arts as well as a fierce protectress, Athena, as the Parthenos, became not only an image of feminine beauty but also a source of power and wisdom in a realm beyond the practical.

To an ancient traveler arriving in Athens, the Parthenon and its sculptures must have appeared radically new and different in style, so strong was the contrast with archaic temples. It is important to remember that for Greeks of the fifth century B.C., an interest in contemporary arts must have been one of the chief reasons for traveling to Athens in the first place. Aeschylus, Sophocles, and Euripides had been surprising and delighting audiences at Athens throughout the period of the Acropolis reconstruction by making use of new modes of expression. So had painters and sculptors. The murals and statue groups made for the agora and other public places after the city began to recuperate from the effects of the Persian wars looked very different from the archaic works of art that had been destroyed or looted. Perhaps more than any other factor, Attic tragedy, with its moving poetry and its wonderful spectacle, had made the quality of originality in artistic expression a natural and expected part of intellectual life in Athens. It was Pheidias who, in the Parthenon, developed the potentialities for creativity and expressive power in monumental art on a level equaling that of dramatic poetry. While the structural scheme of the Parthenon remained clearly within certain traditional formal contexts, the effect of the building upon the observer, like the effect of the latest play by Euripides, carried with it the impact of something excitingly different—a spirit that could be distinctly felt as a kind of freedom from tradition (compare figs. 5 and 6).

The originality of the Parthenon must be understood not as an isolated phenomenon, but against its proper background, a background of vigorous intellectual and cultural activity. In this respect, it may be useful to recall the revolutionary changes occurring simultaneously in other fields of art. For example, it was at Athens, during the middle and latter part of the fifth century B.C. that the art of painting seems to have undergone the most drastic transformation of its entire history; here, for the first time, the archaic flatness of the picture plane was shattered. Some quite basic revision of aesthetic and perceptual principles seems to have affected the spatial and pictorial context of forms painted on a flat surface, rendering most earlier concepts of plane decoration obsolete and inappropriate. In place of two-dimensional designs we begin to find compositions of figures seen in light and shade, in striking contrast to earlier practice; and in all the arts the representation of character—what Aristotle called *ethos*—showed an awareness of mood and purpose far beyond the reach of the archaic styles.

The beginnings of these important changes in the arts were taking place throughout those years when Pheidias and his colleagues on the Parthenon project were serving their artistic apprenticeships. Pheidias himself was undoubtedly at the center of a group of artists just beginning to become aware of the expressive possibilities of a drastically altered way of seeing things, a formal context that fully involved the principle of the third dimension. This same group of artists, with Pheidias in charge, embarked, as we have seen, on the rebuilding of the Parthenon in accordance with an entirely new plan. The design for a version of the Acropolis temple that had been created a generation earlier was deemed unusable. Theirs was a new starting point in the literal sense. They must have set about their task in the full knowledge that not only a new Acropolis would take shape under their hands, but a whole new world of art.

By the time the Parthenon was completed in 432 B.C., a new approach to form in sculpture had, indeed, become established, and there can be little doubt that it was in the creation of the Parthenon that the main principles of that approach were formulated. From its zenith here, classical Greek art has had many reincarnations—in ancient Rome, in Renaissance and Baroque Europe, in nineteenth-century France, and in America. As a principle of education, especially the education of the architect, the importance of the classical tradition has already been cited in the comments of Le Corbusier. More surprising, perhaps, is the fact that contemporary painters and sculptors of the highest originality—men like Picasso and Henry Moore—still find inspiration not only in the spirit of classicism, but in the details of the ancient monuments themselves, especially in their pictorial motifs. With astonishing regularity the classical model, in the words of Whitney Oates, "either in theme or motif or subject matter or content, by its very vitality or livingness, has found re-expression." [14]

14. Whitney Oates, ed., *From Sophocles to Picasso* (Bloomington, Ill., 1962), p. 15. This volume of essays is the record of a symposium, "The Present Day Vitality of the Classical Tradition," held on the campus of the University of Illinois by the American Council of Learned Societies. Of special interest to our discussion here are the two essays by Otto J. Brendel: "The Classical Style in Modern Art" (pp. 71 ff.) and "Classical and Non-Classical Elements in Picasso's *Guernica*" (pp. 121 ff.).

II

Ancient literature is of little help to the art historian in solving the problems of the Parthenon since most of the writings we might find useful have vanished. That there once existed a considerable contemporary literature of both a technical and critical nature cannot be doubted. The titles of the lost writings on the art and architecture of the classical period have survived in the bibliographies of later authors. For the Parthenon, Vitruvius, writing in Augustan Rome, mentions a book written by its architect, Ictinus, in collaboration with an associate named Karpion.[15] Another author, Silenus, is credited with having written a book on measurements and proportions of Doric buildings.[16] Aside from a few passages in the Vitruvian text that might be based on earlier writings, no ancient descriptions or critical evaluations of the Parthenon written by professional architects or other qualified experts have survived. The few precious fragments of description that have come down to us are by ancient writers who may qualify, perhaps, as "nonprofessional" critics. These fragments reveal a number of very interesting facts. First of all, it seems clear that ancient observers understood quite well the dual nature of the challenge that faced Pheidias and his colleagues as they assembled on the Acropolis in 448 B.C. to take up the task of reconstruction. On the one hand, as we have seen, the intellectual climate of mid-fifth-century Athens demanded an artistic performance of inventiveness and originality. On the other hand, the artists were certainly well aware that a sense of the continuity and sanctity of the ancient religious precincts on the Acropolis might find expression only by means of the repetition of traditional motifs. Plutarch, in an often-quoted passage, emphasizes this dualism; he speaks of the freshness and newness of the Acropolis buildings, making, at the same time, a special point of the fact that, to the Greeks of the fifth century B.C., the structural forms retained somehow a sense of being "ancient."[17] Plutarch also stresses the timelessness of the Acropolis buildings and their mysterious power of regeneration. In the same passage, written more than five hundred years

15. Vitruvius, *On Architecture*, VII, praef. 12. It has sometimes been suggested that Karpion is an error in transcription for Callicrates.

16. Vitruvius, *loc. cit.* The name of Silenus as the author of *De Symmetrius Doricorum* is mentioned only in Vitruvius. Nothing is known of his life, and it is impossible to guess the date of his work. *RE*, 2, III, 1, 55.

17. Plutarch, *Life of Pericles*, XIII, 11. Cf. J. J. Pollitt, *The Art of Greece 1400–31 B.C.*, Sources and Documents in the History of Art Series (Prentice Hall, 1965), p. 116.

after the completion of the Parthenon at a time when Roman architecture had only recently produced a whole new repertory of monumental forms, Plutarch remarks, "It is as if some ever-flowering
life and unaging spirit had been infused into the creation of these
[Acropolis] works." While not employing the term *classical*, Plutarch's statements show an awareness of the concept of classicism as
an art-historical phenomenon. (Plutarch sees the Periclean Acropolis as
something traditional yet new, something alive yet unaging, something that could be continually inspiring.)

Another fragment of an ancient treatise gives us an impression of
Athens at about the end of the second century B.C., when the city,
having lost most of its commercial and political importance, had
already assumed the role it was to have under the Romans—that of a
university town and center for the arts:

> The road to Athens is a pleasant one, running between cultivated
> fields the whole way. The city itself is dry and ill-supplied with
> water. The streets are nothing but miserable old lanes, the houses
> mean, with a few better ones among them. On his first arrival a
> stranger would hardly believe that this is the Athens of which he
> has heard so much. Yet he will soon come to believe that this is
> Athens indeed. A music hall, the most beautiful in the world, a
> large and stately theater, a costly, remarkable, and farseen temple
> of Athena called the Parthenon rising above the theater, strike
> the beholder with admiration.[18]

This passage draws our attention to something that, when we study
the Parthenon in photographs, we may easily forget—the importance
of its position on the Acropolis (figs. 2, 4, 9). The significance of the
building as a [dominating feature of the city as a whole] impresses
every visitor to Athens. What strikes us most in the setting, even
today, is the isolated grandeur of the temple on top of its jutting
rock. [The enormous Acropolis rock, which raises the sacred precinct aloft, places the Parthenon in a commanding position with
respect to the entire countryside.] This fact probably constituted one
of the greatest challenges of all to Pheidias and his circle—greater
than their awareness of the artistic meaning their work would naturally acquire for future generations. The cliffs of the Acropolis,
rising abruptly from the surrounding plain, seem to be architectural,
like an enormous podium (fig. 2), an impression that is reinforced
when the Acropolis is viewed against the background of more gently

18. Once attributed to Dicaearchus, a pupil of Aristotle, this passage is
assigned by Frazer and others to a later writer, probably of the period
between 164–86 B.C. Cf. J. G. Frazer, *Pausanias' Description of Greece*
(London, 1897), p. xliii, n. 1.

sloping mountains in the distance. The Acropolis cliffs had always been held in immense reverence by the Greeks of Attica. The primitive belief that the steep rock faces were inhabited by superhuman forces, a belief no doubt belonging to remotest antiquity, was still a theme of classical poetry. When Euripides described a scene in Attica, he was apt to characterize the setting not by means of its famous buildings, but by calling up a powerful image of the landscape: "the Rock of Pallas, which looks down on this land." [19]

But the architects of the Parthenon did not attempt to repeat architecturally the theme of unlimited supernatural power as they found it expressed in the Acropolis cliffs, though perhaps they might have done so. Instead, they created an effect that brings that raw surge of power under control. The temple structure contrasts with the rough, jagged grayness of the mighty rock. With its luminous, finely drawn columns holding the rugged cliffs in check, the Parthenon becomes expressive of the might of rationalism. We seem to see in tangible form a spiritual concept that might be described as wisdom, the quality personified by Athena. Athena's temple, crowning her rock, represents the antithesis of the unruly forces manifest in the cliffs below. The colonnades express the beauty of a logical arrangement. Their contrast with the cliffs seems to accentuate the unpredictability of wild nature, reminding us that without the control of reason, primeval power is both ugly and dangerous. At the same time, they are an extension of the cliffs, appearing to draw energy from some point deep inside the core of the rock, transmitting to the entire architectural and sculptural composition a sense of the vitality belonging to the supernatural powers dwelling within its mass. There is a temptation to see in this a demonstration of the ancient philosopher's concept of inspiration, which always included an element of the irrational. For Plato, artistic inspiration begins with a touch of madness, a special state of mind brought on by means of contact with the powers of a god or by a vision of the supernatural. The raw power of the rock can be seen and felt in the columns of the Parthenon, but it is a power which has been transformed by human hands into an image of beauty. Beauty was thus equated with the control of wisdom over brute force, and in this way it is linked with Athena, the personification of wisdom and the protectress of the city.

So finely modulated are the architectural forms of the Parthenon that many writers have likened the building to sculpture (see Mavrikios, pp. 199–224).[20] To appreciate the quality of the sculptural

19. Euripides, *Hippolytus*, 29.
20. For example, Berve and Gruben, *op. cit.*, pp. 376 ff.

expression achieved in the Parthenon it is helpful to remember that Ictinus, in other building projects, was elsewhere capable of giving the Doric order an entirely different expressive content. His temple of Apollo at Bassae, for example, expresses a mood very unlike what we see at Athens. The coarser texture and darker color of the stone employed for the columns, whose outlines seem brittle and hard; the narrower plan; the absolute lack of any visible horizontal curvature in the stylobate all result in a feeling not so much of beauty, but of strength. Here is something determined, awesome, and somehow forbidding—qualities suitable for the dwelling place of Apollo. The temple at Bassae, because it lacks the refinement of the Parthenon, has sometimes been considered inferior to the temple on the Athenian Acropolis, perhaps an early work by Ictinus; but the frieze within the cella is clearly later than the Parthenon frieze, and there are, according to Dinsmoor, a number of architectural features that probably postdate the Parthenon as well.[21] Many of those who have stood before the temple at Bassae, in its lonely setting of wild Arcadian mountains, feel that its clarity of formal expression is no less successful than in the Parthenon, suggesting equally well the mature performance of a skilled architect.[22] By comparison with the Parthenon, the performance is different, perhaps less beautiful in an absolute sense; but it is by no means less moving. Ictinus and his colleagues in the fifth century B.C. learned to vary the elements of temple architecture in such a way that the motifs could be employed to produce a distinct impression of ethos (in the Aristotelian sense). The spiritual presence of the god to whom the temple was to be dedicated could be felt in the designs of the buildings. In the handling of architectural form, Ictinus could—and did—distinguish between a determined, unyielding Apollo on the one hand and a wise and graceful Athena on the other.[23]

21. William Bell Dinsmoor, *The Temple of Apollo at Bassae*, Metropolitan Museum of Art Studies, IV (New York, 1933). Dinsmoor is undecided about the date of the design. He suggests that Ictinus may have originally designed the temple when he was a younger man but, being called away to Athens to work on the Parthenon, postponed construction of certain parts until after the Parthenon was completed.

22. Like the Parthenon, the temple at Bassae shows signs of experimentation. For example, it has the earliest extant Corinthian capital, and its interior frieze, now in the British Museum, is one of the most original and moving of classical sculptures.

23. Vincent Scully (*The Earth, the Temple and the Gods: Greek Sacred Architecture* [New Haven, 1963], p. 176) points out that a contrast between male and female qualities may be seen in peripteral temple designs. In his treatment of the Parthenon, Scully sees a blending of both male and female elements.

Analogies between sculpture and architecture are often made in discussions of the Parthenon, and they serve a useful purpose; but we must occasionally remind ourselves that, in certain ways, such analogies can be quite misleading. Especially when we rely on photographs in our studies, we should recall that the primary realities of monuments like the Parthenon are, indeed, architectural, not sculptural. Much more than for any work of sculpture, our actual perception of the Parthenon has to do with the massiveness of stone and its use in forms that project themselves over the whole environment. The Parthenon is, to some extent, in control of our feelings and even our movements wherever we may be in the city of Athens. Our perception of the composition involves continuous movement, time, sequence, and memory in a manner that belongs strictly to architecture. Our position relative to certain motifs within the architectural complex, our experience of scale, our glimpses of sky and of surrounding terrain—all of these form a series of impressions that follows the order and the logic of architecture, a predetermined sequence destined to reach a climax in the final revelation of the cella and its statue (figs. 42–43).

Today, our first uninterrupted view of the west façade of the Parthenon is from the Propylaea (fig. 1). In antiquity, however, a visitor to the Acropolis would not have seen the complete façade from so great a distance.[24] An inner precinct wall originally enclosed the Parthenon terrace, separating it from other parts of the Acropolis sanctuary. Moreover, it is important to remember that as a tourist in antiquity, on passing through the Propylaea, one would have encountered an imposing array of statues and dedications in the immediate foreground (fig. 8), among them the colossal bronze statue of *Athena Promachos*.[25] Only after passing through a second gate-building leading through the precinct wall of the Parthenon itself would it have been possible to have an uninterrupted view of the entire architectural composition (fig. 7). From this second gate, our point of view in antiquity would have differed in several ways from the manner in which we first behold the structure at the present time. The position of the inner gateway would have forced us to approach the building at a somewhat different angle, the columns of the north flank receding away from us in a much sharper perspective than they do now, as seen from the Propylaea. Directly in front of us would have been the flight of giant steps, forming a base for the

24. G. P. Stevens, *The Setting of the Periclean Parthenon, Hesperia,* Supplement III (Princeton, 1940).
25. Pausanias I, 28, 2.

western terrace, forcing our glance upward and increasing our awareness of the raised position of the temple.[26] As we approach, the frieze within the peripteron becomes visible (fig. 16), and its sculptured horsemen are as much a part of our impression of the temple design as the metopes and pediments Because, in antiquity, we would initially have been so much closer to the steps and stylobate, the awesome height and the mass of the marble forms would have seemed greatly magnified and our sense of the structure more strongly mingled with the secondary impressions of texture, color, and decorative accents.

The decisive step in the sequence of experiences that make up our perception of any architectural design comes only when we find ourselves standing on the same stretch of ground on which the supports of the building rest, when no further obstacle remains between us and the edifice. Ordinarily, the supporting elements of a building are as much a part of the design as the structure itself. And so it was for the Parthenon. Its terrace was narrow and confined, especially on the north, so that this decisive step, this single impression of the whole ensemble from the foundations up, was reserved until the last possible moment. Only at close range would the stone architraves (fig. 12) have seemed at last to acquire their proper relation to a supporting ground. At the same time, once one stands on the temple platform there is an unavoidable exhilaration in the awareness of being high up on a mountaintop, above the city. The experience is overpowering, and from now on we are under the spell of the weight and mass of the stones, of the dynamics of pure construction, in a world both removed from and dominating reality.

This experience of structure in a Doric temple often takes the modern viewer by surprise. By contrast, in our modern skyscrapers, the real foundations of buildings are mostly hidden deep underground, and towering structures of enormous weight appear to float entirely in air. In the Parthenon, the terrace, the podium, the steps, and even the bedrock itself form a group of elements that are of the greatest importance to the design. The bedrock of the Acropolis slopes downward under the Parthenon from northeast to southwest. When it was decided by the Periclean builders to widen the plan of the older temple, it became necessary to cut away an outcropping of rock on the northeast to make way for the lowest course of

---

26. This effect was no doubt heightened by the change in level upward from east to west in the platform of the Parthenon: G. P. Stevens, "Concerning the Impressiveness of the Parthenon," *AJA*, LXVI (1962), pp. 337–338.

stones in the platform. Everywhere else, the platform is raised up artificially. On the west, the flight of high steps, its rate of climb far too great to afford access from that direction, is precisely controlled to enter smoothly into the rhythms of the superstructure, thus forming a monumental transition from bedrock to stylobate. The stylobate itself, on which the fluted column drums rest, is not flat. It is a carefully tailored surface, specially prepared (like a modern shaped canvas) to enhance the qualities of the composition, its subtle upward curve transmitting energy through the columns to the entablature above. This horizontal curvature actually begins not in the stylobate, but below the stylobate in the foundations. But the curvature is most noticeable in the stylobate, which directly receives the downward thrust of the column drums. The curves of the stylobate seem to express a feeling of communication between the bedrock and superstructure, an interchange or mingling of forces.

We read in Dinsmoor's description of the Parthenon that horizontal curvature in peripteral temples may have originated to help in the draining of rain water; but such a purpose can be served equally well in a platform that slopes downward from the cella to the outer edge of the crepis along straight lines. The slope, to function well, need not be curved. Therefore, as Dinsmoor himself later shows, there seems little reason to doubt Vitruvius when he tells us that horizontal curvature served an optical, not a functional, purpose: "The level of the stylobate must be raised along the middle by the *scamilli impares*, for, if the stylobate is laid perfectly level, it will look to the eye as though it were slightly hollowed." [27] Vitruvius promises to explain the *scamilli impares*, but that portion of his work has been lost. [28]

The distinguishing features of the Parthenon plan are strikingly revealed in any comparison with other great fifth-century temples,

27. Vitruvius, III, iv, 5.

28. G. P. Stevens, in his article "Concerning the Curvature of the Steps of the Parthenon," has attempted to reconstruct the formula (*AJA*, XXXVIII [1934], pp. 533–542 and pl. 37). Although Vitruvius implies that horizontal curvature became canonical in later structures of the peripteral type, examples showing curvature are very rare. It has been observed in the architraves of the Propylaea, but not in the stylobate. Goodyear, in *The Greek Refinements* (London and New Haven, 1912), tried to show that horizontal curvature characterized all ancient architecture, but his claims have not withstood criticism. See, for example, the refutation by A. Von Gerkan of Goodyear's description of horizontal curvature in the temple at Cori: *RM*, XL [1925], pp. 167 ff. Dinsmoor (infra, p. 181) lists the most significant examples of horizontal curvature, which include the temple of Athena at Corinth and the stylobate prepared for the older Parthenon. Cf. Dinsmoor's explanation of the *scamilli impares* of Vitruvius (infra, pp. 181 f. and n. 13).

such as the temple of Zeus at Olympia.[29] At first glance, it is obvious that the rhythm of the peristyle in the Parthenon penetrates the cella in a manner that is totally unprecedented. Especially instructive is, of course, the contrast between the plan of the Periclean Parthenon and its predecessor, the older Parthenon (text fig. 2), the plan of which probably dates to the 480s B.C. The changes introduced by the Periclean architects were made primarily in the cella, which was greatly widened. The character of this innermost sanctuary as a functional space was so differently conceived that it evidently became impossible to carry out any such transformation of this area without introducing corresponding changes in the entire sequence of architectural motifs, starting with the widening of the peristyle façades. We may observe in the plan of the Periclean temple how these façades were altered. Not only was the number of columns increased from six to eight, expanding the rhythm of the peristyle, but the ratio between the diameters of the columns and the spaces of the intercolumniations was changed, making the colonnades somewhat more dense. According to Dinsmoor, from this new ratio of 9:4 a new proportional system was applied throughout to the other parts of the building, bestowing on the design a much greater sense of unity.

When we study the interior plan of the older Parthenon, we see that as far as the shape of the cella is concerned it is very similar to the long, narrow cella buildings in other fifth-century temples predating the Periclean structure. In the Periclean design the traditional emphasis on the longitudinal axis in the cella is finally relaxed: the space within the cella is wider in proportion to its length; and there is more space behind the interior colonnades, a feature already introduced in the older Parthenon. The increased depth of the side aisles in the Parthenon already gives the spatial environment within the cella a more dynamic, three-dimensional character; but the architectural meaning of this space with respect to its axis was decisively altered by the introduction in the Periclean design of the transverse colonnade, connecting the longitudinal colonnades across the rear of the cella, thus creating a continuously flowing, three-sided composition. In the older Parthenon as well as in the temple of Zeus at Olympia and in the temple of Aphaia at Aegina, the interior colonnades terminated uncomfortably in the rear wall of the cella. This

29. Such comparisons are made in the following works: Robert L. Scranton, "Interior Design of Greek Temples," *AJA*, L (1946), pp. 39–51; Carl Weickert, "*Erga Perikleus*: Studien zur Kunstgeschichte des 5. Jahrhunderts, II," *Abhandlungen der deutschen Akademie der Wissenschaften zu Berlin* (Berlin, 1950).

only added to the tunnellike atmosphere of the traditional cella design. The transverse colonnade in the interior of the present Parthenon revolutionized the character of the enclosed space.

The same "modernization" of the cella also was introduced into
the Hephaisteion in the Athenian agora, the first design for which
evidently predated the Parthenon. Dinsmoor considers it likely that
"the entire cella building [of the Hephaisteion was] redesigned in
emulation of the new contemporary design for the Parthenon.
. . . "[30] Although the Hephaisteion may have had the first example of the transverse colonnade, [31] Dinsmoor's main conclusion seems
valid. We deal with an invention characteristic of a whole pattern of
architectural innovations developed in connection with the revision
of an earlier plan for the Parthenon. Such an invention might have
been simultaneously applied to other buildings, such as the Hephaisteion, that were then under construction. Indeed, the discussions that led to these changes may have started considerably earlier
than 448 B.C., and there is no reason why such discussions might not
have affected other structures in and around Athens before the re-
visions of the Parthenon itself were actually carried out. But it seems
quite likely that it was the problem of what to do about the partially completed Parthenon, still in ruins, that stimulated controversy
in the first place, causing change in a wider context. The actual sequence in which the changes were executed in various buildings is a
matter of relatively minor importance. As in the case of the horizontal curvature, examples earlier than the Parthenon can, indeed,
be found, but what matters is that in the Parthenon such things were
made more effective so that they could be clearly read as marking a
turning point in the history of art.

When it was finished and in position, the gold and ivory cult
statue of the *Athena Parthenos* by Pheidias, now known only
through ancient copies (figs. 43, 44),[32] repeated the three-sided
spatial movement of the cella colonnade, which was, in effect, a
background for the statue. With its right hand outstretched to hold a
winged Victory and its left hand extended downward to steady the
great shield at its side, the statue provided a sequence of forms

30. William Bell Dinsmoor, "The Internal Colonnade of the Hephaisteion," *Hesperia*, XXXVII (1968), p. 159.

31. Herbert Koch, *Studien zum Theseustempel in Athen* (Berlin, 1955),
pp. 66 ff.; Francis C. Penrose, *An Investigation of the Principles of Athenian
Architecture* (New York and London, 1888), pl. 36.

32. A recent study on the statute is that of W. H. Schuchhardt in
Antike Plastik II (1963), Teil 3, pp. 31 ff.

describing a wide semicircular volume, like an apse, adding to a sense of release from the longitudinal axis.

The cella of the Parthenon, from wall to wall, was the widest known in Greece. Its walls were pushed so far outward that the peripteron corridors on the long flanks of the temple had to be narrowed. In fact, the great peripteron halls outside the cella walls are narrower in the Parthenon than the side aisles within the cella—a strange reversal, as Carl Weickert points out, of the ratio common in all other comparable Doric temples.[33]

It is important to notice in our study of the Parthenon plan that while the design of the Periclean structure called for many innovations, certain striking departures from fifth-century practice were already present in the plan for the older temple. The most conspicuous of these is the architectural treatment of the pronaos and opisthodome, the two "porches" of the Parthenon. The temples at Aegina and Olympia and a number of other fifth-century examples all follow a standard rule, which calls for two columns *in antis,* forming a room at either end of the temple, a space clearly discrete from both the peristyle on the one hand and interior chambers on the other. The antae or side walls of the traditional porch are created by continuing the walls of the naos (or cella) so that they embrace the porch columns. Such porches were usually closed off by means of grilles (openwork screens) inserted between the columns and the antae. In older temples the amount of space within the pronaos and the opisthodome was substantial, so that they seem like additional rooms. The point to be noticed is that in both the Parthenon and in the plan of its predecessor, these porch chambers follow a design that seems to be a departure from earlier practice. The side walls of the porches all but vanish, the depth of the space diminishes, and in place of a pair of columns *in antis* there are now freestanding colonnades extending across the full width of the naos and the opisthodome. These colonnades, four columns wide in the older Parthenon and six columns wide in the Periclean Parthenon, appear to detach themselves completely from the interior chambers of the temple. Light can enter the porches from the sides, behind the end columns. The space within the porch is no longer a discrete chamber. Instead, the form of the porch colonnades, as revised, provides a transition between the peristyle colonnades and the interior of the cella. In his study of temple interiors, R. L. Scranton describes this situation in the following manner:

33. Weickert, *op. cit.,* p. 6.

... the pronaos columns of the Parthenon repeat the peripteron façade; the pronaos itself is open and narrow, corresponding to the peripteron halls. The columns are little more than a screen, but are clearly integrated to the naos. . . . Thus there is an integration and harmonization between the spaces and design of the peripteron and those of the naos. . . . Entering from the front, one would pass through the octastyle façade, cross transversely the peripteron corridor, then pass through the hexastyle façade of the pronaos, and cross transversely the shorter pronaos. He would feel the spaces to be similar, but, as it were, gathering themselves in for the entrance. [Once within the cella] the recollection of the exterior would cushion, so to speak, the sense of confinement. It would permit a certain recoil, and it would in general achieve a sense of unity of the major parts of the building.[34]

This unity between interior and exterior features, as Scranton describes it, constitutes the most significant architectural innovation of the Parthenon. However, we must also mention the fact that, but for a difference in the number of columns, the same general conditions apply to Hill's plan of the older Parthenon. In both plans the treatment of the porch columns as an architectural screen fundamentally reinterpreted the relationship between the prismatic core of the cella building and its encircling peristyle colonnade. But the change was gradual. The revision of the design of the peripteral temple took place step by step, as the problems of the Parthenon were analyzed. It began in the older Parthenon, and was enlarged upon by the architects of the Periclean project, who carried the transformation to its natural conclusion. The final design of the Periclean temple abolishes the old-fashioned insistence upon a strict, longitudinal axis within the cella and relieves the sudden contrast from light to dark. By introducing a transverse colonnade in the interior, there was created within the cella an effect that was an appropriate answer to the sequence of architectural experiences set in motion by the octastyle façade, the freestanding columns of the porches, raised a step higher than the peristyle colonnades, providing an ideal transition between the exterior of the building and the more fully articulated interior chambers.

III

The Venetian bombardment of the Turkish fortifications on the Acropolis in 1687 caused an explosion of such violence within the

34. Scranton, *op. cit.*, p. 35.

cella of the Parthenon that the entire roof was blown off the building and the cella walls were almost completely demolished. Parts of
the opisthodome and its porch on the west together with the western
and eastern ends of the peristyle remained standing, but most of the
columns of the north and the central part of the south flank were
knocked down along with their entablature blocks and sculptured
metopes.[35]

The violence of the explosion seems incomprehensible. According to a story told later in Venice, the Turks had moved their supply
of gunpowder into the Parthenon (which was then serving as a
mosque) in the belief that the Venetian attackers would not fire
upon a building that had once been a church dedicated to the Virgin
Mary. The Venetians are said to have learned of the gunpowder
from a Turkish deserter, whereupon they determined to destroy the
Turkish garrison's potential to wage war. Venetian artillerymen
tried in vain for hours to score a direct hit on the Parthenon. Eventually, despite a deplorable lack of skill, they succeeded. Two days
later the Turks surrendered, and the Venetians, under their leader,
Francesco Morosini, occupied the ruined Acropolis. The irony of
the story is that after a short stay the Venetians decided to abandon
the town, and Athens fell once again into Turkish hands.

All this is related by J. M. Paton in his introduction to a Gennadeion Monographs publication of the original manuscript of an
eyewitness account of the tragedy written by a Yugoslav member of
the Venetian attack force named Cristoforo Ivanovich, presented in
this volume in translation (pp. 124–128). Paton comments upon the
fact that in view of the subsequent withdrawal of the Venetians, the
destruction of one of the most perfectly preserved and beautiful
ancient monuments served absolutely no military or strategic purpose.
The Venetian destruction, moreover, did not end with the explosion.
Before their withdrawal, an attempt was evidently made to remove
the central figures from the west pediment of the Parthenon in order
to carry them back to Venice. We may suppose that Morosini
decided to follow the example of his thirteenth-century name-
sake, who, after the capture of Constantinople in 1204, carried
back to Venice the four magnificent bronze horses belonging to an
ancient quadriga that are now standing above the façade of Saint

35. The north flank was later rebuilt by Greek authorities. More recently, the Greek Archaeological Service mounted a project to dismantle
and rebuild the colonnade strictly following ancient methods. It is this
restoration we now see on the north flank of the temple: Nicolas Balanos,
The Reconstruction of the Monuments of the Acropolis (Athens, 1949)
and *Les Monuments de l'Acropole: Relèvement et conservation* (Paris, 1938).

Mark's cathedral. Or it may be that the Venetians proposed to emulate the ancient Romans, who carried in triumph through the streets of Rome famous works of art from the conquered cities of Greece. Among the statues that disappeared from the pediment on this occasion were the famous horses of Athena from the scene of the goddess's contest with Poseidon for the city of Athens. It is said that the tackle being used to lower the statues from the pediment slipped and that the statues were hopelessly ruined when they came crashing to the ground, where they remained in fragments. The French, too, around 1800, are accused of dropping and ruining a piece of Parthenon sculpture, a metope, in the course of lowering it from the building. It seems certain, at any rate, that many losses were the result of looting and careless handling in the years immediately following the Venetian bombardment.

Earlier events in the history of the Parthenon after the close of antiquity are not as generously chronicled as is the explosion of 1687.[36] Little of importance in the way of graphic or documentary evidence concerning the Parthenon survives from the entire range of centuries between the end of classical antiquity and the 1670s, when drawings of the Parthenon sculptures—the so-called Carrey drawings—were commissioned by the Marquis de Nointel. At some period long before the disappearance of the sculptures of the west pediment in the seventeenth century, the central part of the east pediment, including the figures of Zeus and Athena, were removed. These figures, too, have vanished except for small fragments. In a way, their loss is the most serious of all, for they formed the centerpiece of the sculptural composition over the main entrance to the temple, the most conspicuous feature of the eastern façade; and while we have a drawing by Carrey that preserves the design of the western pedimental group, there is no such record of the central motif of the eastern pediment since the statues had already disappeared before Carrey's day. The scene represented in the eastern pediment, according to Pausanias, was the birth of Athena, a composition that Evelyn B. Harrison attempts to reconstruct (see pp. 225–311).

It seems likely that the damage to the eastern pediment dates to the time when the Parthenon was first converted to the service of Christianity. This event undoubtedly took place sometime soon after an imperial Roman decree in A.D. 435 required all buildings of pagan worship to be either converted and rededicated as churches or suffer

36. The history of the Parthenon from the end of antiquity through the Turkish occupation is treated in detail by Michaelis, *op. cit.* Cf. W. Judeich, *Topographie von Athen,* 2nd ed. (Munich, 1931); Jean Baelen, *La Chronique de Parthénon* (Paris, 1956).

destruction. Structural changes to the Parthenon, no doubt carried out by Byzantine architects, must have included the closing up of the eastern entrance to the cella and the construction on that end of the building of an apse.[37] A new entrance was cut into the cella from the west, leading from the room that one enters after passing through the western porch (opisthodome). This four-columned room, whose precise function in antiquity has never been determined, now became the narthex of the church, which was dedicated to Saint Sophia; and the six great columns of the opisthodome gave the portals of the church an impressive monumental frame.

It is difficult to envisage what may have happened to the eastern end of the Parthenon when the apse of a Byzantine church replaced the pronaos. The two central columns of the pronaos were actually incorporated into the masonry of the apse, but beyond that the archeological evidence is uncertain. It seems unlikely that extensive renovation of this kind could have been carried on in this portion of the building without seriously disturbing both the frieze in the architraves of the pronaos colonnade and the statues in the center of the pediment.[38] It is difficult to believe, however, that the sculptures removed in the course of renovation would have been simply discarded or destroyed. Many fragments of the east frieze have, in fact, been recovered (figs. 34–42), and it is certainly possible that additional pieces of the sculptures of the eastern façade may yet reappear.

Almost nothing is known of the history of the Parthenon during the "Dark Ages," which were nowhere darker than at Athens. From time to time, Athens came under the domination of warring knights from western Europe; but these knights did not always visit the city itself or live there. By the Middle Ages the place had become a backwater, far from the scenes of combat and diplomacy where the fate of Greek cities, especially during the Crusades, was often held in the balance. In 1204, Burgundian and Lombardic soldiers captured the Acropolis, but made their headquarters at Thebes. Under their control, the Parthenon became a Roman Catholic church dedicated to the Virgin Mary, and a Catholic archbishop replaced the Greek Orthodox leader.[39] The Acropolis assumed at this time some-

37. Martin Luther D'Ooge, *The Acropolis of Athens* (London, 1908), pp. 307 ff.

38. Cf. William Bell Dinsmoor, "New Evidence for the Parthenon Frieze," *AJA* (1954), pp. 144–145. For speculation on the loss of the pedimental statues, see B. Sauer, *Der Laborde'sche Kopf und die Giebelgruppen des Parthenon* (Geissen, 1903), pp. 27 f.

39. William Miller, *The Latins in the Levant* (London, 1908), pp. 6 ff., 232 ff.

thing of the character it must have had during the Dorian migrations. It was a medieval citadel, part fortress, part religious sanctuary, and part princely residence and court. During this period, the population of Athens dwindled to the size of an unimportant village, perhaps less than five hundred families remaining in the area of the old town surrounding the Acropolis. Here goats and sheep grazed, climbing over the partially buried ruins of classical structures. To the people of the town, the Periclean temple was now a church within the stronghold of a foreign garrison; and it soon became a forgotten relic.

The situation at Athens changed again in the early Renaissance. In 1387, the citadel was occupied by a Florentine adventurer named Raniero Acciajuoli, who founded a dynasty of Athenian dukes. Proclaiming himself Nerio I, he converted the Propylaea, whose open colonnades were now walled up, into a palace worthy of a monarch. It is during the tenure of a successor, Nerio II (1435–51), that we receive a ray of light concerning the condition of the Acropolis and the Parthenon in the Renaissance. An Italian traveler named Ciriaco d'Ancona visited the Florentine court at Athens perhaps on more than one occasion during the second quarter of the fifteenth century, and has left us a record of his stay.[40]

Ciriaco made drawings to illustrate his letters and descriptions of ancient monuments in Greece. The drawing reproduced in our text fig. 4 (from the Hamilton folio in Berlin) was long considered to be an original drawing of the Parthenon by him.[41] It is from a kind of scrapbook of odds and ends collected for the antiquarian Petrus Donatus, bishop of Padua during the first half of the fifteenth century. The drawing is now considered by some to be a copy.[42] Its authenticity is reaffirmed by Charles Mitchell in an article written especially for this anthology (see pp. 111–123). Among the more interesting examples of poetic license taken in rendering the details of the temple are the wings given by Ciriaco to the figures in the west pediment, making them into typical Renaissance cherubs.

Although unreliable in detail, the Ciriaco drawings are an early hint of the new archeological interest in classical antiquity that was to sweep Europe during the following centuries. Unfortunately, by

40. Paul McKendrick summarizes our knowledge of Ciriaco in his article "A Renaissance Odyssey: The Life of Cyriac of Ancona," *Classica et Medievalia*, XIII (1952), pp. 131 ff. A more detailed and recent study is that by E. W. Bodnar, "Cyriacus of Ancona and Athens," *Collection Latomus*, XLIII (1960).

41. A. Michaelis, "Eine Originalizeichnung des Parthenon," *Archaeologische Zeitung*, XL (1882), pp. 367 ff.

42. Bernard Ashmole, "Cyriac of Ancona," *Proceedings of the British Academy*, XLV (1959), pp. 25 ff.; cf. E. W. Bodnar, "Athens in April, 1436: I," *Archaeology*, XXIII (1970), pp. 96 ff.

the time this movement was properly under way, the Acropolis had been closed to foreign visitors. The Turks took control of Athens not long after Ciriaco's visit. In the 1460s Mohammed II took up residence in the citadel and had the Parthenon converted into a mosque. Visitors were henceforth rarely permitted beyond the reconstructed fortress gates to the Acropolis.

Moslem control of the ancient sanctuary on the Athenian Acropolis resulted in no immediate damage to the Parthenon. A minaret was added where the Christian bell tower had stood, but there were no important structural changes carried out within the temple as there had been under early Christian rule. Only after the explosion caused by the Venetian artillery bombardment of 1687, when the stones of the Parthenon lay scattered over the citadel, were there serious losses. Since the Turkish rulers of Athens had no special interest in the conservation of classical monuments, there was no effort to safeguard the fragments or to restore them to the structure. A smaller mosque was eventually built amidst the ruins of the vast ancient structure, and many of the fallen parts that would have been worth saving, such as the sculptured metopes from the destroyed flanks, simply disappeared, no one knows precisely how. Some fragments of the sculptures seem to have been quarried for new construction. Such a fragment was found in the 1950s in the walls of a house demolished by the American excavators in the agora.[43]

As interest grew in the fate of the Acropolis buildings on the part of artists and connoisseurs in western Europe, occasional visitors were permitted to enter the citadel by the local Turkish authorities at Athens. Such visitors seem to have carried off souvenirs in the form of fragments of the sculptures, some of which have since reappeared in various European collections.[44]

43. Evelyn B. Harrison, "A New Parthenon Fragment from the Athenian Agora," *Hesperia*, XXIV (1955), pp. 85–87.

44. A fragment of a pedimental horse from the Parthenon was discovered among the miscellaneous sculptures in the storage rooms of the Vatican Museums as recently as 1947: H. Speier, "Framento di una Testa di Cavallo Proveniente dai Magazzini dei Musei Vaticani," *Rendiconti della Pont. Accad. Rom. Arch.*, XXIII–XXIV (1947–48), pp. 57 ff. Together with small fragments of Parthenon metopes discovered earlier, this piece is now on exhibition in a special room in the Vatican Museums behind the Etruscan collection. Other Parthenon sculptures, apart from the main group in the British Museum, are in museums in Paris, Palermo, and Athens. The head of the horse in the Vatican is certainly from the Parthenon but appears to be a repair executed during the Roman period. Information on all these fragments is collected in the recent catalogues by Frank Brommer: *Die Skulpturen der Parthenon-Giebel*, 2 vols. (Mainz am Rhein, 1963); *Die Metopen des Parthenon: Katalog und Untersuchung*, 2 vols. (Mainz am Rhein, 1967).

Toward the close of the eighteenth century there emerged a comprehensive program of conservation for the monuments of the Acropolis. Realizing that continuing losses and damage to the monuments could not be avoided, the English peer Lord Elgin envisaged nothing less than the making of a complete set of drawings and casts of all extant sculptures and architectural decorations of the Parthenon. Europe at that time was at the height of the Napoleonic wars, and Lord Elgin was in competition with the French for access to the classical remains of the Acropolis. The victory of the British forces over Napoleon in Egypt resulted in improved relationships between the Turkish and British governments, and after years of delay Lord Elgin was suddenly granted a free hand to carry out his plans on the Acropolis. It was his original intention to re-create the Parthenon in plaster casts in order to make available in London as complete and accurate a record as possible of the art of the high classical period. Elgin had in mind the classical education of British architects and artists of the future as well as the preservation of monuments that were rapidly disappearing. For the purpose of making casts, scaffolding was erected along portions of the Parthenon still standing, and artists were brought to Athens from various parts of Europe to carry out the work. The interesting and complex story of how Lord Elgin's agents at Athens came to remove the ancient stones themselves is recounted by Jacob Rothenberg in this anthology (pp. 128–170).

Considering the serious losses resulting from the destruction of the Parthenon during the Turkish-Venetian conflict and the subsequent looting of its ruins throughout succeeding generations, it is a matter of extreme good fortune that we possess a set of drawings of the sculptures dating from the period before the explosion. These drawings, said to be by the artist Jacques Carrey, a student of Charles Le Brun, are now preserved in the Bibliothèque Nationale in Paris.[45] The drawings of the Parthenon were executed in 1674, when Carrey (or another artist) was brought to Athens by the Marquis de Nointel, an enthusiastic admirer of Athens and its antiquities who must be

45. The drawings are reproduced in Henri A. S. Omont, *Athènes au XVIIe siècle: Dessins des sculptures du Parthénon attribuées à J. Carrey* (Paris, 1896). There is now a handsome new edition on the drawings: Theodore Bowie and Dieter Thimme, eds., *The Carrey Drawings of the Parthenon Sculptures* (Bloomington, Ind., 1971). Little is known about the career of Jacques Carrey. Among the few works attributable to him, apart from the drawings of the Parthenon, are six large panels that he painted for the church of Saint Pantéléon at Troyes. The tradition connecting Carrey with the drawings has been seriously questioned, but his name continues to be used, sometimes in quotation marks.

counted among the first modern Europeans to conceive and carry out, at his own expense, a genuine archeological project on the Acropolis.[46] We know fourteen of the metopes of the Parthenon, which later disappeared, some 48 feet of the frieze, and some of the lost figures of the pediments only by means of the drawings made under Nointel's patronage on this occasion.

Evidently it was the Marquis de Nointel's intention to have his artists produce a complete set of drawings of the Parthenon sculptures, thus anticipating the idea of Lord Elgin. If so, some drawings were already lost by 1770, when the remaining group became a part of the French royal library. The drawings are executed in red chalk, the figures appearing against a background shaded in pencil. This combination reproduces so badly in photographs that a certain clumsiness of line in the originals often appears worse than ever in photographic reproductions. The artist's main difficulty in drawing the pediments seems to have arisen from the simple fact that he could not always see the bases of the pedimental statues from any given viewpoint and was, therefore, unable to render effectively the placement of feet and other supports. His angle of view seems different for different figures, as though he moved from one place to another in the course of rendering a single pedimental composition. This gives the drawings of the pediments an effect of awkwardness that sometimes destroys our confidence in them. Nevertheless, comparisons between his figures and the extant fragments of pedimental statues have often proved useful; and it has been found that his renderings may be relied on for certain purposes: the general poses, drapery, design, degree of preservation—in short, everything but style and angle of view. The drawings are invaluable for any attempt to discuss the lost portions of the pediments. The Carrey drawings were also useful in the analysis of a group of statuettes of the Roman period from Eleusis, some of which are copies of Parthenon statues.[47]

One of the most important of the missing episodes in our knowledge of the development of the classical style in Greece is the story of the planning of a thematic program for the sculptures of the

46. The Marquis de Nointel's interest in classical antiquity is shown in a portrait of him, now in the museum at Chartres, in which he is depicted against a background of the city of Athens (Omont, *op. cit.*, pl. 30).

47. The manner in which the Carrey drawings may add to our knowledge of the Parthenon sculptures is well demonstrated in the following studies: Evelyn B. Harrison, "U and Her Neighbors in the West Pediment of the Parthenon," in *Essays in the History of Art: Presented to Rudolf Wittkower*, ed. Douglas Fraser et al. (London and New York, 1969), pp. 1 ff.; Rhys Carpenter, "New Material for the West Pediment of the Parthenon," *Hesperia*, I (1932), pp. 1 ff.

Parthenon. In thematic content, no less than in formal treatment, the sculptures of the Parthenon set new standards. Yet on the planning of the themes our ancient sources are silent. Perhaps the most surprising innovation in the thematic content of the sculptural program is the inclusion in the frieze of a depiction of a contemporary event—the Panathenaic procession.

From its very beginnings, Greek art demonstrates a degree of ambivalence with regard to the depiction of contemporary scenes. The funerary games shown on vases of the geometric period might represent either contemporary princely celebrations or those of legend, for example the games in honor of Patroclus in the *Iliad*.[48] It seems possible to see them from both points of view, and perhaps this was, in fact, the intention. By the archaic period, however, in the works of certain artists, we can observe a clear sense of delight in themes evidently informed by the observation of everyday life; but the ambivalence remains. For example, scenes of arrival or farewell of a warrior, which must have been familiar in Greece, were treated by many archaic vase painters; yet Exekias, in the well-known amphora in the Vatican,[49] creates an aura of remoteness and mystery around his figures that somehow removes them from the realm of the ordinary. As we look at his picture, what seemed at first to be a familiar scene begins to take on a different meaning. In the actual depiction, the warrior becomes not an ordinary youth, but Castor (one of the Dioscuri), and his mother, tenderly offering him a flower, becomes Leda. Exekias provides labels for his figures, so that we are in no doubt as to their identity. But even without the labels the identity of the family would be suggested by something in the pictorial style, and it might occur to us to wonder over the seeming conflict between the prosaic human nature of the action portrayed and the great fame and immortality of the actors. In archaic painting, some special pictorial quality instinctively applied has blended these conflicting elements into a single poetic statement, but by the middle of the fifth century B.C. the possibility of following two alternative paths in art provided the basis for a controversy that had become explicit. In the Parthenon we see the first attempt, on the level of monumental art, to make a clear distinction between the pictoral techniques of allegory on the one hand and naturalistic representation on the other. Both methods were applied in the sculptures: naturalism in the frieze, allegory in the metopes and pedi-

48. John Carter, "The Beginnings of Narrative Art in the Greek Geometric Period," *BSA*, LXVII (1972), pp. 25 ff. (with earlier bibliography).

49. J. D. Beazley, *The Development of Attic Black-Figure* (Berkeley and London, 1951; 2nd ed., 1964), pp. 65 ff., pl. 28, 29.

ments; and each method, as developed in the Parthenon, was different in its own way from traditional forms of Greek pictorial narrative.

In the Parthenon frieze, the kind of detail that the artist selected concentrates our attention on the accidental and the momentary (figs. 17–42)—the way an offering bearer sets down his burden for an instant to get a better grip, the way a sacrificial beast strains impatiently against his bonds, the way the horses of the cavalrymen rear up or dart forward as the movement of the long procession speeds up or slows down. At the same time, the figures in the frieze are idealized. The human figures have a touch of the godlike, while the gods are shown in casual poses and seem human. In other words, although undoubtedly a representation of a real event, there is an ambiguity that allows us to read a variety of interpretations into what is shown, as in earlier examples of genre scenes in Greek art.

The Panathenaic procession, which was one of the most important social and religious events in Athenian life, is known to us through ancient writings, in which many of the details of the procession are recorded.[50] During the Panathenaea, musical performances and games were dedicated to the patron goddess as well as religious ritual in one form or another; but the Panathenaic procession was the chief pageant of the festival and the prelude to its most important ceremony. The main feature of this ceremony was the presentation to Athena of a new peplos,[51] the traditional garment of Attic women. As was true many centuries later at Chartres,[52] a garment belonging to the goddess played a central role in the religious rites celebrated on the Acropolis. But while Mary's tunic at Chartres was a relic of what was in that day great antiquity, Athena's peplos was not. A new one was woven for each succeeding festival by a group of specially selected maidens, the Arrhephorae, who resided, while they labored upon it, within a sacred enclosure near the Erechtheum. This peplos was a work of art in its own right, bearing scenes of battle between the Olympian gods and the giants.[53] So that it might

50. References collected by L. Deubner, *Attische Feste* (Berlin, 1932).
51. A peplos is a large rectangle of cloth folded around the body, clasped over each shoulder, and belted, with an overfold.
52. Robert Branner, ed., *Chartres Cathedral*, Norton Critical Studies in Art History (New York, 1969), p. 70. A garment said to have belonged to the Virgin Mary is still displayed at Chartres and is considered one of the most precious and holy relics in France.
53. For an interesting description, see Louis de Ronchaud, *La Tapisserie dans l'antiquité* (Paris, n.d.). In a lecture entitled "Le Péplos d'Athéné, la décoration interieure du Parthénon resititué d'après un passage d'Euripide," published separately after its reading in Paris in May, 1885, Ronchaud suggests that large tapestries like the peplos of Athena may have been of great importance as hangings in ancient temple décor.

be admired by the spectators crowding the route of the procession, it was displayed by hanging it from the spars of a ship which was drawn on wheels through the city.

The Parthenon frieze shows various participants in the Panathenaic procession. Athenian youths riding horses and others driving chariots follow along behind officials who will perform the sacrificial rites. Included among the officials we see musicians and the attendants who lead the sacrificial beasts. In the frieze, the procession has divided at the southwestern corner of the Parthenon, part of it moving along the north flank, another part along the south flank, to meet at the eastern terrace. There is a clear suggestion of the slowing down of the procession as it arrives at its destination. Some of the horsemen pause; others race ahead to close their ranks. On the east, the procession has arrived and the ceremonies are already in progress.

The east frieze (figs. 34–42) presents many difficulties in interpretation. Included among the assembled witnesses are the Olympian gods (figs. 36–41), seated and relaxed as they prepare to view the solemn sacrifices.[54] In the center of the frieze, above the entrance to the cella and situated between two groups of gods, is the so-called "cult scene" (fig. 42), which affords a view into the temple, where a peplos (perhaps the old peplos, as Carpenter suggests) is being folded and put away for safekeeping. Outside, a signal is given (fig. 34) and the sacrifices are about to begin [55] (see Philipp Fehl, pp. 311–321).

Recently, a theory that has gained much ground is that the Parthenon frieze represents not a contemporary procession of the Periclean Age, but an older one, taking place in the days of the legendary kings and peopled with mythological characters.[56] Advocates of this interpretation explain that certain crucial items are missing from the representation of the procession in the frieze, such as the ship. R. Ross Holloway lists three other categories of officiates known from ancient writings to have participated in the procession but who are not shown in the Parthenon frieze.[57] These are

---

54. George Wicker Elderkin, "The Seated Deities of the Parthenon Frieze," *AJA*, XL (1936), pp. 92–99.

55. Cf. A. Furtwängler, *Masterpieces of Greek Sculpture* (1895), pp. 427 ff.

56. Chrysoula Kardara, "Glaukopis, the Archaic Naos and the Theme of the Parthenon Frieze," *ArchEph 1961* (1964), pp. 115 ff. (in Greek).

57. R. Ross Holloway, "The Archaic Akropolis and the Parthenon Frieze," *Art Bulletin*, XLVIII (1966), p. 223. Holloway also points out some of the flaws in Miss Kardara's attempt to identify various deities and heroes (such as Poseidon and Theseus) among the processional figures in the frieze.

the basket carriers, the Athenian hoplites, and the female water carriers (the latter having been replaced in the frieze by youths). In any case, their absence does not seem sufficiently conspicuous to force us into a search for a complex mythological and historical allegory when we deal with a representation that is so clearly naturalistic in its artistic statement and so obviously not in need of labels. The sense of immediacy and the clarity of action that we see in the frieze itself suggests something actual and uncomplicated, witnessed by men as well as by the gods, within the context of a single occasion, just as the pediments, in the manner of classical drama, portray unique cosmic events played out in the course of a single day.

A detail in the frieze that has puzzled everyone is the representation in the "cult scene" of maidens carrying what seem to be stools. (They appear to the left of the group folding the peplos of Athena, fig. 42.) An ingenious explanation of the presence of these stools has been given by Dorothy Burr Thompson,[58] whose theory is that the stools are part of the spoils taken from the invading Persian armies, perhaps part of the furniture belonging to the Persian king—his golden footstools, in fact. These objects were probably stored in the Parthenon and carried in the Panathenaic procession. If this theory is correct, it removes one of the last obstacles to an interpretation of the frieze as a representation of a contemporary scene.

Among the many unsolved problems concerning the sculptures of the Parthenon are those that pertain to the metopes (figs. 56–63). The Parthenon creates so strong an impression of unity and harmony in all of its aspects that we are led to expect a kind of logical continuity of both style and theme throughout the structure and its decorations. The metopes reinforce such an impression. In the temple of Zeus at Olympia, only the metopes of the pronaos and opisthodome received sculptural decoration, and the labors of Heracles provided a perfect theme for the entire series. In the Parthenon a different tradition was followed—applying sculptured reliefs to the exterior metopes of the peristyle, in this case ninety-two in all; and there arose the difficulty of finding a suitable theme for so great a number of designs. Obviously, no one legend would suffice; yet the earlier practice of mingling different themes seemed to be out of the question here. The solution was to find a group of legends in which a single allegorical meaning could be seen. The result is a kind of history of ancient mythological warfare that involved the history of Athens and its gods and heroes, with scenes of battle from various

58. Dorothy Burr Thompson, "The Persian Spoils at Athens," in *The Aegean and the Near East: Studies Presented to Hetty Goldman* (Locust Valley, N. Y., 1956), pp. 281–291.

conflicts: the war between the gods and giants; the war between the Greeks and the Amazons; the war between the Lapiths and the centaurs; and the sack of Troy. What ties all these scenes together is the symbolism of the Parthenon itself. The temple is a celebration of the survival of the Athenians, through the intercession of Athena, in the face of an overwhelming eastern force that had destroyed their city and threatened them with annihilation. Their victory over the Persians, though not itself represented in the sculptures, continues the series of famous conflicts in which the Greeks wage war against the forces of barbarism. Civilization, personified by Theseus, confronts primitiveness, in the shape of such savages as Amazons and centaurs—a clear allusion to the real intrusion of fearsome hordes from the East.

The organization of this thematic material in the metopes seems to follow a logical order. The most important war, the battle between the giants and the gods, led by Zeus, was placed on the main eastern façade over the entrance to the cella. On the west is the battle between the Amazons and the Greeks, led by Theseus. But matters are less clear with regard to the two long flanks since so many of the metopes are destroyed. The metopes from the southern flank that are actually preserved represent the fight between the Lapiths and centaurs; others, known through the Carrey drawings, also fit in with this theme. Although the assumption is sometimes challenged, most authorities now regard the south metopes as having represented this one story.[59] More vexing is the problem of the vanished metopes of the north flank, where some critics have seen a duplication of the Lapith theme of the south side of the temple but with a reordering of the individual scenes. Among the fragments that do survive from the north, however, are scenes that unmistakably represent episodes from the Trojan War. A. H. Smith, writing in the early part of this century, favored such an interpretation; and in a more recent work on Greek sculpture by Georg Lippold, the subject of the north metopes is given as the Iliupersis (the fall of Troy) according to the Homeric account.[60] Thus, despite the difficulties,

59. P. Eckstein, "Die Südmetopen des Parthenon und die Carreyschen Zeichnungen," *JdI*, LXVIII (1953), pp. 79–97. A complete re-examination of the metopes as they are preserved was published in catalogue form by Brommer, *Die Metopen des Parthenon, op. cit. (supra*, n. 44). See his bibliography on pp. 241 f.

60. The suggestion of an Iliupersis theme originated with Carl Robert, "Die Iliupersis des Polyghot," *Winckelmann-Programm*, XVII (Halle, 1893), p. 60. A. H. Smith discusses it in *The Sculptures of the Parthenon* (London, 1910), p. 40. Cf. Georg Lippold, *Die Griechische Plastik*, Handbuch der Archäologie, V (Munich, 1950), p. 149. Brommer, *op. cit.*

most opinion at present is overwhelmingly in favor of a flawlessly unified thematic program in which each set of metopes—north, south, east, and west—was devoted to a single myth.

Without doubt, the most impressive works of sculpture to have survived from the height of the classical period in Greece are the statues from the east pediment of the Parthenon, now in the British Museum. As we have seen, the central figures from this pediment have been lost, and the figures preserved in London are fragments of those from the two ends of the triangular pediment. There have been numerous attempts to reconstruct the whole design of the east pediment of the Parthenon, filling in the central figures, but until the recent reconstruction by Evelyn B. Harrison (pp. 225–311), none of the suggested designs seemed to agree with the realities of the preserved statues. In older reconstructions,[61] there is little sense of interaction between the figures, which seem isolated from each other not only formally, but psychologically also, each one seeming to look inward or to be somehow lost in his own thoughts, like the figures in the race of Pelops on the east pediment at Olympia. Such a design is not Pheidian in feeling. It belongs to an earlier stage of classical style and is in sharp contrast to what we see in the Parthenon statues themselves. In the statues there is an impression not only of rhythmic movement bridging the gaps between the figures, but of actual violence and turmoil, an impulse that must have started in the missing center of the composition and, as Gruben wrote, communicated itself "like a tidal wave . . . to the Gods reclining at the sides." [62] Harrison explains this "tidal wave" as being an emanation of shock waves from the center of the design, where a blow has been struck by Hephaestus, freeing Athena from the head of Zeus. The sudden revelation of a fully armed Athena has instantaneous repercussions over land, sea, and throughout the heavens—in fact, throughout the entire cosmos—these regions being represented allegorically by the figures of deities appearing on either side of the actors in the center. Harrison, in her reconstruction of the design, has captured the excitement we feel in the fragments of the pedimental sculptures, an accomplishment that should have important consequences for any new treatment of the history of classical Greek art.

In her reconstruction, Harrison makes a number of new suggestions concerning the identities of the preserved pedimental fragments. Among the most interesting is the identification of the beau-

---

61. For example, Rhys Carpenter, "The Lost Statues of the East Pediment of the Parthenon," *Hesperia*, II (1933), pp. 62 ff. For additional bibliography on the restorations, see Evelyn B. Harrison's footnotes in this volume.

62. Berve and Gruben, *op. cit. (supra,* n. 3), p. 379.

tiful Laborde head in the Louvre (fig. 54, text fig. 53) as the head of Amphitrite. This head is the only female head belonging to the pedimental statues that has survived, and it is, therefore, of great importance to the study of classical sculpture. Its authenticity does not seem to be in doubt.[63]

When we consider the position of the Parthenon sculptures in the history of art, certain points stand out clearly. The cosmic setting of Athena's birth, circumscribed by the chariots of the rising sun (fig. 45) and setting moon provided a new conception of scale and a new internal temporal and dynamic unity to the scene. Our sense of time and place as a background for events in the context of pictorial narrative seems to have been reinterpreted by Pheidias in accordance with the principles developed by the fifth-century tragedians, intensifying the dramatic impact and the monumentality of sculptural representations. The scope of monumental art was widened, and allegory was placed on a new level where a more abstract symbolic vocabulary might function. Motifs involving a complex dramatic action and including many interlocking figures, in contrast to the calmly posed and isolated groups of the earlier Severe style (the style of the pediments from the Temple of Zeus at Olympia), might now be included in a greatly enriched repertory of allegorical symbols and forms. Pheidias invented the plastic means by which a scene composed of many parts could be transformed into a single powerful image. He showed how draperies could be given a formal value as a unifying principle within a design (fig. 49), and how its rhythms could be controlled and superimposed one upon another in order to suggest overtones of expressive meaning (fig. 52). He showed how even the musculature of a figure could be transformed by means of formal emphasis (figs. 46, 47, 55), resulting almost in a kind of Michelangelesque distortion full of unlimited power. The sense of internal compositional unity is so strong in the pedimental

63. Another head, with certain stylistic similarities to the Laborde head and also of Pentelic marble, was found by Charles Lenormant in 1846, among the collections of the French Royal Library, which were, at that time, in great disorder after decades of neglect. The provenance of the piece has never been discovered, but Lenormant believed it to belong to a nymph from the pediments of the Parthenon. His son, François Lenormant, published it as such: "Tête du fronton occidental du Parthénon," *Gazette Archéologique*, I (1875), pp. 1 ff. This attribution is not valid, and the head, now in the Cabinet des Médailles in the Bibliothèque Nationale in Paris, today bears a label that reads "Tête d'Apollon" and is described in the new catalogue (unpublished) as a work from the late classical period. The Laborde head was discovered in Venice in the nineteenth century and may very well have been carried there by one of Morosini's soldiers.

figures of the Parthenon that it is possible to see this unity as an end in itself, an ideal of architectural sculpture. Yet the dichotomy between form and subject matter, which was a natural result of the Pheidian discoveries, never became an explicit concern of artists in Greece, as it would in the modern period. Curiously enough, an increased awareness of the expressive potentialities of the formal and abstract elements of design had the opposite effect at first. The ambitions of the classical Greek artist with regard to subject matter, his desire to explore the expressive potentialities of traditional themes, seem to have increased, even while the technical powers placed in his hands made it possible for him to go beyond tradition.

Thus Pheidias, in the Parthenon, enabled the sculptor to compete with poetry in the handling of thematic material, and a new relationship between the artist and his audience can be dated from this moment. Beginning with the sculptures of the Parthenon, the attention of the viewer is more directly focused on the formal means appropriate to art and on the sculptural performance per se. At the same time, the demand of the viewer for narrative details in art was reduced as his interest was awakened by the expressive possibilities of the formal aspects of design.

In describing the position of the Parthenon in the history of Greek art it is important to realize that although Vitruvius and other ancient critics considered the design of the building canonical, its special proportional properties were never actually imitated by later Greek architects, any more than was the special music of the sculptures imitated by Pheidias' successors. The achievement of the Parthenon masters did not bring the development of art and architecture to a standstill by inspiring mere imitation. On the contrary, the immediate effect of the Parthenon was to stimulate originality and experimentation. As Charles Picard has said: "There were as many dissidents as there were disciples among the followers of Pheidias." [64]

In sculpture, the most conspicuous example of the way the Pheidian style opened up new paths during succeeding decades may be observed in the handling of drapery (figs. 38, 48–53). The lavish use of drapery in classical works of art, with richly detailed concentrations of folds emphasizing form and movement, is always reminiscent of the art of the Parthenon because it was the sculpture of the Parthenon that most fully suggested the expressive and decorative possibilities inherent in such motifs. [65] Such contemporary and later masters as

64. Charles Picard, *La Sculpture*, vol. III of *Manuel d'archéologie grecque*, 4 vols. (Paris, 1948), pt. I, p. 1.
65. See the chapter on classical draperies in Rhys Carpenter, *Greek Sculpture: A Critical Review* (Chicago, 1960), pp. 109 ff.

Paionios, Scopas, and Praxiteles all seem to have recognized the principle involved without imitating Pheidian rhythms and compositional devices. Each artist invented variations of his own, finding it possible, by altering the formal rendering of draperies in some subtle but decisive manner, to make in his own art a personal statement. The expression of individual artistic personality on this level may be dated earlier, in the generation of Calamis and Myron, but it is in the Parthenon sculptures that we may first recognize a conscious and explicit understanding of the formal means of such expression.

In architecture, the major impact of the Parthenon in the classical period occurred on the level of theoretical principles. The theoretical approach to design in architecture—indeed, the very activity of the architect—now had a new frame of reference that, as in sculpture, included the possibility of a personal statement. The most important and far-reaching new principle of design in the Parthenon was embodied in a more thorough blending of the Doric and Ionic orders, a phenomenon that can be traced back to the second half of the sixth century B.C. Not only was a very prominent feature of the Ionic order—the continuous frieze—introduced unexpectedly into a Doric composition, but the bold contours of the traditional Doric temple were everywhere softened and restrained by a sense of Ionic elegance. Many of the architectural masterpieces of the fourth century B.C. (for example, the tholos at Epidaurus) continued this principle of creating new harmonies by blending the orders, bringing into formal balance architectural and decorative motifs from a variety of different sources.

The design of the Parthenon, with its ideal numerical ratio unifying all the parts of the structure, is as perfect an expression of architectural beauty as Ictinus and Pheidias could make it. Yet a comparison of its design with that of the older Parthenon clearly reveals the manner in which the architects struggled to overcome the traditional formulas that had applied to earlier temples. Here, Greek architects—not for the first time, but more successfully—reacted against the defects of the traditional peripteral form—a closed prism with a longitudinal axis, surrounded by an open colonnade. In the Parthenon they were able to introduce changes that resolved the main difficulties of such a design while retaining the basic tradition. The new design was, in a sense, perfection; yet succeeding generations of Greek artists, while recognizing that perfection, never actually copied it. More important to them than any ideal perfection was the process of change itself.

Thus the Parthenon, like the canon of Polyclitus, did not, in reality, become standard. It had, rather, the character of a gathering of forces, a work in which the most important developments of fifth-century art were embodied and given for the first time a clear and unequivocal statement. The result was a new understanding of the possibilities inherent in such a work, and this in turn produced a series of changes that could only end in infinite variety—the variety of artistic modes of expression that, indeed, characterized the later periods of antiquity. The designers of the Parthenon gave definition to a new concept of art as it had been gradually formulated in earlier generations, a concept that already contained the seeds for many of the forms of artistic expression mankind has witnessed in more recent periods.

V. J. B.

HISTORY, ARCHEOLOGICAL
ANALYSIS, AND CRITICISM

HISTORY

RUSSELL MEIGGS
The Political Implications of the Parthenon—[1963] *

In the following essay, Professor Meiggs reinterprets the ancient literary sources pertaining to the Parthenon and the men who built it. As we read his study it becomes increasingly clear that the Parthenon was planned and constructed against a background of controversial political issues then troubling the Athenian democracy.

WHEN the main Greek army that had been sent forward to hold Thermopylai streamed back through Attica, something approaching panic spread through the demes of the city. Soon afterwards they knew that Leonidas and his three hundred Spartans had been killed to a man, fighting a battle that had become hopeless. Thermopylai had fallen, Boeotia had already medized; within days the Persians would be in Attica and the victors of Marathon could expect little mercy. A total evacuation was ordered, but to most Athenians the order was unnecessary. Men, women, and children, clutching what food and belongings they could, made as quickly as possible for the shore or the Megarian border. All available boats were brought into service; the majority of the population of Attica were ferried to Salamis, Aigina, and Troizen, while the Athenian triremes mustered with the Greek fleet at Salamis. Not everyone accepted the inevitable. Doubtless some old people stayed in their demes to take their chance; but a minority had not given up hope. Rising sharply from the plain was the spreading plateau of their Acropolis. Designed by nature for defence, it was, they thought, impregnable.

* Russell Meiggs, "The Political Implications of the Parthenon," in *Parthenos and Parthenon*, ed. G. T. W. Hooker, supplement to vol. X of *Greece and Rome* (Oxford, 1963), pp. 36–45. Reprinted here by permission of the Clarendon Press, Oxford.

Even the small body who remained loyal to the tyrants when the Spartan army invaded in full force to liberate Athens in 510 B.C. had managed to hold out on the Acropolis and surrendered only because their children had been trapped. Delphic Apollo had bidden the Athenians to rely on their wooden walls. Not everyone was convinced by Themistokles that Apollo meant the fleet.

The Athenian crews, waiting nervously at Salamis to know what moves the Persian fleet would make, saw the smoke rising from the Acropolis. They knew that the deserted city and countryside would be sacked; the swift capture of their impregnable fortress was a shock and a surprise. It meant the end of the great new temple that they were building to Athena, and of much else besides. Bitterness was blurred when the Persian ships sailed into the bay of Salamis and ship grappled ship. In the sweat and excitement of battle the ruin of homes and temples could be forgotten; victory did something to compensate. But only the Persian fleet had been beaten; while a strong Persian army remained in Greece Attica was untenable, unless a large Peloponnesian army moved beyond the Isthmus. It was not until Plataia had been won and Mardonios' army in increasing disorder had retreated through Thessaly and Thrace to Asia that Athenians could return home in security. Thucydides tells us that the returning Athenians found their city razed to the ground but for a few buildings where Persian officers had lodged. A thick layer of ash over the Agora is the clearest archaeological evidence of the thoroughness of the destruction: the lower city at the beginning of 479 must have consisted largely of ash and rubble. On the Acropolis the new temple of Athena, conceived in the glow of Marathon, was levelled to the ground; column drums and blocks of marble were scattered on the site.

In the reconstruction of the city the first public building that was undertaken was for defence. Very little is known of the city walls in the archaic period, but the building of the new walls in 478 is vividly described by Thucydides, and enough remains for the archaeologist to understand the general character of the work. As Thucydides leads us to expect, the surviving remains show clear signs of improvisation and haste. The funerary monuments of the Kerameikos had almost certainly been levelled in the Persian sack; many of them, including fine marble reliefs and elegant archaic dedicatory inscriptions, were incorporated in the walls. The building of the new city walls was accompanied by a hasty repair of the Acropolis defences, and here too material from the sack was used. Looking up from the Agora to the north face of the Acropolis one sees a wall of strangely assorted stones irregularly packed together, but in the irregularity the eye focuses on a stretch of deliberate order. Near the top, embedded in the wall, is a conspicuous line of thick column drums. These are not packed together at random; they are deliberately placed in line to catch the eye. The Athenians knew that these were to have been the columns of their new temple of Athena. This was their war memorial, and on the top the ruined temple remained in ruins. Twenty years later this site still remained in ruins. Why?

The fourth-century orators knew the answer. Before the battle of Plataia the Greeks had sworn that they would not rebuild the temples destroyed by the Persians, but would leave them as an everlasting memorial of the barbarians' sacrilege. The orators could even quote the oath:

> I will not set life before freedom, nor will I desert my leaders alive or dead, but I will give burial to all the allies who die in the battle. And having conquered the barbarians in the war, I will not raze to the ground any city that has fought in defence of Greece, but all those who have chosen the barbarian's side I will tithe. And I will not rebuild any of the temples that have been burnt and destroyed by the barbarians, but I will let them be left as a memorial to those who come after of the sacrilege of the barbarians.[1]

When strong appeals were needed in the fourth century to stir up patriotism a copy of the oath, together with the oath that the ephebes swore, was inscribed on a marble stele and set up in the temple of Ares at Acharnai, where it was discovered a generation ago.[2] This text has no reference to the burnt temples, but since the main purpose of publication was to revive pride in Athenian courage, this omission need cause no surprise; in other respects the inscribed text differs only in minute points from the versions in the orators.

Theopompos, the savage and undiscriminating fourth-century critic of Athenian democracy, ridiculed the oath as one of Athens' many patriotic inventions; and modern scholars, with few exceptions, have been very content to follow his lead. It is true that some of the clauses carry little conviction, but even if the fourth-century version of the oath rings false it does not necessarily follow that no such oath was taken. As excavation extends, the number of religious sites that are found to have remained in ruins until the middle of the century grows impressively. To the temples on the Acropolis must be added, for example, the altar of the Twelve Gods,

1. Lycurgus, *Leocr.* 81.
2. M. N. Tod, *Greek Historical Inscriptions* (Oxford, 1933–48), ii, No. 204.

the temple of Apollo Patroos, and the Metroon in the Agora; a temple of Hephaistos (not quite certainly attested) on Kolonos hill overlooking the Agora; and in Attica a temple of Hera and another of Demeter on the road from Phaleron to Athens, and the temple of Apollo at Sounion. Since the only exceptions so far known are the Eleusinia at Eleusis and Athens, in both of which there was almost certainly new building between the Persian War and the middle of the century, the goddesses of the Mysteries may have been especially exempt from what was otherwise a general rule.

We have to ask, however, not only why the gods were apparently neglected for more than twenty years, but why after such long neglect there was, as it seems, a sudden outburst of temple-building near the middle of the century. Admittedly only one of the new temples can be precisely dated. In the developed Athenian democracy the commissioners appointed by the demos to supervise public building were required to publish their accounts and set them up where everyone could see them, and the surviving fragments of the Parthenon accounts date the first year's expenditure by the commissioners to 447/6. This was the year in which the quarrying of the marble began, though the planning preliminaries may have taken a year or more. It was not until he was appointed by the demos that the architect could get to work securely on his plans, and before work on the building was begun his plans had to be approved. The decision to build the Parthenon could have been taken as early as 448 or 449. Less precision is possible in the dating of the other temples, for we rely on archaeological evidence alone; but there is good reason to believe that the Parthenon was but part of a large-scale building programme. From the pottery associated with the foundations of the temple of Hephaistos, overlooking the Agora, a date *c.* 450 has been inferred, and the style of the building suggests that it was started earlier but influenced by the Parthenon in its later stages. We cannot, however, necessarily conclude that this temple was started earlier, for we are dealing with two different architects. At roughly the same date, to judge by its architecture, a new temple of Ares also was built. It was transferred stone by stone to the Agora in the Roman period, but originally it was built elsewhere in the city or in Attica. A near-contemporary was the temple of Apollo at Sounion, probably by the same architect as the Hephaisteion; and the temple of Nemesis at Rhamnous may be the next and last in his series.

The simplest hypothesis to explain why there was such a long delay in temple building in the period following the Persian Wars is that the Athenians, with the other Greeks, had taken an oath that they would not rebuild the temples destroyed by the Persians. The

simplest hypothesis to explain the outburst of new building in the forties is that peace had been made with Persia, the Peace of Kallias, and
that the Athenians considered that this peace freed them from their
oath. An interesting document reflected in Plutarch's *Perikles* gives
point and conviction to the hypothesis. Chapter 17 of the *Perikles* fits
very loosely to what precedes and what follows. Plutarch has been
describing the greatness of Perikles when he turns aside to quote a
spectacular illustration of his *megalophrosyne:*

> When the Spartans were beginning to resent the growth of
> Athenian power Perikles proposed a decree inviting all Greeks
> wheresoever in Europe or Asia, cities small and great, to send rep-
> resentatives to a congress at Athens to discuss the Greek temples
> which the barbarians burnt, the sacrifices which they vowed to the
> gods when they fought the barbarians but had not yet made, and
> the sea, that all might sail in security and keep the peace. For this
> purpose twenty men over fifty years of age were sent out, of
> whom five were dispatched to the Ionians and Dorians in Asia and
> islanders as far as Lesbos and Rhodes; five to the Hellespont and
> Thrace as far as Byzantium; and five also to Boeotia, Phokis,
> and the Peloponnese, and from the Peloponnese through Lokris to
> the neighbouring country as far as Akarnania and Amprakia. The
> remaining five proceeded through Euboea to the Oitaians and the
> Malian Gulf and the Phthiotians and Thessalians. They were to
> urge them all to come and take part in counsel for the preserva-
> tion of peace and the welfare of Greece.

This is the language not of a literary source but of an inscription, and
it is probable that Plutarch had himself seen and been impressed by
this decree, which is not recorded or reflected in any other literary
source that has survived. He may have seen it while glancing through
Krateros' collection of Attic decrees, or even in a Hellenistic edition
of the decrees of Perikles. There is no proof that the document is
genuine, and there was undoubtedly a disturbing tendency in the
fourth century to fill out Athenian fifth-century history with cir-
cumstantial 'documents'; but the terms of this decree are at least very
plausible and they should be accepted until they are disproved. The
agenda of the congress was therefore to discuss the vows for sacrifices made at the time of the Persian War, the rebuilding of the temples destroyed by the Persians, and the policing of the seas for the
maintenance of peace. The last two problems in particular make better sense if they arise from making peace with Persia. Plutarch tells
us that the Spartans were the first to suspect and refuse the invitation; the congress was not held. We may infer that Perikles could
claim this failure to secure the general co-operation of Greece in

solving common problems as a justification for Athens' taking unilateral action. Another document, reflected in a papyrus fragment from Egypt, tells us that Perikles carried in 450/49 a decree in the assembly that the accumulated reserve of the Delian League, which had been transferred from Delos to the Athenian Acropolis in 454, should be used for the rebuilding of Athens' destroyed temples.

This was a far-reaching decision, and we could expect political controversy: Plutarch records in colourful language a heated debate in the Athenian assembly. Thucydides, son of Melesias, had assumed the leadership of the opposition to radical democracy when Kimon died in Cyprus, and through the early forties fought Perikles for the control of the assembly until the issue was decided by his ostracism in 443. Thucydides and his followers protested vigorously against the use on Athenian buildings of money contributed by the allies for the war against Persia:

> They cried out that the people were dishonoured and in bad repute for bringing the common funds of the Greeks from Delos to Athens; and what could be the fairest of answers to the critics, that it was in fear of the barbarians that they removed them and were guarding the common funds in safety, Perikles had made impossible. 'And Greece seems to be the victim of monstrous and manifest tyranny, when she sees us using what she is forced to contribute for the war to gild and deck our city like a wanton woman, decorating her with costly stones and statues, and thousand-talent temples.' But Perikles pointed out to the people that they owed no account to the allies for the money, so long as they protected them and kept out the barbarians. The allies contributed not a horse, not a ship, not a hoplite, but money only; and this belonged not to those who gave it but to those to whom it was given, provided they fulfilled the services for which the money was given. And when the city was adequately equipped with what she needed for war she should turn her resources to undertakings which would bring undying glory when they were completed, and would provide prosperity while they were being built; for every kind of workmanship would be required, and services of many kinds, which would stimulate all the crafts and give employment to all hands, and so give pay to almost the whole city, decorating and maintaining herself from her own resources.

After an almost imperceptible break Plutarch explains the social and economic aspects of the policy:

> For military expeditions brought good pay to the young and strong; and as he did not want the undisciplined artisan class to be without some share in the rewards, nor to take them while doing

nothing and remaining idle, Perikles carried in the assembly great building projects and undertakings involving many crafts; so the people who stayed at home might take their share of the benefit from the public funds no less than the crews and the garrisons and the expeditionary forces. The raw materials were stone, bronze, ivory, gold, ebony, cypress-wood, and to fashion and work them were the crafts: carpenters, moulders, coppersmiths, stone-workers, goldsmiths, ivory-workers, painters, pattern-weavers, workers in relief. Then there were the men engaged in transport and carriage, merchants, sailors, helmsmen by sea, and by land cartwrights, and men who kept yokes of beasts, and drovers; rope makers, flax-workers, shoemakers, roadmakers, and miners. And each craft, like a general with his own army, had its own crowd of hired workers and individual craftsmen organized like an instrument and body for the service to be performed; so, in a word, the various needs to be met distributed and spread prosperity through every age and condition.[3]

Plutarch enjoyed writing this purple passage, and we can enjoy it too; but the widespread view that it derives from a good contemporary source needs re-examination. Those at least who believe in a Peace of Kallias should scrutinize the credentials of the debate rigorously, for in Plutarch's account there is no clear indication of any peace at all; the natural implication is that tribute is still being paid towards a war that is still being fought. In any debate on the use of the allies' money for Athenian building the peace with Persia, if peace there was, must surely have been a crucial focus of argument. It is not an unfair question to ask who the fifth-century source will have been whom Plutarch directly or indirectly used; for Thucydides assures us that the only Athenian history before his own of the period between the Persian and Peloponnesian Wars was written by Hellanikos, whose account was brief and careless in chronology, and we think we know the other main sources of the period, Ion of Chios and Stesimbrotos of Thasos, who are both quoted by Plutarch. Ion, a tragic poet who had his plays produced at Athens and was given Athenian citizenship, was a versatile writer, who included in his minor writings a collection of anecdotes concerning famous characters and events of his own lifetime. Stesimbrotos wrote a pamphlet *On Themistokles, Thucydides* [son of Melesias], and *Perikles*; the fragments that survive suggest a vitriolic critic of Perikles and Athenian democracy. Stesimbrotos can almost certainly be ruled out, for it would be completely inconsistent with what we know of his writing if he had produced such a favourable picture of Perikles.

3. *Per.* 12.1–7.

The same objection makes Ion an improbable source, for he too seems to have had little love for Perikles. Nor does the recording of a whole debate seem to suit the anecdotal character of his memoirs. He did, however, record Kimon's famous plea in the Athenian assembly when Sparta appealed for help to reduce her helots on Ithome: 'Athens must not allow Greece to go lame nor Athens to lose her yoke-fellow.'[4] It is not impossible that the vivid language of Thucydides' attack stems ultimately from Ion of Chios. Perikles' reply rouses much stronger suspicion. This type of rhetoric does not fit our picture of the Olympian: the allies provide 'not a horse, not a ship, not a hoplite, but only money'; but Chios, Lesbos, and Samos still provided ships when required, and in the fifties some of the allies had provided hoplites. The central substance of the answer could be Periklean, but even so it will have been considerably elaborated. Nor should we be surprised if the source of this speech were found in the fourth century or later. Cicero was at one time satisfied that Roman gentlemen interested in the history of oratory could consult some of the original speeches of Perikles.[5] A hundred years later Quintilian could assume that they were forgeries, and this was no temporary scepticism; Plutarch thought he knew that all that survived of Perikles' writings and sayings were his decrees and a handful of memorable sayings.[6] The speeches in Plutarch probably derive from a later rhetorical reappraisal, perhaps composed when building policies were under discussion. Cicero tells us that Demetrios of Phaleron attacked the extravagance of the Propylaea.[7] The late fourth century, the generation of Theophrastos, would be an appropriate setting for this reconstruction of a famous occasion; but there are other contexts in the Hellenistic period that it would fit just as well.

But even if there is no fifth-century source behind Plutarch's debate, nor even behind the argument and language he attributes to Thucydides, we can at least be sure that the reserve of the Delian League was in fact used for the rebuilding of the Acropolis. It would have been impossible for Athens from her own resources to finance the almost feverish building activity of the forties, and the inscriptions imply that she did not. When the large island of Samos revolted from Athens in 440, more than 1,200 talents were paid out by the treasurers of Athena; and it was the treasurers of Athena who made the most important payments to the commissioners of the Parthenon, and of Pheidias' great chryselephantine statue of Athena. By

4. Plut. *Kimon* 16. 10.
5. Plut. *Per.* 8. 7; Quint. iii. 1. 12.
6. *De Or.* ii. 93.
7. *Off.* ii. 60.

the forties the main Athenian reserve is technically Athena's money; most of it must have come from Delos. That some Athenians should have felt serious qualms about this use of allied money is not unnatural, and even if the arguments attributed by Plutarch to Thucydides' followers are invented in a rhetorical school, they are a convincing invention. But it would be naïve to believe that the moral aspect of the case was the only one that concerned the oligarchs. At the time of the battle of Tanagra in the early fifties, they had realized the strategic implications of the building of long walls from Athens to the Peiraeus, and some of the extremists had even negotiated with Sparta.[8] When Perikles outlined his building policy it was not difficult to see the economic and social implications. The distribution of so much money among the craftsmen and unskilled workers would give them an economic independence which would be politically dangerous. State pay for jury service and state offices was bad enough; state pay for the work of the working class was going too far. It is not surprising that Thucydides' objections were overruled; too many voting Athenians had too much to gain.

Once the principle of using the allies' money for the Parthenon and other buildings had been accepted, other grounds of opposition had to be found by Thucydides. Our only evidence comes from Plutarch, but his account, which is usually neglected, deserves respect. The main ground of attack that led to the ostracism, according to Plutarch, was the extravagance of Perikles' building programme. The speakers of Thucydides' party protested loudly against Perikles. He was, they said, 'draining the city's resources and destroying its revenues'. Perikles' reply is also given by Plutarch: 'He asked them in the assembly if they thought that the expense was heavy, and when they said "Very heavy indeed", he said: "Let the expense then be not yours but mine, and these buildings that we are dedicating will have my name inscribed on them." ' The response was unequivocal: 'They cried out that the expenditure must come from public money and that in guiding their building policy he should spare nothing.'[9] By a nice coincidence a large fragment of an Athenian decree survives which records that, probably, in the thirties, Perikles and his family offered to pay for some building or other public work in Athens, but that the people declined the offer and ruled that the money should come from the tribute paid by the allies.[10] Several modern scholars have seen in this decree the origin of Plutarch's story of Perikles' offer, but we should not follow them. The main objection to this view is not that Plutarch would have mistaken the

8. Thuc. i. 107. 4.
9. Plut. *Per.* 14 1f.
10. *I.G.* i². 54.

context, for such mistakes Plutarch is very apt to make, but that it shrivels the whole point of the story. Perikles is asking the people for a vote of confidence in the detailed public responsibility assigned to the demos by the reforms of Ephialtes. It is no accident that the earliest accounts on marble of public buildings that have survived seem to date from the years following the radical reforms of Ephialtes in 462. They illustrate an important aspect of the principles he embodied. In the years between the invasion of Xerxes and Ephialtes' new laws there was little new public construction in Athens, but most of the buildings we hear of are associated with individual members of distinguished families. The Stoa Poikile, which was probably completed in the sixties, was originally called the Peisianakteion, and Peisianax was an Alkmaionid. It was Kimon who transformed the Academy, planted plane trees in the Agora, and built up the south wall of the Acropolis from the spoils of the Eurymedon. A temple of Artemis of Good Counsel was built by Themistokles. This was still an age of aristocratic patronage, and to Ephialtes and his party such patronage was undemocratic. It was the demos in its assembly that should decide what public buildings were to be built, and who should build them. Commissioners elected by the people should supervise the progress of the work and its financing. Their accounts should be controlled by public auditors chosen by the people, and should be publicly summarized on stone and set up where all who wished could see them.

The fragments of the Parthenon accounts bear witness to the principle of popular control inaugurated by Ephialtes. The assembly's part is more vividly illustrated in the decree that records the decision to build a new temple to Athena Nike in the early forties:

> [Glau]kos moved that a priestess for Athena Nike should be appointed . . . from among all Athenian women, and that the Athenians should provide a doorway for the sanctuary according to a specification to be drawn up by Kallikrates, and the *poletai* should let out the contract during the prytany of Leontis. And the priestess should receive fifty drachmae [a year] and she should receive also the legs and hides of the public victims. And the Athenians should build a temple according to a specification to be drawn up by Kallikrates and an altar of stone. Hestiaios moved that they elect three men to the Boule, and these should work with Kallikrates on the plan and report to the Boule how the work should be leased out.

The spirit of Hestiaios' amendment is perhaps uncertain, but it looks very like the suspicion of the amateur and the administrator for the professional. Whatever the implications of the wording, the procedure is essentially democratic. However much guidance they received from their leaders, the people could have rejected the architect suggested to them, and later they could have questioned in court the account of the commissioners they had themselves chosen.

The Parthenon was the creation of a free democracy, initiated, controlled, and approved by the popular assembly and its judicial organs. The name of Perikles was not inscribed on it; but to all succeeding ages, the Parthenon is a Periklean building. As Thucydides the historian saw, during this brief generation Athens enjoyed the forms of democracy but was guided by a single man's leadership.

Bibliography

There is a good short fifth-century building history of Athens by Ida Thallon Hill in *The Ancient City of Athens* (London, 1953). Some of the political implications are discussed by B. D. Meritt, H. T. Wade-Gery, and M. F. McGregor in *The Athenian Tribute-Lists* (Cambridge, Mass. 1939–53), iii. 275–300. The more controversial issues, including the genuineness of the Plataian oath and the reliability of Plutarch, lightly sketched above, will be more fully discussed in a forthcoming book on the Athenian Empire.

CHARLES MITCHELL
Ciriaco d'Ancona: Fifteenth-Century Drawings and Descriptions of the Parthenon—[1973] *

Apart from Jacques Carrey's precious series of drawings made in 1674, there are only three extant drawings of the Parthenon that date from before the devastating explosion of 1687. They derive from the eccentric fifteenth-century Italian traveler and antiquary Ciriaco d'Ancona. All three drawings depict the west front of the temple. Charles Mitchell examines these drawings in their manuscript context, assesses their accuracy, and discusses their relation to the visits Ciriaco made to Athens in the fifteenth century. Professor Mitchell is chairman of the department of the history of art at Bryn Mawr College.

The first traveler since antiquity to describe the Parthenon, and the first man we know of to record any of its architecture and sculpture in drawings, was the sharp-eyed, eccentric antiquary and papal diplomatic agent Ciriaco d'Ancona (*ca.* 1391–*ca.* 1455). We know for

* Written especially for this volume.

certain that he visited Athens twice. The first visit was in April, 1436, in the course of an extended tour of Greece which brought him back to Venice in August, 1436.[1] In the following year he again visited Greece, making a tour of the Peloponnesus where his last recorded stop was at Mistra in September; and it is possible that he again saw the Parthenon on his way home, though of this we cannot by any means be sure because the next recorded date in his biography is September, 1438, when he was at home in Ancona.[2] His second definitely attested visit to Athens was in February, 1444, when he was on his way to interview the sultan at Adrianople, whence he proceeded to Constantinople in order to discuss the war against the Turks with John VIII Palaeologus, the Byzantine emperor.[3]

Ciriaco made primary records of what he did and saw on his various journeys in a series of diaries or *commentaria*, and he also apparently kept rough notebooks of the *parerga*—drafts of letters, literary extracts, etc.—incidental to his tours.[4] Of his original autograph diaries the only surviving example is a section of Trotti MS. 373 in the Ambrosian Library in Milan, dealing with his journeys in the Peloponnesus in 1447–48. This contains both text and drawings, and it is of the highest value as a touchstone of how Ciriaco would record his archeological finds and observations for his personal use.[5] But as well as being an original recorder of antiquities, he was also an ardent publicist; and he put a great deal of time and energy into making extracts and compilations from his basic records either for his own more permanent and formal literary record or for circulation—sometimes in very fine and elegant form—to his patrons and friends.

1. For Ciriaco, generally see now E. W. Bodnar, *Cyriacus of Ancona and Athens*, Collection Latomus, XLIII (Brussels-Berchem, 1960), *passim*. On his first visit to Athens, *ibid.*, pp. 35 ff., and *id.*, "Athens in April 1436," *Archaeology*, XXIII (1970), pp. 96–105, 188–199.

2. Bodnar, *Cyriacus*, pp. 48–49.

3. *Ibid.*, pp. 51–53.

4. Ciriaco's rough notebook of the Greek tour of 1436 survives in an autograph manuscript: see P. Maas, "Ein Notizbuch des Cyriacus von Ancona aus dem Jahre 1436," *Beiträge zur Forschung . . . aus dem Antiquariat Jacques Rosenthal*, I. Folge, Heft 1 (Munich, 1913), pp. 5–15.

5. On the Trotti MS see R. Sabbadini, "Ciriaco d'Ancona e la sua descrizione autografa del Peloponneso trasmessa da Leonardo Botta," *Miscellanea Ceriani* (Milan, 1910), pp. 183–247 (with illustrations), and Bodnar, *Cyriacus*, pp. 117–118. Ciriaco's fidelity as a draftsman in the Parthenon and other drawings is discussed by Bernard Ashmole, "Cyriac of Ancona," *Proceedings of the British Academy*, XLV (1958), pp. 25–41.

Our evidence for Ciriaco's first visit to Athens comes from four sources. The first is the print of a seventeenth-century transcript by Carlo Morone, the Barberini librarian, from a lost codex that incorporated something very close to Ciriaco's *commentaria* on his Greek tours of 1435–36 and 1436–37, which were evidently extensive with regard to both textual matter and drawings.[6] Morone's exemplar lacked drawings or indications of them in the Athenian section, but it included Ciriaco's description of his arrival in Athens and his sight of the Parthenon:

> On April 7th [1436] I came to Athens, where I first viewed huge walls everywhere collapsed with age; and inside the city and in the country round about I saw incredible marble buildings, houses and sacred shrines, various works of figured sculpture conspicuous for their fine workmanship, and vast columns—all fallen in massive ruins. But what pleased me most of all was the great and marvellous marble temple of the goddess Pallas on the topmost citadel of the city, a divine work by Phidias, which has fifty-eight towering columns, each seven feet in diameter, and is splendidly adorned with the noblest images on all sides which you see superbly carved on both fronts, on the friezes on the walls, and on the epistyles [i.e., metopes].[7]

Second, on folio 25 of MS. 1191 in the Palatine Library in Parma—a codex that contains no drawings but leaves spaces which show that there were drawings or spaces for them in its exemplar—we have a description of the Parthenon very similar to the Morone version except that it is transposed into the third person and gives no date for Ciriaco's arrival in Athens.[8] Third, the first visit to Athens is recorded in a copiously attested tradition of shorter extracts from the 1435–37 journals, a tradition traced back by Mommsen to a lost archetype (the *Antiquum Venetum*), which Bodnar has now convincingly identified as a volume compiled by Ciriaco for a member of the Venetian Contarini family.[9] This volume, as we shall see, was evidently illustrated by drawings. Fourth, there is Hamilton MS. 454 in the Berlin Staatsbibliothek, a splendid antiquarian miscellany

6. [Carlo Morone], *Epigrammata reperta per Illyricum a Cyriaco Anconitano* (Rome [Franciscus Moneta], ca. 1654). (Moneta published a volume of *Inscriptiones antiquae Basilicae S. Pauli ad Viam Ostiensem*, with the same layout and type face, in Rome in 1654.) On Morone see Bodnar, *Cyriacus*, pp. 78–87 and *passim*.

7. Morone, p. 37; Bodnar, *Cyriacus*, p. 35.

8. See Bodnar, *Cyriacus*, pp. 106–110.

9. *Ibid.*, pp. 95–106.

written on vellum, of which the seventh gathering at least (fols. 81–
90) was put together by Ciriaco himself, with the help of another
scribe and probably another draftsman, for presentation to Pietro
Donato, the bishop of Padua (d. 1447).[10] This section of the manuscript consists mostly of extracts, with text and drawings, from the
1435–37 *commentaria*, and the main bulk of its text, along with another isolated entry on folio 121ᵛ, was unquestionably penned by
Ciriaco in the large idiosyncratic hand he customarily used on formal
occasions. On folio 85ᵛ we have a drawing of the Parthenon (text fig.
4) accompanied by a first-person description that is substantially the
same as what we find in Morone, except that it gives April 6 as the
date of Ciriaco's arrival in Athens and makes special mention at the
end of the "scenes of fighting centaurs" carved on the "epistyles." [11]

For Ciriaco's second recorded visit to Athens in February, 1444—
the original *commentaria* being lost and no derivatives of them having
survived—our fullest evidence comes from an anonymous fifteenth-
century transcript of a letter that Ciriaco wrote about a month later,
on March 29, from Chios. It is addressed to his friend and supporter
Andreolo Giustiniani, the Genoese governor of the island, and it tells
how, having re-examined the Tower of the Winds, he had introduced
himself to Nerio Acciaiuoli, the prince of Athens, in the latter's palace on the Acropolis (built into the Propylaea, which Ciriaco much
admired and described in considerable architectural detail) and had
once more investigated the Parthenon:

> But what I most wanted to do on revisiting that splendid citadel
> was more carefully to examine from every angle that most noble
> temple of the goddess Pallas, which is built of solid polished
> marble and which, as we know from Aristotle's words to king
> Alexander, from our own Roman Pliny, and from many other
> good ancient writers, is a wondrous work of Phidias. . . . This
> excellent and marvellous temple survives to this day with fifty-
> eight columns, twelve on each front (so arranged that there are
> double rows of six in the middle at either end), and seventeen
> each side outside the walls, all these columns being five feet in
> diameter. Between the columns along the sides and the inner walls
> are passages for walking, each five feet wide. Above the columns
> are epistyles nine and a half feet long and four feet high, on

10. See Adolf Michaelis, "Eine Originalzeichnung des Parthenon von
Cyriacus von Ancona," *Archaeologische Zeitung*, XL (1882), pp. 367–383;
T. Mommsen, "Über die berliner Excerptenhandschrift des Petrus Dona-
tus," *Jahrbuch der preuss. Kunstsammlungen*, IV (1883), pp. 73–89; Bodnar,
Cyriacus, pp. 84–85 and *passim*.
11. *Epistilia* seems to mean "metopes."

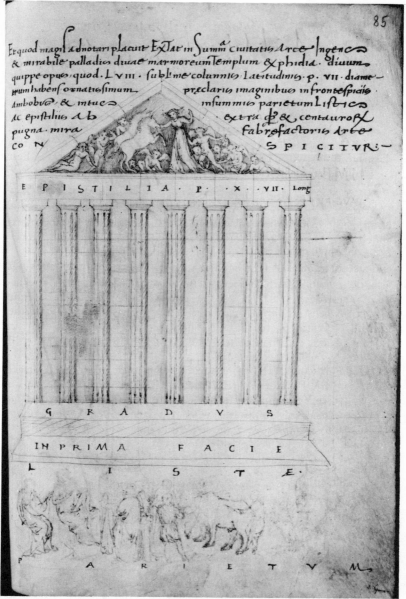

4. West front and parts of the frieze of the Parthenon. Silverpoint and ink drawing by Ciriaco d'Ancona. Berlin, Deutsche Staatsbibliothek, Hamilton MS. 454, fol. 85ᵛ.

which you see superbly carved sculptures of the Thessalian battles of the Centaurs and Lapiths, while on the frieze placed
high on the inner walls about two cubits from the top, that great
artist Phidias has magnificently represented the victories of
Athens in the time of Pericles, each frieze being about the height
of a ten-year-old boy. Finally, on each of the fronts, you look up
at colossal images of men and horses, entirely filling the two
pediments, which fittingly ornament that vast temple. Of this
magnificent work I have taken care to include a drawing, as best
I could, in the journals of my   present travels through Greece.[12]

Now we come to the drawings, taking the Hamilton drawing first
(text fig. 4). Like three other Athenian drawings in this seventh gathering of the manuscript, it is executed in silverpoint with inscriptions
added with the pen.[13] The other three silverpoints depict the Tower
of the Winds (fol. 88[v]),[14] the monument of Lysicrates (fol. 88[v]),[15]
and a seated figure of Homer (fol. 90[r]); and there are other drawings
also, done wholly with the pen, of the now vanished gateway of Hadrian's aqueduct (fol. 85[v]),[16] the peristyle of the temple of the
Olympian Zeus (fol. 87[v]),[17] and one of the giants that stood near the
Odeum of Agrippa (fol. 88[v]).[18] These pen drawings are clearly in
Ciriaco's hand, and their style is thoroughly consonant with the pen
drawings in the Trotti codex.

The Parthenon drawing represents the west front with select
slabs from the Panathenaic frieze below. It is very inaccurate, as we
can easily see by comparing it with whatever fragments survive and
with the remarkably faithful drawing that Jacques Carrey—observing,
like Ciriaco, from below without scaffolding—made of it in 1674.[19]
The order, it is true, is correctly Doric (except for the fluting of the
columns) and the number of the eight columns is faithful too. But

12. For text and commentary see Bodnar, *Cyriacus*, pp. 50–53.

13. I owe many thanks to Dr. Giovanni Mardersteig for his kindness
in sending me the results of his recent examination of the Hamilton codex,
which I know only from photographs, as regards the distinction of hands
and media in its text and drawings.

14. Reproduced by C. Huelsen, *Il Libro di Giuliano da Sangallo Vati-
cano Barberiniano 4424* (Leipzig, 1910), II, pl. N, and Bodnar, "Athens in
April 1436," p. 192.

15. Repr. Bodnar, "Athens in April 1436," p. 104.

16. Repr. Huelsen, II, pl. M; Ashmole, pl. VIIb; Bodnar, "Athens in
April 1436," p. 196.

17. Repr. Huelsen, II, pl. M; Ashmole, pl. VIIIb.

18. Repr. Huelsen, II, pl. N; Bodnar, "Athens in April 1436," p. 104.

19. For Carrey's drawings and other pictorial records of the Parthenon
see Theodore Bowie and Dieter Thimme, eds., *The Carrey Drawings of
the Parthenon Sculptures* (Bloomington, Ind., 1971).

the metopes and triglyphs are omitted; the proportions of the front are wrong; and so are the details of the pediment sculptures. The scene represented is the contest of Athena and Poseidon, with their horses and attendants, for the land of Athens; and, save for Poseidon's horses, this was still more or less intact in Carrey's day. The Hamilton draftsman, however, entirely omitted Poseidon and simply showed Athena—gesticulating in modish fifteenth-century dress, like a lady in some late Gothic Book of Hours—dominating with her horses the center of the pediment, while he fancifully transformed the attendant figures into winged putti. The drawing of the frieze slabs below, on the other hand, if rather cramped, is much more recognizable,[20] which makes it all the more strange that the draftsman of the pediment got it so wrong.

In view of Ciriaco's general accuracy in the Trotti codex and elsewhere, his authorship of the Hamilton Parthenon drawing has been doubted,[21] but there can be no doubt that it is his handiwork. First, he laid out the lines of the pediment, entablature, columns, and stylobate in silverpoint in a bold, amateurish fashion consistent with that of the Trotti drawings; and at the same time he drew the figures in the pediment, meticulously making sure that Athena's left hand, the head of the left-hand corner figure, and the wings of the two figures to the right did not intersect the lines of the pediment which they overlap. The style of the pediment drawing, it is true, is in some ways unlike that of the Trotti drawings, but there can be no question that it is by the same hand as the one that drew the architecture. Next, when front and pediment were drawn out, Ciriaco himself wrote out the descriptive text at the top of the page, fitting the writing to the triangular shape of the pediment but once or twice encroaching on its boundaries with his pen; and at this stage, before or after he wrote out the text, he inserted the explanatory legends in a style of penmanship that is his alone: "EPISTILLA. P.X.VII. Long." [22] across the entablature; "GRADVS IN PRIMA FACIES" across the stylobate; and "LISTAE PARIETVM" to designate the frieze. (The painterly three-dimensional character of the frieze drawing, incidentally, is so radically different from the pediment drawing above that Ciriaco would appear to have assigned it to an-

20. The left group comes from the east frieze, the next from the north frieze, the oxen from the north frieze also, and the horseman to the right probably from the west frieze.

21. See Ashmole, *op. cit.*

22. Cf. the phrase in the letter to Giustiniani (Bodnar, *Cyriacus*, p. 52): "habent et Columnae desuper Epistilia longitudine p. VIIII cum dimidio, altitudine vero IIII."

other more professional draftsman to execute, presumably from his own rougher drawings.) Thus Ciriaco, whose writing is spread over it from top to bottom, was himself undoubtedly responsible for the layout and for most of the execution of the whole page; and, as regards the pediment drawing in particular, we are forced to the conclusion that, working in silverpoint probably a number of years before he wrote the Trotti *commentarium*, he contrived to draw his always perky and puppetlike figures in a manner somewhat different from the one he employed in his private journals. Such archeology, it is true, is repugnant to us; and it exasperated Mommsen.[23] But it is false to expect Ciriaco to have had the scruples of a nineteenth- or twentieth-century scholar. Accurately as he often recorded antiquities in the first instance, the autograph Hamilton drawing proves

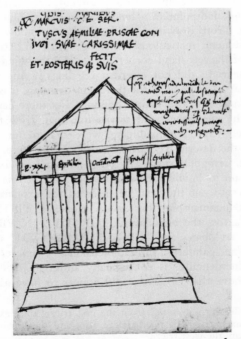

5. West front of the Parthenon. Anonymous drawing after Ciriaco d'Ancona. Marburg, Westdeutsche Bibliothek, MS. Berol. lat. quart. 432 (formerly Manzoni 92), fol. 73ʳ.

23. Mommsen, *op. cit.*, p. 75.

that, for the delectation of a grand patron, he might indulge in playful conceit; and we must recognize this as part and parcel of his vision of antiquity.

A second Parthenon drawing, deriving from Ciriaco (text fig. 5), occurs on folio 73ʳ of MS. Berol. lat. quart. 432 (formerly Manzoni 92) in the Westdeutsche Bibliothek in Marburg—a coarsely and hastily transcribed fifteenth-century antiquarian miscellany which includes a number of Ciriacesque inscriptions and drawings that seem to belong to the Contarini tradition of shorter extracts from the 1435–37 *commentaria*.[24] Wretched as it is, this Manzoni codex is singularly valuable for two reasons. In the first place, it contains three Athenian drawings—the Parthenon, the Olympieum (fol. 78ᵛ),[25] and the gateway of Hadrian's aqueduct (fol. 79ʳ)[26]—that occur in the Hamilton manuscript but not in the other representatives of the tradition of shorter extracts. This suggests that there were drawings in the archetype. In the second place, its drawings of the Olympieum and of Hadrian's aqueduct, for all their incidental scribal errors and crudities of draftsmanship, are more accurate and fuller in explanatory legends than the Hamilton drawings of these monuments.[27] This strongly suggests that the Manzoni drawings— and the Parthenon drawing in particular—are as near as we can get to the original drawings Ciriaco made in April, 1436.

The legend attached to the Manzoni drawing (text fig. 5) briefly summarizes the fact that it was an admirable Pheidian temple of Pallas with fifty-eight columns, each 7 feet in diameter, and that it was adorned with beautiful sculptures;[28] and although the inept draftsman has arbitrarily given the west front of the temple eleven columns instead of eight, the proportions of pediment, columns, and stylobate are generally similar to those in the Hamilton drawing. This indicates that the drawing Ciriaco made in 1436 was similarly proportioned. The Manzoni drawing, however, has no sculpture in the pediment and the explanatory legend across the entablature is different from what we find in the Hamilton drawing, though not inconsistent with it: p.xxi. [a misreading of "xvii"?] /Epistilia/Occidentalis/Facies/Epistilia. This suggests, perhaps not conclusively, that the archetypal drawing was also without figure drawing in the pediment and that it was similarly inscribed.

24. For the Manzoni codex see Huelsen, II, pp. 42-43, and Bodnar, *Cyriacus*, pp. 128–129.
25. Repr. Huelsen, II., fig. 44, and Ashmole, pl. VIIIa.
26. Repr. Huelsen, II., fig. 43, and Ashmole, pl. VIIc.
27. See Huelsen, II, p. 43, for the legends.
28. *Ibid.*, p. 42, for the text.

Third, we have to consider a further Ciriacesque drawing of the Parthenon which differs quite substantially from the Hamilton and Manzoni versions (text fig. 6). This is in Barberini MS. Lat. 4424 in the Vatican Library—the so-called sketchbook of the architect Giuliano da Sangallo.[29] The main bulk of this large folio volume, which Sangallo began to compile in 1465, consists of plans, elevations, and details of antique—and a few modern—Roman buildings drawn with pen and wash by his own hand. But folios 28 and 29, rectos and versos, are quite unlike the rest of the book in matter, layout, and style, and they derive without question from Ciriaco. Here the drawings are again in the hand of Giuliano, but the written matter appears to be in the hand of his son Francesco (b. 1494), which would date the execution of the folios to the early years of the sixteenth century.

6. West front and parts of the Parthenon frieze. Drawing after Ciriaco d'Ancona. Sketchbook of Giuliano da Sangallo. Rome, Vatican Library, Barberini MS. Lat. 4424, fol. 28ᵛ (detail).

29. The substantive publication is Huelsen, *op. cit.*, with a facsimile of the whole in vol. I.

Folio 28ʳ (apart from a fanciful drawing of a Nereid and a couple of Athenian steles) is occupied in the upper half of the page by a large and skillfully contrived, though somewhat amateurish, western elevation of the interior of the Hagia Sophia in Constantinople—a city which, after earlier visits in 1418 and 1425 that can be discounted here, Ciriaco next visited in 1444 and (for a longer stay) at the turn of 1446,[30]—while the lower half of the page shows an equally impressive bird's-eye view of the exterior of the church.[31] Folio 28ᵛ, in two crowded columns, shows alternating descriptions and drawings, in typical Ciriacesque fashion, of sites and monuments he visited in Greece in 1436; and the drawing of the Parthenon appears in the lower half of the right-hand column sandwiched between a drawing of the walls of Eretria in Euboea above it and a drawing of the gate-way of Hadrian's aqueduct in Athens below. Folios 29ʳ and 29ᵛ (apart from a typically Sangallesque plan of Sant' Andrea in Rome at the bottom of folio 29ᵛ) record Athenian and other monuments, in-cluding two which Ciriaco did not see until 1437. The descriptions of the monuments on the two folios are phrased in the third person throughout, and all are undated. What we have here, then, is a copy of a single composite third-person set piece (unless it is conflated from a number of such set pieces) that incorporated materials rang-ing in date from 1436 to 1444, if not later.

Now let us analyse the Parthenon drawing. The descriptive mat-ter above the drawing is practically identical with the Hamilton and Morone versions, except for the transposition of the wording into the third person and the omission of any date. In general layout it is patterned on the same lines as the Hamilton drawing, with the west front shown above and the same selection of frieze slabs below; but the details are very different. The proportions of the pediment and columns are now more authentic, but the columns have acquired composite capitals instead of Doric ones. The pediment is again sculptured, and although Poseidon is still omitted, Athena now wears a more classical dress and the attendant figures are a little closer to the originals and have shed their incongruous wings. The frieze groups, too, are rather better spaced out and clarified. The most con-spicuous difference, however, is the inclusion of six metope sculptures from the south side, at least two of which can be confidently iden-tified.[32] But these metopes are strangely set up in a row above and

30. For the visits to Constantinople see Bodnar, *Cyriacus*, pp. 53–54.
31. Ashmole, pl. XV, reproduces this page, and folio 28ᵛ on pl. III.
32. The first in the row seems to be south metope no. 1 (Frank Brom-mer, *Die Metopen des Parthenon: Katalog und Untersuchung*, 2 vols. [Mainz am Rhein, 1967], pl. 163); the last in the row south metope no. 32 (Brommer, pl. 236).

behind the pediment, and they stand on a row of Composite columns, two of which are just indicated behind the pediment while the outer ones extend on either side and have curiously molded socles projecting from their bases in a way which bears no relation at all to the appearance of the actual building. Finally, there is a different set of explanatory inscriptions. The architrave of the front is inscribed "P.IΛ" [33] and "OCCIDENTALIS FACIES" in a way that partly squares with the Manzoni drawing. Below the metopes, the inscription "P.IΛ/EPISTILIA" is the reverse of what we find on the architrave in the Hamilton drawing. And above the metopes are two inscriptions that appear neither in the Hamilton nor in the Manzoni drawing: "Columnae. p. XVII" and "Ab omni parte templi centauri in foribus." How are we to account for these differences?

Some of them can be demonstrably explained away as inventions imported by Sangallo. What he seems to have had before him was a drawing of the temple front and another drawing—either on the same same sheet or on another—diagrammatically displaying the metopes of the south side. He then conflated and interpreted these data in the light of the Roman antique he already knew, drawing heavily on his knowledge of Roman gateways, triumphal arches, and sculptured attics.[34] From Rome—who knows?—he may have derived the more authentic classical proportions of the Parthenon front, rather than from Ciriaco himself. From Rome he clearly derived the molded pedestals at the bottom of the big columns supporting the row of metopes.[35] And in his own drawings of Roman buildings we find almost exact parallels to the Composite capitals,[36] and to the way he indicates the beginning of fluting at the tops of the columns.[37] But this still leaves us with the more or less faithful drawings of the metope sculptures—which do not occur in the Hamilton or Manzoni drawings—to explain; and it is important to remember that Sangallo could not possibly have invented them himself. He could have got them, at that time in Italy, only from the drawings of Ciriaco. What, precisely, was his source?

This brings us to our last problem, which unfortunately cannot be solved conclusively. Did Sangallo's exemplar or exemplars spring

33. Michaelis is probably right to read this as "P.17."
34. Cf. Sangallo's drawings of the Porta Maggiore (Huelsen, I, fol. 5ʳ), the arch of Constantine (*ibid.*, fol. 19ᵛ), the arch of Septimius Severus (*ibid.*, fol. 21ᵛ), and especially the Borghettaccio on the Via Flaminia (*ibid.*, fol. 36ᵛ).
35. Cf. the monuments cited in the foregoing note.
36. Cf. those in the drawing of the Porta Maggiore (Huelsen, I, fol. 5ʳ).
37. Cf. the drawing of the temple of Augustus at Pozzuoli (Huelsen, I, fol. 6ᵛ).

from Ciriaco's first visit to Athens in 1436, or possibly from another sight of the Parthenon on his return from the Peloponnesus in 1437–38? Or did it derive from Ciriaco's second and more careful inspection of the Parthenon in 1444? The arguments in favor of the former hypothesis are strong. The general layout and the still largely fanciful pediment sculpture in the Sangallo drawing are plainly akin to those of the Hamilton drawing, which illustrates the 1436 visit, though the only strict *terminus ante* for its execution is 1447, when Pietro Donato died.[38] The drawing occurs on a page of monuments which Ciriaco inspected in 1436. The description, though undated and in the third person, corresponds with the 1436 descriptions we find in Morone and in the Hamilton codex, not with the fuller specifications of 1444 reflected in the letter to Andreolo Giustiniani. The explanatory inscriptions, moreover, while adding new information ("Columnae p. XVII" and "Ab omni parte centauri in foribus"), are quite consistent with what occur in the Hamilton and Manzoni drawings. All this suggests that the Sangallo drawing derives from materials dating from 1436—in which case, to save the appearances, we have to presume that these included a drawing of the metope sculpture which Ciriaco for some reason withheld from his presentation piece for Pietro Donato. The arguments for connecting the Sangallo drawing with the 1444 Athenian visit, on the other hand, are not negligible. Sangallo's exemplar was probably, if not certainly, an integral body of material of dates ranging from 1436 to 1444 or later. In 1444, as we know from the letter to Giustiniani, Ciriaco made a closer and more accurate survey of the Parthenon than he had done in 1436, paying special attention (as Sangallo's drawing does) to the sculpture as well as the architecture; and on that occasion he made another drawing of the building. The fairly accurate proportions of the Sangallo drawing, as well as the metope sculpture, could possibly derive from that drawing. And, finally, the extra inscription "Columnae p. XVII" in the Sangallo drawing—expanding "p." into "peristili"—accords well with the new information given in the Giustiniani letter which stated that the Parthenon had seventeen columns on either side. The only safe conclusion, however, is a *non liquet*; and, whatever the true answer, Jacques Carrey's drawings must still remain the best evidence we have as to what the west front, the frieze, and the metopes of the Parthenon looked like before the Venetians blew up the Turkish powder magazine in 1687.[39]

38. Bodnar (*Cyriacus*, p. 50, n. 3) reasonably suggests 1442–43 as a likely date for the transcription of the Hamilton excerpts, and perhaps sometime before 1444 as a possible date for the composition of the Contarini volume (*ibid.*, p. 106).

39. For information and discussion I am most grateful to Prof. Bernard

CRISTOFORO IVANOVICH
[An Eyewitness Account of the Bombardment of the
Acropolis—1687–88] *

A fleet and an army under the command of Francesco Morosini, a
Venetian nobleman, arrived at the port of Athens on September 21,
1687, whereupon the Turkish garrison at Athens immediately took
refuge behind the strong walls of the Acropolis and prepared for a
siege. Five days later, on September 25, an explosion in the Parthenon
reduced the venerable structure, until then in an almost perfect state
of preservation, to ruins, blowing off the roof, destroying almost the
entire cella, and knocking down all but a few columns of both the
north and south peristyles. Cristoforo Ivanovich, one of Count
Morosini's aides, later became a writer of some reputation in Venice;
and among his unpublished manuscripts, he left us a detailed history
of the campaigns of Morosini in which he had taken part, including
the siege of Athens. This is his version of the events leading up to
the explosion. The pages preceding the place in the story where our
selection begins describe the voyage of Morosini's fleet from Venice
along the coast of Greece and the Peloponnesus, and some earlier
skirmishes with Turkish forces along the way.

His warrior mind never tiring of exercising itself in military affairs, the captain general [Morosini] summoned the war council to
determine what was left to be carried out in the month and a half of
campaign that still remained. The decision of that council was to ex-
ploit the present favorable circumstances of the consternation of the
enemy army, which, scattered after the defeat suffered in the fields
of Patras at the hands of our victorious forces, found itself reduced
in Thebes to only ten thousand men, and to direct those forces to the
taking of the fortress of Athens [i.e., the Acropolis]. The idea was
that, with Achaea, too, subjugated, in addition to the acquisition

Ashmole, Fr. Edward Bodnar, S.J., Fr. Peter Levi, S.J., Dr. Giovanni
Mardersteig, Mr. John Mitchell, and Prof. C. M. Robertson, and to my
colleagues Profs. Carl Nylander, Machteld Mellink, Brunilde Ridgway, and
Russell Scott.

   * From Cristoforo Ivanovich, "Istoria della Lega Ortodossa contro il
Turco," in *Venetians in Athens, 1687–1688: From the Istoria of Cristoforo
Ivanovich*, ed. James Morton Paton, Gennadeion Monographs, I (Harvard
University Press for American School of Classical Studies at Athens, 1940).
This translation, by Rodney Guirasch, was made from Paton's published
version of the Italian text, courtesy of the American School of Classical
Studies at Athens.

remarkable in itself with respect to the fertility of the land and to the flourishing commerce which maintained that port, the conquered kingdom of the Morea would be made safe from enemy invasions, at the same time as future peace and tranquillity would be established for its subjects.

Consquently, on the twentieth of September, the army, consisting of eight thousand infantrymen and six hundred horses, having embarked aboard galleys, sailed all that night with a favorable wind in the direction of Porto Lione [i.e., the Peiraeus, Athens' port], where it landed the following morning and disembarked without enemy interference or the least loss of time. This port was so called because of a marble lion 10 feet in height that stood on its innermost banks. It is situated on the northern shores of the Saronic Gulf. Its entrance is somewhat narrow and, farther in, is very deep and capable of floating many ships. Menesteo [Menestheus] [1] is said to have departed from here to go to Troy with the ships, and before him Theseus when he went to pay the penalty to Minos for the death of Androgeus.[2]

At the appearance of this army the foremost Greeks of the city went to humble themselves before His Excellency the captain general, and with expressions of complete devotion to his revered name, they offered their riches and their very lives for the greater glory of the Republic. They were received kindly, inspired to faithful vassalage, and assured of paternal affection and suitable protection from the Turks. From these Greeks it was learned that the Turks were skilled in the handling of arms, six hundred strong in the fortress and firmly resolved to defend themselves, encouraged by the hope of being relieved by the seraschiero [Turkish commander]. Hearing this news, His Excellency ordered the army to march without delay into the Borgo [the lower town of Athens] about 5 miles from the seacoast and situated at the foot of the mountain of the fortress, especially since the Turks, who used to inhabit the former, had withdrawn out of fear into the latter. Count Chinismark promptly carried out the order with the march of the men, Field Quartermaster General Dolfino assisting him, and advanced about 2 miles into an olive wood on the evening of the twenty-second [of September].

On the twenty-third he sent to the field four light cannons, two newly invented heavy cannons, and four mortars, all of which were

1. In mythology, the original leader of the Athenian forces sent to Troy, but killed early in the Trojan War [Ed.].
2. Androgeus, son of King Minos of Crete, on his way home after winning the contests in the games at Athens, was killed because of his friendship with members of an Athenian revolutionary faction [Ed.].

drawn by the galley crews. The army pushed on to the Borgo without any obstruction from the enemy, who was closed up in the fortress. The general drew up the attack the same day, and at the timely arrival of the above-mentioned cannons and mortars, they began to fire on the fortress with the assistance of the captain general himself, who had decided to move to the field to be better able to oversee the undertaking. From the continuous shelling, the besieged suffered considerable damage to the narrow enclosing wall of the fortress. His Excellency, informed that the Turks' ammunition, together with their principle women and children, were in the temple of Minerva [Athena], the latter believing themselves safe there on account of the thickness of the walls and vaults of this temple, His Excellency ordered Count Mutoni to direct his fire at that part. Even from the beginning a certain disorder appeared in the tossing of the bombs, which were falling outside, and this was because of the inequality of the weight which varied 130 pounds from one to the next; but through practice and adjustment not a single one fell outside, so that one of them, striking the side of the temple, finally succeeded in breaking it. There followed a terrible explosion in the fire of powder and grenades that were inside, and the firing and the reverberations of the above munitions made tremble all the houses of the Borgo, which seemed a great city, and put a tremendous fear in the besieged. In this way that famous temple of Minerva, which so many centuries and so many wars had not been able to destroy, was ruined.

While the siege continued vigorously, the enemy reinforcements, consisting of two thousand horses and one thousand infantrymen, had been sighted in those fields at dawn on the morning of the twenty-eighth, and Count General Chinismark in his experience considered it proper to go to meet them, such being the earlier intention of the generalissimo in case the Turks should appear; wherefore, taking the cavalry and marine infantry, he set himself against them, and at the mere sight of the Christian troops the Turks took headlong flight. In the meantime, Field Quartermaster General Dolfino, heedless of his own safety and often exposing himself to musket fire in order to speed up the work of the cannons and bombs, sought to press the fortress ever more strongly and to force the Turks to surrender. Mutoni, informed by a Greek that some women of the Aga Khan had withdrawn into a house, directed fire at it, and a bomb made such a slaughter of them that the fortress, terrified and still despairing of the aid that had fled, agreed to show the white flag and to surrender; this was at 10:00 P.M. of the same day.

General Chinismark approached the fortress to hear the Turks' intention, which was to surrender on terms, no longer being able to stand the heat of the fire that was burning in several places in the fortress. The prince of Turin, who was present, had one of his slaves ask them if they had been afraid of the bombs; and one of them, enraged, replied that if it hadn't been for them, the fortress wouldn't have surrendered. And the Turk was right about this. The fortress is situated at great height upon a *grebbano*, a kind of very hard stone, and is inaccessible on three sides and impenetrable by any mine.

The terms of their surrender were established: they were to leave all their weapons in the fortress, leave with their women and children and with those possessions that each could carry from the fortress to the sea in a single trip, and to hire three foreign vessels for their embarkation and voyage to Smyrna. The complete surrender agreement was sent to the captain general in the port, *with five leading Turks* [Ivanovich's italics], who were *treated courteously* and by whom, on the thirtieth of September, the paper was signed. These Turks were held as hostages aboard the galleass *Quirini* until the completion of the surrender. His Excellency decided to go to the field on October 1 with many nobles, all on horseback, and also to the Borgo to observe the necessary affairs and to give appropriate orders. He remained there all that day and that night returned to his generalship. So on the third of October the Turks set sail and the Republic took possession of this impregnable fortress. About three thousand came out, including about six hundred men-at-arms. Another three hundred of the force of this garrison, inspired by the true light of Heaven, chose to stay to cleanse the impurity of their souls in the waters of Holy Baptism.

Then, by order of the captain general, Daniel Dolfino IV, who from the time of the attack until the end gave numerous demonstrations of his courage, ability, and experience in the above-mentioned position of field quartermaster general extraordinary, took over the government and the administration of the city and the so impressive fortress. The other field quartermaster general, Zorzi Benzon, also distinguished himself during the same period, in the superintendence of the cavalry, with similarly attested displays of courageous zeal. The nobles who also underwent the hardships of the campaign with great merit, Nicolò Capello II, Andrea Pisani, Alessandro Valier, Ferigo Marcello, and Pietro Emo, followed their worthy example. The superintendent, Count San Felice Mutoni, immortalized the custom and use of bombs in full witness of his great experience. His Excellency had the *condottiere* of the men-at-arms, Count Tomeo Pompei, enter the fortress, where it was necessary to spend a few days to clear it of the great number of enemy bodies killed by the fire and at the same time to purge it of the wreckage.

The famous temple of Minerva, destroyed and crumbled by the bombs on account of the burning of all the grain and other food provisions that the enemy had stored in it, was composed of the finest marble and supported by thirty-two columns, and had already been converted by the Turks into a most magnificent mosque.

[EDITOR'S NOTE: The *Istoria of Cristoforo Ivanovich* goes on to describe the movements of Morosini and the Venetian army in Greece in a series of actions against the Turks, and the battles between European troops and Turkish forces in Hungary.]

JACOB ROTHENBERG
The Acquisition of the Elgin Marbles,
the Years 1799–1806—[1967] *

> After the destruction of the Parthenon in the Venetian bombardment of 1687, the Turks, regaining control of the Acropolis, made no effort to restore or rebuild the temple and life went on as usual around the fallen stones and column drums. With the reawakening in Europe of interest in the monuments of antiquity during the course of the eighteenth century, an effort was made to preserve what was left of the Parthenon by making drawings and plaster casts of the sculptures and architectural motifs, a process that had already begun before the explosion with Carrey's drawings under the patronage of the Marquis de Nointel. Intending to provide English schools of art and architecture with a complete set of drawings and casts of the Parthenon sculptures, the British ambassador to Turkey, Thomas Bruce, seventh Lord of Elgin, sent a group of artists and technicians to Athens at about the turn of the nineteenth century. In the following selection, Professor Rothenberg re-examines the correspondence between Lord Elgin and those close to him during his tenure as ambassador in Istanbul and, later, during his imprisonment in France, putting together a vivid account of Elgin's growing determination to remove rather than merely to copy the sculptures of the Parthenon. The controversy surrounding his removal of the sculptures from Athens began almost immediately, even while the removal was in progress, and it has continued to rage to the present day. Rothenberg provides a new perspective by which to judge Lord Elgin's actions in order to re-evaluate the issues in this controversy.
>   Jacob Rothenberg is professor of art history at the City College of the City University of New York.

It was in the year 1799, upon his appointment as Ambassador to Constantinople, that Lord Elgin first conceived of a program of anti-

* Chapter 5 of Jacob Rothenberg, "*Descensus ad Terram:* The Acquisition and Reception of the Elgin Marbles," Ph.D. diss. Columbia University, 1967. By arrangement with the author.

quarian pursuits in Greece. The idea was proposed to him by Thomas Harrison (1744–1829), an architect working for him in Scotland,[1] that casts from actual Athenian monuments [2] might serve as a valuable addition to the general knowledge already available through the publications of Stuart and Revett, Chandler, Le Roi, and others. An unsuccessful attempt to interest the government in financing such a project [3] led Elgin to approach a number of individual artists, especially J. M. W. Turner, already well known as a topographical draughtsman,[4] but Turner's conditions and demands were beyond Elgin's resources. Unable to make arrangements with English artists,[5] Elgin proceeded to the Continent and upon arriving in Sicily met Giovanni Battista Lusieri, a painstaking Neapolitan artist, skilled in picturesque views,[6] with whom he soon reached an agreement. Lu-

1. Harrison is noted for his bridge at Lancaster (1783–1788), his Grosvenor Bridge at Chester (1827–1832), and his Court House at Chester (1793–1820), the last built in pure Greek Doric style. He also designed Elgin's house at Broomhall. (See H. M. Colvin, *Biographical Dictionary of English Architects*, London, 1954, pp. 268–269.)

2. Harrison was particularly interested in casts of the corner Ionic capitals of Greek temples which had been drawn by Stuart and Revett (see *The Antiquities of Athens*, Vol. I, London, 1762, Ch. II, Pl. VII) and were noted for their unique form. He also urged that reproductions of Periclean sculpture be brought back from Greece for English artists to study. (See A. Michaelis, "Die Aufnahme der Elgin Marbles in London," *Im Neuen Reich*, VII, Leipzig, 1877 [I], p. 85.)

3. In London Elgin communicated with Lord Grenville, Mr. Pitt, and Mr. Dundas, who felt that expenses of an indefinite nature, with little chance of success at the time, were not justified. (See Arthur H. Smith, "Lord Elgin and His Collection," *Journal of Hellenic Studies*, Vol. XXXVI, 1916 [hereinafter referred to as *JHS*, XXXVI], p. 166.)

4. Turner was then 24 years old, but as early as 1790 he had exhibited architectural renderings in water color at the Royal Academy. (See T. S. R. Boase, *English Art, 1800–1870*, Oxford, 1959, p. 34.)

5. Elgin also approached the topographic artist William Daniell, the water-colorist Thomas Girtin, and the young architectural student Robert Smirke to join his company of draughtsmen, but they rejected his offer. Elgin, in turn, rejected Richard Smirke, the brother of Robert. (See "The Farington Diary Typescript," British Museum Department of Prints and Drawings, pp. 1533, 1539, and 1564; entries of April-May, 1799.)

6. The traveler, H. W. Williams, in a letter of May, 1817, from Athens, gives this estimate of Lusieri's drawings:

> They are upon a considerable scale . . . not less than 7 or 8 feet . . . he has even one of Constantinople 18 feet by 3 or 4 feet. . . . He takes an incredible amount of time in doing them. . . . I have more than once presumed he carried details a little too far, further indeed than nature seems to authorize . . . exciting painful feelings on reflecting on the wearisome toil and trouble such outlines must have cost him. On examining the subject from which several of his outlines have been made, I confess I could not perceive the minutiae described in them

sieri was engaged to head an entire artistic commission of unprecedented make-up, whose remaining members were procured from Naples and Rome by William Richard Hamilton (1777–1855), Elgin's private secretary and adviser, who played a major role in the acquisition and eventual purchase of the marbles by Parliament. The five others employed in the group, besides Lusieri, were: Feodor Ivanowitsch, called the "Calmuck," a Tartar native of [Astrakhan], trained in Karlsruhe and Rome, who was hired as the sculptural draughtsman; [7] Vincenzo Balestra and Sebastian Ittar, two architectural draughtsmen; and Bernardino Ledus and Vincenzo Rosati, two *formatori*, or moulders of casts. It is the composition of this group, more than anything else, that makes clear Elgin's original intentions to make reproductions and drawings of ancient monuments, rather than to remove pieces of sculpture or architecture from them. However, circumstances were soon to arise that prevailed upon him to change his mind.

After several months of delay and preparation in Sicily and Italy, Hamilton and the other members of the group left for Constantinople in April, 1800. Arriving there in May, they were given final instructions by Lord Elgin, and shortly thereafter departed for Athens, which they reached on July 22, 1800. There they presented letters of introduction from Elgin to the British consul, Logotheti. But their intentions to take casts of structural or sculptural details on the

---

which has led me to suppose he must have used a telescope. . . . I saw only one coloured drawing by Lusieri and that consists of a few columns of the Temple of Minerva. It is a meritorious work of art, as far as relates to breadth of effect and truth of light and shade, without mannerism or fallacious touching. The colouring, however, is rather heavy and seems to be shaded with Indian ink, which loses its clearness where there is any depth of shadow . . . (*Travels in Italy, Greece, and the Ionian Islands*, London, 1820, II, pp. 331–334).

But E. D. Clarke disagrees with Williams on Lusieri's color: "It may be said of Lusieri, as of Claude Lorrain, 'if he be not the Poet, he is the Historian of Nature.' By some his compositions have been deemed to be too laboured; but his coloring is exquisite" (*Travels in Various Countries of Europe, Asia, and Africa*, London, 1812–1816, Vol. III, p. 469).

7. Hamilton reported to Elgin that he was forced to choose a foreigner because of the lack of available talent. "It was singular that all Rome could not afford a single 'desinateur de figures' that was even of ordinary ability" (*JHS*, XXXVI, p. 172). A criticism of the Calmuck's abilities is given in the notes of "W.K.F." (Weimarische Kunst-Freunde) annexed to C. A. Böttiger's *Denkschrift über Lord Elgin's Erwerbungen in Griechenland*, Leipzig and Altenburg, 1817, pp. 62–63: "The Calmuck is a man gifted with a great deal of talent whose clear drawings nearly always indicate taste and mind. But I think he has hardly sufficient knowledge and accuracy to let one look for the highest standard of accuracy and truthfulness of style."

Acropolis, as they had planned, were immediately thwarted by the Turkish authorities. According to Lord Elgin's later testimony before the Select Committee of Parliament, his workmen were permitted access to the Acropolis only for the purpose of drawing, and that at an expense of five guineas a day.[8] Under these conditions, nine months passed, from August, 1800, to April, 1801, with relatively little accomplishment on the temples within the fortress. During this period, repeated attempts were made, without success, to secure from Constantinople, *firmans*, or permits, to cast details of these temples.[9]

In May of 1801 the situation further deteriorated. Owing to a suspicion that French troops were about to invade Greece, the Turkish governor at Athens withdrew from Elgin's company all access privileges to the Acropolis for the purpose of drawing or casting.[10] The rumor turned out to be unfounded, but it was not until the middle of June that Lusieri, with the help of the British consul, Logotheti, managed to regain admission to the Acropolis. Some mitigation of the restrictions on casting, although they did not apply to the Parthenon itself, seems to have accompanied this return, but not without continued exposure to Turkish harassment and extortion. Yet the pleasure with which such progress was greeted is thus registered in a letter of Mary Nisbet, Countess of Elgin, to her father, whose initial reservations about the entire Athenian project she had apparently shared, but who had changed his mind after a visit to Athens in May:

> You know I was always against the *formatori*, and I remember you did not admire the idea of them; so I feel the greatest comfort at your approbation of their work. After having been at such an expence it is certainly very pleasing to hear things are done in so superior and masterly a stile. . . . Elgin is going immediately to get the proper Firmaun for Minerva's temple. . . .[11]

8. See *Report from the Select Committee of the House of Commons on the Earl of Elgin's Collection of Sculptured Marbles*, London, 1816 (hereinafter referred to as *Report*), p. 33.

9. Lusieri visited Elgin at Constantinople early in 1801 to see if he could break the stalemate. Elgin supposedly procured some kind of *firman* which he sent to the British consul, Logotheti, in Athens, but it seems never to have arrived. In April we find Lusieri still pleading with Elgin for the procurement of such documents. (*JHS*, XXXVI, pp. 185–186)

10. See William St. Clair, *Lord Elgin and the Marbles*, Oxford, 1967, p. 87.

11. See *The Letters of Mary Nisbet of Dirleton, Countess of Elgin*, arranged by Lieutenant-Colonel Nisbet-Hamilton Grant, London, 1926 (hereinafter referred to as *Letters, Countess of Elgin*); Letter of Lady Elgin to her father, June 14, 1801.

It was not in Elgin's mind, however, that the idea of removing the Parthenon sculptures was born,[12] but in that of Dr. Philip Hunt, chaplain to his Embassy, who, along with Hamilton, guided the operations of the company of artists and workmen during Elgin's absence from the scene.[13] The intense attraction Hunt felt for the Athenian monuments—an enthusiasm which Lusieri shared—already is communicated in a letter to Elgin of May 22, 1801, in these words:

> Of the temples of Minerva, Theseus, and Neptune I can say nothing that would convey an idea of the effect they produce. They must be seen to know what the union of simplicity and beauty is capable of; and after having feasted the eyes with those exquisite specimens of Athenian architecture, every deviation from them, even the edifices of Rome itself, will almost disgust. Lusieri, tho' born on the banks of the Tiber, and attached as he was to the proud remains of the Mistress of the World, is now an enthusiastic admirer of the Doric Buildings here and turns with disgust from the works of Hadrian or Herodes Atticus and everything on the Roman model.[14]

Hunt goes on in the same letter to raise again the matter of a broader *firman*. He presses Elgin thus:

> Positive *Firmans* must, however, be obtained from the Porte to enable the Architects and Modellers to proceed in their most interesting labours. . . . Till those *Firmans* are obtained, the bas-reliefs and the Groups on the Metopes (of the Parthenon) can neither be modelled or drawn.[15]

Hunt's patience was obviously running out. Frustrated by the delay which such written communication entailed and piqued by the example of Fauvel who had already acquired a few pieces of the

---

12. Elgin insisted in his testimony to the Parliamentary Committee that he had no intention originally of removing any sculpture until he became aware of how destructive the Turks had been: " . . . it was no part of my original plan to bring away anything but models." (See *Report*, p. 41; also see William R. Hamilton, *Memorandum on the Subject of the Earl of Elgin's Pursuits in Greece*, Second Edition, corrected, London, 1815 [hereinafter referred to as *Memorandum*, 1815], p. 16. There are two earlier editions of the *Memorandum* [see note 147], as well as a German edition by C. A. Böttiger [see note 7].)

13. "The removals only took place," says St. Clair, *op. cit.*, p. 92, "as a result of a series of accidents all of them involving the Reverend Philip Hunt." Also see A. Michaelis, *A Century of Archaeological Discoveries*, New York and London, 1908, p. 28.

14. *JHS*, XXXVI, p. 188.

15. *Loc. cit.*

Parthenon sculptures for Choiseul-Gouffier [see note 24], he made, two bold decisions which helped break the deadlock. He decided to go to Constantinople himself in June to see Elgin. He also made up his mind to ask for a *firman* of more inclusive scope than had formerly been requested. The conditions, which he apparently induced Elgin to apply for, are set forth in a written memorandum of July 1, 1801, signed by Hunt, and contain the first mention of the acquisition or removal of sculptures:

> Mr. Hunt recommends that a *Fermaun* should be procured from the Porte addressed to the Voivode and Cadi of Athens as well as to the Disdar or governor of the Citadel, stating that the artists are in the service of the British Ambassador Extra-Ordinary and that they are to have not only permission but protection in the following objects: (1) to enter freely within the walls of the citadel, and to draw and mould with plaster the ancient Temples there, (2) to erect scaffolding and to dig where they may wish to discover the ancient foundations, and (3) liberty to take away any sculptures or inscriptions which do not interfere with the works or the walls of the Citadel.[16]

Furthermore, Hunt, anticipating some duplicity on the part of the Turks, urged Elgin to ask for a literal translation to accompany the order.[17] Shortly before the submission of these requests there came a most advantageous turn of events for Elgin in the political relations between England and Turkey. The British won a decisive military success against the Napoleonic forces which had invaded the Turkish dominion of Egypt.[18] As a result, the antipathy of the Turks to Elgin's Athenian pursuits vanished almost overnight, and straightaway an official letter, or *firman*, complete with Italian translation, addressed to the Cadi, or Chief Judge, and to the Voivode,

16. *Ibid.*, p. 190.
17. *Report*, p. 141.
18. The French had entered Egypt in 1798. In the spring of 1801 their garrison at Cairo was besieged by three converging columns of Anglo-Turkish forces, one from Rosetta, one from Syria, and one from Qusair on the Red Sea. When the first two of these met at the Nile a few miles north of Cairo, the Mameluke beys, the local rulers of Egypt, threw their support to the Anglo-Turkish side. On June 17, 1801, the French commander at Cairo, seeing the futility of his position, surrendered. The British then attacked the French forces at Alexandria. When a rescue attempt from Toulon failed, General Menou, Commander-in-Chief of all French forces in Egypt, capitulated to the British General Hutchinson. (See J. C. Herold, *Bonaparte in Egypt*, 1962; also, J. Marlowe, *A History of Modern Egypt and Anglo-Egyptian Relations, 1800–1956*, Second Edition, 1965, p. 21.)

or Governor, of Athens, was issued at Constantinople early in July
of 1801 by the Caimacan Pasha, who was filling the office of the
Grand Vizier at the Porte during that Minister's absence in Egypt.[19]
The manner in which the *firman* was drawn up indicates that Elgin
must have submitted Hunt's memorandum to the Porte verbatim. It
not only grants permission to Lord Elgin's company, as Hunt had
requested, to enter and leave the Citadel at will, and to measure,
sketch, cast, and excavate around the structures and monuments
contained therein, but also contains a final and crucial clause to the
effect that "when they wished to take away any pieces of stone with
old inscriptions or figures thereon, no hindrance or opposition be
made thereto." [20] It was on the strength of this clause that the acquisition of the Parthenon sculptures by Elgin was made possible.

Elgin himself attributed the issuance of the *firman* entirely to the
political situation. He says,

> In proportion with the change of affairs in our relations toward
> Turkey the facilities of access were increased to me and to all
> English travellers, and about the middle of the summer of 1801
> all difficulties were removed; we then had access for general
> purposes. The objections disappeared from the moment of the
> decided success of our arms in Egypt. . . . Yes, the whole system
> of Turkish feeling met with a revolution in the first place from
> the invasion of the French, and afterwards by our own conquest.[21]

Lady Elgin, in a letter to her father of July 9, 1801, expresses her own
jubilation and the delight of the company in the new decree, whose
terms she recounts as follows:

> I am happy to tell you Pisani has succeeded à merveille in his
> *firman* from the Porte. Hunt is in raptures for the *firman* is per-
> fection and P. says he will answer with his whiskers that it is
> exact. It allows our artists to go into the citadel, to copy and

19. See *Report*, Appendix No. 10, pp. xxiv–xxvi, for a complete English
translation of the *firman*.
20. The *firman* grants Elgin's workmen full liberty in "going in and out
of the citadel of Athens; or in fixing scaffolding around the ancient Temple
of the Idols; or in modelling with chalk or gypsum the ornaments and visible figures thereon, or in measuring the fragments and vestiges of other
ruined edifices, or in excavating, when they find it necessary, the foundations, in search of inscriptions among the rubbish . . . and that they be not
molested, and that no one meddle with their scaffolding or implements, nor
hinder them from taking away any pieces of stone [qualche pezzi di pietra]
with inscriptions or figures." (See also A. Michaelis, *Ancient Marbles in
Great Britain*, Cambridge, 1882, pp. 134–135.)
21. *Report*, pp. 32, 40.

model everything in it, to erect scaffolds all round the Temple, to dig and discover all the ancient foundations and to bring away any marbles that may be deemed curious by their having inscriptions on them, and that they are not to be disturbed by the soldiers, etc. under any pretense whatsoever. Don't you think this will do? I am in the greatest glee, for it would have been a great pity to have failed in the principal part, after having been at such an expence. . . .[22]

It is significant that although Lady Elgin refers to the taking of stones with inscriptions, she makes no mention of the removal of sculptures from the temples. It would seem that she herself neither saw any such implication or intention in the final clause of the *firman*, nor anticipated that it would soon come to that. Apparently she was content to read the document as granting the fulfillment of Elgin's original plans. Indeed the permission to take sculptures affixed to the temples resulted largely from the fact that the Voivode at Athens, to whom the *firman* was addressed, under the additional incentive of presents given to him by Hunt, either chose, or was induced, to take a very liberal rather than a narrow interpretation of the last words of the directive concerning the removal of figured or inscribed stones.[23]

Hunt lost no time in putting the conditions of the newly granted *firman* to a test:

When the original was read to the Voivode at Athens he seemed disposed to grant any wish of mine with respect to Lord Elgin's pursuits, in consequence of which I asked him permission to detach from the Parthenon the most perfect and as it appeared to me the most beautiful Metope. I obtained that permission and acted upon it immediately. I had one carefully packed and put on board a Ragusan ship which was under my orders from which it was transferred to a frigate and sent to England. The facility with which this had been obtained induced Lord Elgin to apply for permission to lower other groups of sculpture from the Parthenon, which he did to a considerable extent. . . .[24]

22. *Letters, Countess of Elgin;* Letter of Lady Elgin to her father, Belgrade, July 9, 1801.

23. Hunt reports that gifts of brilliant cut-glass lustres, firearms, and other pieces of British manufacture were given to the Voivode, but no money, at the time the *firman* was presented (*Report*, p. 146; Michaelis, *Ancient Marbles . . .* , p. 135). The crucial role which Hunt played in maneuvering the Turkish Voivode into allowing Elgin's party to remove sculptures from the buildings is well detailed in St. Clair (*op. cit.*) pp. 92–97.

24. *Report*, p. 142. Hunt recounts the removal of the first metope again in his letter of 1805 from France to Lady Elgin's mother:

Thus did the marbles come into Lord Elgin's possession.

Elgin's communications with Lusieri, directly after the granting of the *firman*, reveal clearly that the new liberties did not in any way

---

The first acquisition we made at Athens was the most perfect of the Metopes from the ruins of the Parthenon on which I recollect Mr. Nisbet and yourself rivetting your eyes with so much admiration. This was the first of them that had been so successfully lowered—M. de Choiseul-Gouffier's attempt to secure one had merely been connived at and for want of time and cordage and windlasses it fell from a considerable height and was broken into fragments.

(*Letters, Countess of Elgin*, p. 331.)

Choiseul-Gouffier was the French Ambassador to the Porte and Elgin's strongest official competitor for the acquisition of Greek antiquities. The incident here related by Hunt refers to South Metope No. VI, now in the Elgin Collection. His statement that it fell and shattered in the attempt to lower it from the structure does not agree, however, with the account given in the papers of Louis-François-Sebastian Fauvel, the principal agent-collector of antiquities in Athens for Choiseul-Gouffier. Fauvel claims that it was blown down during a hurricane which broke it into three pieces. (See *Revue archéologique*, Series III, XXVI, 1895, p. 29.) These were acquired by Fauvel in 1788 and shipped out of Athens in 1803, but with the outbreak of war, the French boat carrying the metope was intercepted by a British frigate and its cargo confiscated to Malta. By order of Admiral Nelson, the cases were sent to London where they became confused with Elgin's shipments and were acquired by him upon his return in 1806. All attempts made by Elgin to return the metope to Choiseul-Gouffier, after discovering that it belonged to him, failed, and it passed into the Elgin Collection after Choiseul's death in 1817. In any case, Hunt, who arrived in Athens in 1800, could not have witnessed the lowering or fall of this metope, and is apparently repeating hearsay. Neither could Hunt have witnessed the acquisition of a second metope for Choiseul, No. X, now at the Louvre * * * , which may also have fallen from the temple and was shipped to France in 1788 by Consul Gaspary (see *Bulletin de la Société Nationale des Antiquaires de France*, 1884, p. 57). This metope was sold at the auction of Choiseul's collection in 1818 and purchased by the Louvre (see J. J. Dubois's *Catalogue d'antiquités égyptiennes, grecques, romaines, et celtiques . . . formant la collection du feu M. LeComte de Choiseul-Gouffier*, Paris, 1818, p. xiii). Considerable confusion was caused by this chain of circumstances in the following century. Most writers, failing to realize that there were two different metopes involved, mistook them for one and the same, until A. H. Smith's account clarified the situation (see *JHS*, XXXVI, pp. 355–365). That both these metopes were already down from the Parthenon is furthermore proven by a reference in 1795 by an English traveler, Colonel Morritt of Rokeby, to only fifteen Lapith and Centaur metopes remaining on the south side at that time (see *The Letters of John B. S. Morritt of Rokeby, Descriptions of Journeys in Europe and Asia Minor in the Years 1794–1796*, edited by G. E. Marindin, London, 1914, p. 174). Since, altogether, eighteen of the south metopes survive, the two Choiseul ones in question must have been off the structure by the time of Colonel Morritt's visit.

alter the original plans and purposes he had in mind. In a letter of July 10, 1801, he urged his chief artist to see to it that the moulders continued making casts of architectural details:

> Besides the general work . . . it would be very essential that the Formatori should be able to take away exact models of little ornaments or detached pieces if any are found which would be interesting for the arts. The very great variety in our manufactures, in objects either of elegance or luxury, offer a thousand applications for such details. A chair, a footstool, designs or shapes for porcelain, ornaments for cornices, nothing is indifferent, and whether it be in painting or a model, exact representations of such things would be much to be desired. . . .[25]

It is significant to note here that Elgin places the instructional and inspirational advantages that would accrue to the industrial and applied arts of England from having copies and models of Greek design made available to them above the private satisfaction or gain that he might derive from possession of the original pieces. Furthermore, as the letter proceeds, Elgin implies a distinction between personal plans for his estate at Broomhall and the future disposition of the Parthenon sculptures or other antiquities being gathered for him:

> . . . Balestra has with him several drawings of my house in Scotland and some plans of the site on which it is intended to build here. . . . The plans . . . should be known to you. This building is a subject that occupies me greatly and offers me the means of placing in a useful, distinguished and agreeable way the various things you may perhaps be able to procure for me. . . .[26]

From what follows, however, it is obvious that Elgin is referring not to the Parthenon sculptures, but to supplies of raw marble or other structural material from which to fashion his house:

> The Hall is intended to be adorned with columns—the cellars underneath are vaulted expressly for this. Would it then be better to get some white columns worked in this country? . . . Or to look out for some different kinds of marble that could be collected together in course of time, and decorate the hall (in the manner of the Great Church at Palermo) with columns all different from one another . . . supplementing them with agates and other rare marbles which are found in Sicily and are worked in small pieces? . . . In either case I should wish to collect as much marble as feasible. I have other places in my house which need it and be-

25. *JHS*, XXXVI, p. 191.
26. *Ibid.*, p. 192.

sides one can easily multiply ornaments of beautiful marble without overdoing it. . . .[27]

Lest there be any confusion in Lusieri's mind between this project and the Parthenon remains or other Greek antiquities, he concludes with this pointed admonition:

These reflexions only apply to unworked marble. You do not need any prompting from me to know the value that is attached to a sculptured marble or historic piece. . . .[28]

This letter, following immediately on the heels of the new *firman*, contains no mention of domesticating any part of the Parthenon sculptures at Broomhall. On the contrary, it suggests that, in Elgin's view, pieces of antique statuary, having archaeological or historical value, must serve a higher purpose than the mere adornment of a private residence. This is perhaps the first indication given us by Elgin of the civic or cultural purposes he was already contemplating regarding the disposition of any original antiquities he might acquire during the period of his ambassadorship. It was an aim he was to repeat more outspokenly on several later occasions. Thus, in a letter of December 18, 1801, from Constantinople, by which time a number of pieces of the Parthenon sculptures had already been acquired, Elgin clearly implies his intention to make his collection available to the nation:

The scale I am upon is the result of much enquiry from scientific and practical artists—and has been carried through with great trouble and expence. But as I have, in so far succeeded, I may be allowed to feel more anxiety than I dare express to see what I have got safely removed. I am flattered with hopes the whole will constitute a very great national acquisition.[29]

In this respect, Elgin differs markedly from other collectors, such as Colonel John B. S. Morritt and Count de Choiseul-Gouffier. The former, a countryman of Elgin, had unsuccessfully attempted, a few

27. *Loc. cit.*
28. *Loc. cit.*
29. This letter, most of which concerns arrangements for shipping some of his marbles out of Malta, is in the collection of Elgin papers and correspondence at Broomhall, Scotland, and remains unpublished. There are four volumes of bound letters headed as follows: "Elgin Papers, Vol. I, Lord Elgin to Lusieri, 1799–1819"; "Vol. II, Lord Elgin to Hamilton, 1812–1836"; "Vol. III, Hamilton to Lord Elgin, 1799–1833"; "Vol. IV, Letters from Artists and Connoisseurs." In addition, there are two other volumes, one labeled "Philip Hunt and the Artists," the other, "Letters of S. Logotheti, 1799–1811." Finally, there is a trunk containing unbound letters and manuscripts.

Jacob Rothenberg   *139*

years before Elgin's arrival, to procure some of the metope and frieze
plaques of the Parthenon for the purpose of adorning his private residence at Rokeby, while the latter, as French Ambassador to the
Porte, had coveted the Parthenon sculptures for the embellishment
of his own neoclassical palace in France before seeing them fall into
Elgin's possession. Choiseul-Gouffier, in a letter of April 26, 1816, to
Elgin, regarding the casts of the Parthenon and Theseum frieze procured for him by Fauvel and with which he had to content himself in place of the originals, betrays his thwarted ambitions thus:

> Lord Elgin a le bonheur de posséder un grand nombre des
> marbres originaux de ces plâtres. C'est un trésor inappréciable;
> pour moi, je m'estimerari heureux d'en recouvrir les copies et de
> pouvoir completer ainsi la décoration de l'asyle modeste où je
> cherche à me consoler de mes pertes.[30]

In actuality, this "modest sanctuary" of which Choiseul speaks was a
magnificent structure modeled on its various façades after diverse
monuments of Athens and Palmyra, with its interior, done in pure
Greek taste, designed for the reception of sculptural decoration.[31]

Once again, in a note of 1802, appended as a postscript to a letter
of the Countess of Elgin to her mother, Elgin divulges an essentially
cultural, rather than acquisitive, program in his antiquarian pursuits:

> All I can say is to express a belief that the object has been attained
> and that when all arrives safe in England I shall be able to shew
> a compleat representation of Athens.[32]

Apparently, Elgin had by now established in his mind the goal of
maintaining at all cost the unity and availability of the collection,
endeavoring to bring to literal fruition Peacham's dream of two centuries before, "to transplant old Greece into England." [33] With this
bold and unprecedented plan to lay before the public a whole series
of original Greek sculptures and details of architecture, all deriving

30. *JHS*, XXXVI, pp. 357–358. [Editor's translation: "Lord Elgin has the
good fortune of possessing a great number of the marble originals from
which the casts were taken. It is a priceless treasure. As for myself, I am
happy to have the casts and thus the means to complete the decoration of
the modest sanctuary in which I expect to console myself for my frustra-
tions."]
31. Described in Dubois's *Catalogue* . . . , p. xiii.
32. *Letters, Countess of Elgin*, p. 179; the letter, from Athens, is dated
April 19, 1802.
33. The phrase was first used by Peacham in reference to the antiquarian
activities of Thomas Howard, Earl of Arundel, England's first collector of
Greek statuary (see *The Compleat Gentleman*, second edition, London,
1634, pp. 107–108).

from the same buildings, British antiquarianism, hitherto limited to the piecemeal acquisition and domestic consumption of individual and scattered pieces mostly of Greco-Roman origin and invariably restored by modern hands to make them more suitable for the sculpture galleries or interior adornment of neoclassical palaces, entered an entirely new phase and opened an archaeological frontier whose possibilities for the study and understanding of classical style and for standards of taste in general no one, not even Elgin, could possibly have foreseen.

The removal of the Parthenon sculptures, as well as details of other monuments on the Acropolis, proceeded with dispatch from the end of July, 1801, onward, with Lord Elgin, who was away from the scene on diplomatic duty, kept informed by communications from Lusieri, Hunt, and Hamilton. The acquisition of the first two metopes from the south side of the Parthenon brought this glowing comment from Lusieri:

> If I said all I could, I should not say anything in comparison with their merit. I am sure there is nothing so perfect of this kind in all the universe.[34]

Around this same time, excavations which had begun at the west end of the temple, in hope of unearthing some of the missing pediment pieces, were crowned with success. These endeavors yielded part of the torso of the central figure of Poseidon [see text figs. 50, 51].[35] Hunt, obviously still under the influence of Spon and Wheler's mistaken iconography, as indeed were Hamilton, Lusieri, and the rest of the company as well, referred to this statue as a "naked Jupiter."[36] Also recovered from this excavation (and presently in the Elgin Collection) were the torso of Hermes [see fig. 55] and the remains of several female statues of the west pediment, among them the so-called Iris, Amphitrite, and sea-nymph[37] [see figs. 48, 52, 53]. Hunt

---

34. The first two metopes were removed on successive days, July 31 and August 1, 1801 (*JHS*, XXXVI, p. 197).

35. Our last record of the Poseidon figure before its recovery, in part, by Elgin's workmen occurs in Dalton's drawing of the west pediment in 1749, where the headless torso is shown having collapsed onto the floor of the pediment just a bit left of center. * * * From its precarious position in the drawing we must presume its having fallen to the ground some time thereafter where the lower part of its body already lay (see *A Collection of Fifty-two Engraved Plates from Drawings by Richard Dalton of Antiquities in Sicily, Greece, Asia Minor, Egypt*, London, 1751–52, Plate III). * * * Stuart and Revett make no mention of it in the *Antiquities of Athens*, II.

36. *JHS*, XXXVI, p. 197.

37. All identifications of Parthenon sculptures referred to herein are those of the British Museum.

registers his astonishment at finding the drapery of the feminine figures "so light and elegant as to resemble the finest muslin" and showing all the contours of the form underneath. Seeing it as no one else
before him had been able to, with the possible exception of Fauvel,
Hunt marvels at the illusionistic transparency, the uncompromising
and revealing naturalism of the drapery treatment in the pediment
forms. But this nonrationalized, nonstylized, almost "unclassical"
empiricism, found at the peak of Greek classical style, took Visconti,
Canova, and Quatremère de Quincy by complete surprise, on the one
hand because they had not really anticipated such complete maturity
of technique in the Phidian period, and on the other because its
alarming truth to "common nature" clashed fundamentally with their
dearest canons of classical ideology. Neither Hunt nor Lusieri, however, was as yet aware of the implications of these discoveries for the
understanding of classical sculpture or Phidian style. They had no
guides or precedents by which to judge, other than the systematic
and gracefully contrived draperies of the Greco-Roman statuary already known to them. Thus, Lusieri showed his appreciation of one
of these statues of the west pediment group unearthed at the foot of
the temple by rating it superior to the celebrated Flora at Rome.
It was the figure which Hunt called a *Victory* but which was
in all likelihood the presently named *Iris* of the Elgin Collection [see
fig. 48],[38] corresponding to the first figure on the south (right) side
of the west pediment in "Carrey's" drawing.

It was not long before Lusieri, as he continued acquiring metopes
and expanded his operations to sawing off frieze sections of the Parthenon, raised a question which was to concern Elgin seriously in the
next few years: the matter of restoration. In a letter of October 26,
1801, he comments to Elgin that for the full enjoyment of the fragments of sculpture, they must be restored at Rome. He suggests that
the work might be done by one of the *formatori*, Ledus, but that he
would have to work under the direction of Mr. Canova, the most
famous sculptor of the age.[39] Whether the intention to restore the
marbles had already entered Elgin's own mind before this, there
seems to be no telling, but this is the earliest mention of the idea in
any of his preserved correspondence with his company. At any rate,
it struck a responsive chord in Elgin, who continued to harbor the
hope that it could be done, and afterward proposed it to Canova

38. Hunt, echoing Lusieri, repeats this evaluation in his letter of 1805 to
Lady Elgin's mother: "Lord Elgin has had the satisfaction of recovering the
greater part of the statue of Victory in a drapery which discovers all the
fine form beneath, with as much delicacy and taste as the Flora Farnese . . ."
(*Letters, Countess of Elgin*, p. 334).
39. *JHS*, XXXVI, p. 203.

when he saw him in Rome in 1803. In this, Elgin was only following the example of practically all 18th-century collectors who submitted their antiquities to Roman sculptors and craftsmen for restoration before taking them home. Not all of Elgin's company, however, shared the opinion that this should be done. Hamilton, in particular, was definitely opposed to it and in a letter of August 8, 1802, to Elgin, makes his reservations clear:

> Lusieri speaks to me frequently of his Expectation that you intend to send the mutilated originals which are carried away from Athens to Rome to be restored—I cannot think it will ever be worth while to risque such valuable monuments in a place where all that is precious is every moment in danger of falling into other hands; besides the Expence—the time such an operation would take and many other considerations, among which it may be said that few would be found who would set a higher value on a work of Phidias or of one of his Scholars, with a modern head and modern arms than they would in their *present state*.[40]

Hamilton's remarks, which indeed anticipate Canova's judgment, may be the earliest objection on record to the intended restoration of the Parthenon sculptures. As such, they are fraught with significance for the coming change in the standards for evaluating antiques which the ultimate decision not to restore these marbles brought about. Hamilton was not entirely correct, however, when he assumed that few would have valued a restored over a mutilated Phidian piece. Not only was his view contrary to the standards and procedures of most collectors regarding damaged antiques, but in the debate over the Elgin Marbles after their arrival in London, a considerable number of British dilettanti and collectors—Richard Payne Knight, the Earl of Aberdeen, and John Morritt among them—deplored the ruined state of the pieces and maintained that their condition lowered their monetary value.[41] Notwithstanding Canova's ruling, Sir George Beaumont (1753–1827), painter, critic, and prominent patron of the arts, who held a respected position as an arbiter of taste in painting somewhat comparable to that of Richard Payne Knight in matters of ancient art,[42] recommended in 1808 that the marbles be

40. *Ibid.*, p. 227.
41. Knight makes frequent reference to the mutilated state of the Elgin Marbles throughout his testimony to the Parliamentary Committee as a factor to be taken into account in their monetary evaluation. (See *Report*, pp. 92–104, *passim;* also see the testimonies of Aberdeen and Morritt, *ibid.*, pp. 127, 132.)
42. For a record of his relationships with artists, see "Sir George Beaumont and His Circle," *Exhibition Catalogue of the Leicester Museums and Art Gallery*, June, 1953, with introduction by P. A. Tomory. (Also see Boase, *op. cit.*, pp. 36–37, 149, 203–204.)

restored on aesthetic grounds, maintaining that in their present state the sight of such disfigured parts of limbs and bodies and stumps of arms excited disgust rather than pleasure in the minds of people in general.[43] Furthermore, when the Aegina marbles, the next great series of original Greek sculptures to be procured from one temple, were discovered in 1811 and ultimately purchased by Crown Prince Ludwig of Bavaria, they were taken to Thorwaldsen in Rome to be restored.[44]

It should be noted that Hamilton's objections to the restoration of the Elgin Marbles seem based as much on practical considerations as on purely artistic ones. Apart from the time and expense involved, he was afraid mainly of losing the marbles to the French if the objects were brought to Rome. His fears were based on the confiscations which had already attended the Napoleonic conquests. In November, 1799, when he was in Rome gathering the company of artists for Elgin, Hamilton had written him: "The French have taken away from Rome all the valuable statues—sixty-two choice pieces from the Vatican alone among which are the Torso, Apollo of Belvedere, Laocoon, Meleager, etc.—besides the best from other museums." [45] In the unstable political situation which attended the Napoleonic victories of the next few years, it is not impossible that, had the Elgin

43. See J. Farington, *The Farington Diary*, edited by J. Greig, third edition, New York, 1923, vol. V, p. 72; entry of June 3, 1808. Elgin may have attempted to interest British artists around this time in making preparatory studies, most likely in the form of sketches or models, for restoration of the marbles, as we learn from a letter of Haydon to Elgin of December, 1808 in which the young artist says:

> You said you intended to offer premiums to those who would produce the best restorations. Now, to restore the mutilated parts of any figure, as they ought to be restored, pre-supposes a thorough knowledge of the character of what remains. This could not be expected from students on their first admission. I would venture, therefore, to propose that a twelve-month should be given to them to model and investigate before they commenced restoring, and then I think your Lordship would have a better chance of their succeeding. . . .

(See Benjamin Robert Haydon, *Correspondence and Table Talk*, London, 1876, Vol. I, p. 256.)

Nothing seems to have come of Haydon's suggestion, and we may conjecture that the reluctance of such masters as Canova and Flaxman to accept the challenge may have changed Haydon's mind, or inhibited lesser artists and students from making the attempt.

44. See Michaelis, *A Century of Archaeological Discoveries*, p. 34.

45. *JHS*, XXXVI, p. 171. In 1799, Visconti went to Paris to devote himself to the Musée Napoléon (Michaelis, *A Century of Archaeological Discoveries*, p. 23). It was to Hamilton that the return of works of art taken by Napoleon from Italy was chiefly due in the settlement after Waterloo.

Marbles gone to Rome to be restored, they might have suffered the same fate.[46] Indeed, a considerable number of them almost did, without ever leaving Athens. When war broke out between England and Turkey in 1807, and French power in Athens was restored, Lusieri had to flee, leaving behind many cases of the Parthenon sculptures and other antiquities gathered by Elgin's company, which, under French instigation, were sequestered by the Vizier. Only the impossibility of transporting them overland by mule, and the unavailability of French shipping at the time, prevented them from actually being sent to Paris.[47]

As antiquarian policy, however, Hamilton's flatly stated view—that any piece of sculpture by Phidias, or even one done by his students, however mutilated it might be, was more valuable in its original form than it would be were it completely restored—struck the first blow against subjecting the Elgin Marbles to another kind of mutilation perhaps even worse than that which they had suffered by centuries of exposure and spoliation. For, the ultimate decision to leave this great and singular body of sculpture entirely untouched established once and for all, in practice, a principle already expounded by many in theory, namely, that the historical authenticity, genuineness, and purity of an antique work of art are more important and valuable than its cosmetic properties, its display appeal, or its commercial salability as interior decoration or furniture.[48] Nevertheless, it was still Lusieri's suggestion to restore

46. Napoleon had invaded Italy in 1796 and the French forces had already taken possession of Rome before Napoleon set sail for Egypt in 1798. The unstable Italian republics set up by the French at Naples, Rome, and Milan fell in 1799 when the Austro-Russian forces defeated the French in the war of the Second Coalition, but Napoleon regained control of Italy upon his return from Egypt by his victory over the Allied forces at Marengo and by the Treaty of Luneville (February, 1801). Power was completely centralized in his hands when he dissolved the Italian (Cisalpine) Republic of 1802 and personally assumed the crown as King of Italy on May 26, 1805, establishing his stepson, Eugène Beauharnais, as puppet viceroy. (See R. J. Rath, *The Fall of the Napoleonic Kingdom of Italy (1814)*, New York, 1941, pp. 13–19.)

47. Michaelis, *Im Neuen Reich*, VII, p. 86.

48. Although the practice of restoration continued unabated throughout the 18th century, obesrvations on its evils had already been made by such authors as Casanova and Cavaceppi. The latter, in the last volume of his *Raccolta d'Antiche Statue, etc. Restaurate da Bart. Cavaceppi, Scultore Romano*, Rome, 1768–1772 (Vol. III), urged only limited, insignificant additions to antiquities, observing that the beauty and historical value of a fragment make it worthy of collecting for its own sake. The restorer is seen essentially as a repairman, who must be guided by the archaeologist. Others, including Visconti, Missirini, Caylus, Barthélémy, and Grosley, took an even more purist, anti-restoration position, asserting that the fragment had nothing to gain from modern additions. But among collectors there was no

the marbles that attracted Elgin, and Hamilton's forbearance had to await the confirmation of Canova, a much higher authority in such matters.

In the meantime, in accordance with the adage that nothing succeeds like success, Elgin, tasting the heady wine of Lusieri's acquisitions over the previous six-month period, began to shift his demands from casts to originals. In a letter of December 26, 1801, he writes:

> I should wish to have of the Acropolis, examples in the actual object of each thing, and architectural ornament—of each cornice, each frieze, each capital—of the decorated ceilings, of the fluted columns, specimens of the different architectural orders and of the variant forms of the orders—of metopes and the like, as much as possible. Finally, everything in the way of sculpture, medals, and curious marbles that can be discovered by means of assiduous and indefatigable excavation. This excavation ought to be pushed on as much as possible, be its success what it may.[49]

The letter is accompanied by a list of presents which are being sent for the Turkish officials, in connection with which Elgin admonishes Lusieri, "I beg you to be careful as to the distribution of these articles. I shall regret nothing that assists my acquisitions in Greece." [50]

Elgin's requests break down into two distinct parts. First, he wants Lusieri to get representative examples of all architectural members and details, but just one of each kind, presumably ("examples in the actual object of each thing and architectural ornament," he says). This is clearly in line with his plan later to exhibit to the British public as complete an image as possible of Periclean architectural and sculptural style. In a sense, it may be regarded as a kind of romantic attempt to bring Stuart and Revett's illustrations to life, to present one great cross-section of Greek classical taste and design, paralleling the drawings in the *Antiquities of Athens*. Second, and equally important to Elgin, is the desire to rescue from oblivion whatever fragments had already disappeared from the structures and lay buried in the ground, strewn in the surrounding debris, or incorporated in the walls of Turkish buildings and fortifications. Here we have the urge of the archaeologist, and it became stronger in the 19th century than it had ever been before,[51] to rediscover and preserve the

---

widespread or consistent acceptance of these principles before the 19th century. (See S. Howard, "Bartolommeo Cavaceppi, 18th Century Restorer," doctoral dissertation, Univ. of Chicago, Aug., 1958, pp. 210–211.)

49. *JHS*, XXXVI, p. 207.

50. *Ibid.*, p. 208.

51. The 19th century was to become the great age of archaeological discovery, studded with spectacular and often unexpected finds—among

past, no matter what the cost, or how small the chances of success, as Elgin himself put it. This, too, is not without its romantic overtones, for here Elgin is seen somewhat in the guise of the knight-crusader who personally accepts the challenge and responsibility, at much risk and expense to himself, of saving man's past from the ravages of time or the hands of the Philistine.[52] Yet, it is both ironic and tragic to note that this very urge to preserve somehow brought about its opposite, the need to destroy. For, while Elgin could in all good conscience implore Lusieri to dig up whatever scraps were to be found, he could at the same time, and with apparently the same nobility of intention and self-righteousness, sanction the cutting down and sawing off of sculptural decoration that had remained undisturbed on the Parthenon and the Erechtheum for more than two thousand years.

Lusieri seems to have responded immediately to Elgin's fervor with some romantic suggestions of his own. He conceived of the possibility of recreating the Caryatid Porch of the Erechtheum by the ingenious device of removing one of the Caryatid maidens and reproducing the others from it. He tells Elgin in a letter of January 11, 1802, "The five Caryatids are exactly similar and the base, cornice, and the upper part are in a pitiful state. It will not be difficult by means with which I am acquainted to get the best of these Caryatids, to have it restored at Rome, and afterwards to have it moulded. In this way your Excellency might have this little monument quite complete." [53] Lusieri's suggestion was, in fact, only a more modest alternative to an earlier and more radical scheme proposed by Hunt in a letter of July 31, 1801: "If your Lordship would come here in a large Man of War that beautiful little model of ancient art (the Porch of the Maidens) might be transported wholly to England. . . ." [54]

---

them the finding of Troy by Schliemann, the discovery of the Rosetta stone and the decipherment by Champollion of the hieroglyphs, the finding of the Aegina and Phigaleian marbles by Cockerell and company, and the unearthing of the ancient sites of Assyria, Babylonia, and Sumeria by Botta, Layard, Koldewey, and others. The impetus which Elgin's deed gave to the archaeological "rescue," or resurrection, of the past should not be overlooked.

52. "Lord Elgin's salvaging and transport of the Parthenon sculptures was a feat of archaeological romanticism no less inspiring than Byron's daydreams of a Greek liberty," say Saxl and Wittkower (*British Art and the Mediterranean*, London, 1948, p. 77).

53. *JHS*, XXXVI, p. 209.

54. *Ibid.*, p. 196. The French apparently had similar ambitions for the Temple of Theseus. (See J. C. Hobhouse, *Journey Through Albania and Other Provinces of Turkey in Europe and Asia . . . during 1809 and 1810*, London, 1813, I, p. 286.)

Although the transplantation and reconstruction of Greek temples in England does not seem to have been part of his original plan, Elgin was at first strongly attracted to Hunt's idea.[55] But strong Greek and Turkish opposition led him to abandon the notion. Lusieri's suggestion, that only one of the figures be removed, prevailed. What probably helped ease Lusieri's conscience was the impression that he was not the first to violate this structure. One of the Caryatids, that of the rear east corner of the Porch, had already disappeared long before the arrival of Elgin's company, and was mistakenly believed to have found its way to Rome.[56] That is why Lusieri refers in his letter to five such figures (see above), not to six. But the missing Caryatid was, in fact, rediscovered at its original site during the Erechtheum excavations of 1837.[57] The Caryatid taken by Lusieri, however, was from a more prominent position, the second from the west corner of the front row. To make matters worse, it was initially replaced by a rude and unsightly pier of rubble. It was this act of confiscation, more than any other, that brought severe censure down upon Elgin's head and later led an indignant traveler, said to be Lord Byron himself, to carve into the west wall of the temple cella the satirical and much-quoted line, "Quod non fecerunt Goti, fecerunt Scoti." [58] William

55. Elgin writes to Lusieri, December 26, 1801, "I name very especially the temple of Pandrosus. I flatter myself that you have already thought of ways of transporting it. If Captain Lacy is with you, with the means that Mr. Hamilton will have supplied, such as levers and so forth, perhaps you could get down the statues one after another, and put them on my brig, and by degrees, transport the whole to Zea . . . (*JHS*, XXXVI, p. 207).

56. This Caryatid is already missing in Richard Dalton's drawing, made in 1749, of the Erechtheum as seen from the southeast (reproduced in G. P. Stevens and J. M. Paton, *The Erechtheum*, Cambridge, 1927, Pl. L, 1.) Thought to have been vandalized, it was for many years confused with a Greco-Roman copy of an Erechtheum Caryatid in the Vatican Museum which was mistaken for this lost original (see L. Ross, *Archäologische Aufsätze*, I, 1855, pp. 121–122).

57. In these excavations the torso and several fragments of the lower part of this long-absent Caryatid were found buried, leading to the supposition that the statue may have fallen when struck by a Venetian bomb in 1687. The head, however, was missing, the markings at the neck indicating that it may have been cut off and removed rather than destroyed by the fall. In 1846–47, under the direction of the French architect, A. Paccard, this Caryatid was restored, not too successfully, by the Italian sculptor Andreoli and replaced in its original position. However, only the ancient torso from neck to hips was used, the eight to ten fragments of the lower part being too unsubstantial to be reassembled with sufficient strength to bear the weight above. (See Stevens and Paton, p. 567.)

58. (See *Childe Harold*, Canto II, 12.) There is some disagreement on both the placement and authorship of this inscription. It is mentioned in

Wilkins, the British architect who later gave testimony to the Parliamentary Committee, and who had visited Athens in 1802 at the height of Elgin's operations there, suggests that had the Erechtheum been suffered to remain untouched, Elgin might have escaped all criticism.[59] The traveler, Edward Dodwell, who was in Athens in 1801, implies the same when he says that had the temples been left alone and had only that sculpture been removed which had already fallen, the British Museum would still have been sufficiently enriched for the improvement of national taste, while casts would have answered every purpose of the originals which were taken.[60]

1834 by Sir Grenville Temple (*Travels in Greece and Turkey*, I, p. 81), who attributes it to Byron but describes it as being carved on the masonry pier substituted for the Caryatid taken by Elgin; while Hobhouse (*Journey Through Albania*, p. 345) locates it "on the plaster wall on the west side of the chapel," but makes no mention of Byron as the author. (Also see A. Michaelis, *Der Parthenon*, Leipzig, 1870–71, p. 81.) The quote comes from a story of a Greek historian (Zosimus) who relates that Alaric, either terrified by the phantoms of Minerva herself and of Achilles striding toward the walls of Troy, or struck with reverence for the temple, had spared the treasures and people of the venerable city. (See J. G. Gennadios, *Lord Elgin and His Predecessors in the Archaeological Invasion of Greece and Especially Athens, 1440–1827*, 1930, p. 79, note. Original in Greek.) There are other versions of the epithet. A similar one was used against the Barberini, with this variation: "Quod non fecerunt barbari fecerunt Barberini," one of the satirical *pasquinades* (affixed to the ancient group then called "Pasquins") on the occasion of Urban VIII's use of bronze from the Pantheon for the Baldacchino in St. Peter's.

59. W. Wilkins, *Atheniensia, or Remarks on the Topography and Buildings of Athens*, London, 1816, p. 144, note.

60. E. Dodwell, *A Classical and Topographical Tour Through Greece during the Years 1801, 1805, and 1806*, London, 1819, I, p. 323. It is interesting to note that two contrasting proposals were made by Englishmen for rectifying the Caryatid removal by Elgin. Dodwell suggested the replacement of the original and substitution of a cast of it in the Elgin Collection: "Would it not be worthy of this country . . . to restore the column of the Erechtheum and the dismantled entablature, which might be done without any serious expense? Our Museum would only be deprived of that single column which might be replaced by a cast answering fully to the purpose of the original" (*ibid.*, I, p. 354). H. W. Williams, on the other hand, suggested that the reproduction be sent back to Greece, and the original retained: "I have been tempted to wish we could send from home a fac-simile by Coade of the Caryatid now in the British Museum and remove the wretched support which is constantly reminding one of what the Turks had spared" (*op. cit.*, II, p. 307). Of the two ideas, it was the one of Williams that was ultimately adopted when in 1846–47 a terra-cotta cast of the Elgin Caryatid, which had been presented by the British Government, was set in place of the masonry pier erected by Lusieri. This, in turn, was replaced in 1912 by a copy made of Portland cement (see Stevens and Paton, *op. cit.*, pp. 568, 235, note 3). But Williams' further suggestion, that this procedure also be used to replace the metopes and frieze sections taken by Elgin, bore no fruit.

It would seem that much of the criticism of Elgin at this time came from his own countrymen who happened to be present in Athens during the years 1801 to 1803 and therefore could witness the proceedings in a way he himself, being away most of the time, could not. In addition to Wilkins and Dodwell, the traveler Edward D. Clarke, the young architect Robert Smirke, and the nobleman-antiquarian Lord Aberdeen were also on hand and registered their objections. Clarke aroused resentment against Elgin when he later published his indignant eye-witness account of how the workmen injured the adjacent parts of the architecture in dislodging one of the Parthenon metopes, and in removing the Selene horse-head from the corner of the east pediment. Of the metope Clarke writes:

> We saw this fine piece of sculpture raised from its station between the triglyphs, but the workmen endeavoring to give it a position adapted to the projected line of descent, a part of the adjoining masonry was loosened by the machinery and down came the fine masses of Pentelican marble, scattering their white fragments with thundering noise among the ruins. . . .[61]

Conscience-stricken over this, Lusieri on two occasions apologized to Elgin.[62] Clarke also makes a point of contrasting the irresponsibility of Elgin's undertaking to the painstaking care being exercised by Lord Aberdeen in his excavation and restoration of the Pnyx,[63] and finds Aberdeen all the more laudable for his opposition to the deplorable operations of Elgin's company.[64] Robert Smirke, whose Grecian tendencies were later to show themselves in his design for the main façade of the British Museum, was only about 21 years old when he was in Athens in 1803,[65] sketching and studying Greek

61. E. D. Clarke, *op. cit.*, II, ii, p. 483.
62. In a letter to Elgin of September 16, 1802, Lusieri says, "I have, my Lord, the pleasure of announcing to you the possession of the 8th metope, the one where there is a Centaur carrying off the woman. The piece has caused much trouble in all respects and I have been obliged to be a little barbarous" (*JHS*, XXXVI, p. 232). In another letter to Elgin of October 28, 1802, he again confesses his guilt when he says, "I must do more still and I much want to try it so that some of the barbarisms that I have been obliged to commit in your service may be forgotten" (*ibid.*, p. 236).
63. An open theatrical area erected shortly after 507 B.C. by Cleisthenes in Athens, on the northeast rocky slope of the hill, to accommodate about 5,000 citizens, and enlarged about a century later. (See W. B. Dinsmoor, *The Architecture of Ancient Greece*, third edition revised, London and New York, 1950, pp. 119, 206–207.)
64. Clarke, *op. cit.*, III, p. 465, note.
65. Smirke was abroad in Italy and Greece from 1801 to 1805. An original representation by him of the west front of the Parthenon as it appeared at this time is in the British Museum, Department of Greek and Roman Antiquities (Folio 41e, "Miscellaneous Prints of the Parthenon").

architecture. In notes to a journal he kept of his trip,[66] he seems torn between his desire to see the marbles rescued for England and the painful sight of the damage inflicted on the architecture in extricating them. He comments:

> Though I was at first pleased with the Idea of our Country coming in possession of such valuable remains, particularly as I have heard much of the French intending to procure them and of their having already made application to the Porte for that purpose; yet I could not but feel a strong regret when I considered their being taken as a sort of signal for the annihilation of such interesting monuments. It particularly affected me when I saw the demolition made to get down the basso-relievos on the walls of the Cella. The men employed were laboring long ineffectually with iron Crows to move the stones of these firm built walls. Each stone as it fell shook the ground with its ponderous weight with a deep hollow noise; it seemed like a convulsive groan of the injured spirit of the Temple.[67]

As Smirke indicates, Elgin was obviously much concerned at this time with the intentions of the French, who were, he feared, on the point of increasing their own efforts to acquire the marbles or to interfere with his operations. He writes to Lusieri on August 9, 1802:

> It seems clear to me that the French have it in their minds to occupy themselves immensely with Greece both in the matter of the arts and in politics. I have reason to believe, that from the moment that the Ambassador and the Consuls go to their posts in these countries, artists will be sent into Greece not without the hope of preventing the completion of my work and of my collections and not even without the hopes of presenting the same subjects to the public before my works can appear.[68]

Meanwhile, deterred neither by such suspicions of French intrigue nor by the criticism of other English travelers in Athens, the work of gathering the sculptures had continued unabated. On May 10, 1802, Lusieri reported the lowering of the Selene horse-head [fig. 45] from the east pediment and his intention to lower the other figures of that pediment in the course of that week.[69] Before September 12, the two

---

For a reproduction of this drawing see F. Brommer *Die Skulpturen der Parthenon-Giebel*, Mainz am Rhein, 1963, Pl. 66.

66. The original notebook, titled "Diary of Robert Smirke, Notes Referred to in My Journal of My Tour Through Greece," is in the Library of the Royal Institute of British Architects, London.

67. Smirke, "Diary," p. 46, note 23.

68. *JHS*, XXXVI, p. 227.

69. *Ibid.*, p. 216.

draped figure groups, that of Persephone and Demeter [see fig. 51] and that of Hestia, Dione, and Aphrodite, also known as the "three Fates" [see fig. 50], had been acquired. Some time after October 8, the Ilissus of the west pediment [see fig. 46] was down, and by the end of November all of the remaining figures of the east pediment had been removed.[70] Also, Lusieri tells us that Feodor the Calmuck, the sculptural draughtsman of the company, had finished his detailed drawings of the frieze [71] * * * and would soon be ready to experiment on engraving them. Besides this, he had collaborated with the architectural draughtsmen on two large elevation drawings of the Parthenon, one of the east façade on which he had rendered a complete conjectural restoration of the pediment and metope sculptures * * * , the other of the south side on which he had drawn on a small scale a restored version of all 32 metopes * * * .[72] On the pedimen-

70. A letter of Hamilton to Elgin, dated September 12, 1802, speaks of efforts to get the two Groups from the Fronton (meaning the east) on board a Hydriote vessel for shipment (*ibid.*, p. 231). A letter of Elgin to Lusieri of October 8, 1802, urges the procurement of the figure of the man (meaning the Ilissus) from the west pediment (*ibid.*, p. 234). A letter of Lusieri to Elgin, dated November 16, 24, and 28, 1802, refers to the extant east pediment figures as "now in your possession" (*ibid.*, p. 238).

71. Letter of Lusieri to Elgin, October 28, 1802 (*ibid.*, p. 235). The Calmuck's original drawings of the Parthenon frieze as well as of the south metopes in the Elgin Collection exist in the British Museum, Department of Greek and Roman Antiquities, Folio 41e, "Elgin Drawings," Vol. 4. This volume contains 80 detailed drawings, mostly in pencil (and a few in sepia wash) of relief sculpture from the Parthenon, Theseum (Hephaesteum), and Temple of Athena Nike. Included in the Parthenon drawings, among others, are a complete rendition of the west frieze and all of the metopes in the Elgin Collection. This letter also mentions that the Calmuck was doing a large rendering of the west pediment (on which, following Spon and Wheler's mistaken inversion of the pediment themes he was representing a restored version of the Birth of Minerva) and a long drawing of the side of the temple showing the metopes, neither of which was yet completed. Of these two the latter drawing survives (see note 72), but that of the west pediment restoration seems to have disappeared.

72. Letter of Lusieri to Elgin dated November 16, 24, and 28, 1802 (*ibid.*, p. 238). The originals of these two drawings are in the British Museum, Department of Greek and Roman Antiquities, Folio 41e, "Elgin Drawings," Vol. 3, containing, among others, six large drawings pertaining to the architecture and sculpture of the Parthenon. Plate II of this volume is a south elevation of the Parthenon done entirely in line, showing in continuous sequence the restored metopes each about one inch in size. Plate III is a restoration of the east façade labeled "Prospetto del Lato del Est del Tempio di Minerva," of which the architectural parts (probably by Balestra) are in sepia tone while Feodor's sculptural details of the pediment figures and metopes are all in line. Two of the other Parthenon plates in this volume show details of sculpture by Feodor. Plate V is a restored version of the north corner showing a part of the terminal north metope, drawn to a size

tal drawing, using the extant figures, but unfortunately still following the reversed iconography of Spon and Wheler, he had represented, Lusieri informs us, the dispute of Minerva and Neptune. Not quite satisfied with the Calmuck's performance, Lusieri criticized his figures in these drawings for being "a little heavy, and though well understood, . . . wanting in that delicacy that always marks the work of the ancients." [73] It was intended by Elgin that Feodor should go to London to superintend the engraving of his drawings, [74] but after protracted negotiations this plan seems never to have been consummated. [75] Overshadowed by the arrival of the originals Feodor's drawings of the Elgin Marbles were apparently forgotten. [76] Casting operations had also proceeded with uninterrupted zeal during this period and by October 28, 1802, an impressive quantity of architecture and sculpture had been moulded including the entire west frieze and the best preserved parts of the north frieze of the Parthenon, six Parthenon metopes, all the different ornaments of the Erechtheum portico, cella, and Pandroseum, the bust of a Caryatid, the east frieze of the Theseum (Hephaesteum), and the entire frieze of the Monument of Lysicrates. [77]

---

of about six inches in height. Plate VI is an elevation of the interior of the west portico labeled "Dinanzi del Tempio di Minerva" showing the complete west frieze on a scale of about one inch in height, comparable to Stuart's engraving of the same in the *Antiquities of Athens*, II, Ch. I, Pl. IV.

73. *JHS*, XXXVI, p. 238.

74. After some dilatoriness on the part of the Calmuck and threats by Lusieri to send his drawings to Rome to be engraved by Camuccini or Piale (*ibid.*, pp. 230, 232) an agreement was reached on April 11, 1803, between Feodor and Elgin binding him to come to England and engrave his drawings there (*ibid.*, p. 255). The plan is corroborated by the anonymous author of an article called "Letter from a Foreign Gentleman in Rome Relative to Lord Elgin's Collection of Grecian Antiquities and Lord Hamilton's Late Travels in Greece," in the *Monthly Magazine*, Vol. XVI, no. 104, part II, August 1, 1803, p. 16, who speaks of meeting Lord Elgin's company of artists there and says, "Mr. Feodor is going to England to superintend the engraving of his drawings."

75. In Lord Elgin's statement of expenses drawn up in 1811 (see *Report*, Appendix no. 5) he says his draughtsman spent two years in England, but this has never been corroborated and there seems to be no further information on it. Apparently Feodor's drawings were never engraved. Later, in 1806, he went to Karlsruhe where he became court painter. (See Thieme-Becker, XI, pp. 337–338.)

76. Some of his work was published much later. Reproductions of the restored versions of metopes I–XIV from his east façade rendering appeared in A. H. Smith, *Sculptures of the Parthenon*, London, 1910, pp. 37–40; see also Koch, *Studien zum Theseustempel*, Pls. 202–204, for his drawings of the Hephaesteum frieze.

77. *JHS*, XXXVI, p. 236.

During this period of intense activity on the Parthenon, Elgin himself had been kept mostly at Constantinople and other parts of the Near East by his official duties. He was able to visit Athens only in the spring of 1802 and again in January, 1803. In his race against the French, he bent every effort toward arranging for the transportation out of Athens of the marbles already acquired. Shipments of the Parthenon sculptures to England, usually by way of Malta or Alexandria, where stops were made to pick up other acquisitions made by Elgin's agents, began in March of 1802.[78] The first pieces arrived at Plymouth on August 12 of that year. The London *Observer* of August 22 carried a notice that fifteen large cases shipped from Egypt by Lord Elgin had arrived and that among the objects opened for inspection was a "most beautiful specimen of Greek sculpture, the figure of a centaur."[79] With this terse and innocent reference to one of the south metopes the public received its first word of what was destined to grow into a veritable avalanche of comment, analysis, and debate in the London press and periodicals. During the next decade (1802–1812) shipments of the Elgin Marbles continued to arrive in various British ports,[80] but before 1806 the

78. In his letter to Lusieri of August 9, 1802, Elgin writes: "After having considered all the circumstances that can affect my operations in Greece I have determined to send my brig again to Athens to take thence absolutely everything that the captain can put on board the ship. He will transport them to Malta whence he will go to Egypt, if the objects that Mr. Hunt took to Alexandria were not yet shipped to England." (*Ibid.*, p. 227).

79. *Ibid.*, p. 295.

80. For a complete listing of all shipments of the Elgin Marbles and the vessels and dates involved, see *ibid.*, pp. 293–294. The Napoleonic wars added to Elgin's difficulties in procuring vessels and the collection had to be shipped in scattered lots, arriving in England over a period of ten years (1802–1812). At least 22 ships had been used in the Elgin operations by 1815 (see *Letters, Countess of Elgin*, p. 82). Only one major mishap attended all these voyages. On September 17, 1802, the *Mentor*, loaded among other things with about 11 cases of sections from the Parthenon frieze, sank in a storm off the shores of Cerigo on its way from the Piraeus to Malta. Eventually, more than two years later, and at considerable expense for salvage operations, all the cases were recovered, as Lusieri reported to Hamilton on October 24, 1804. Thus, none of Elgin's acquisitions of original sculpture was lost. (See *JHS*, XXXVI, pp. 240–260 for the complete story of the *Mentor*.) Of the pediment figures the Selene horse-head was the first to arrive in England, some time in the latter part of 1802. The chief surviving pediment figures (the Dionysus, the Hebe, the Persephone-Demeter group, and the three "Fates," of the east pediment, and the Ilissus and Hermes of the west pediment) shipped out of the Piraeus to Malta on board the *Braakel* in February of 1803 (*ibid.*, p. 254). They left Malta, arriving in England on board the *Prevoyante* in January, 1804. From 1804 to 1812 shipments of the marbles from the Piraeus to Malta continued to be made, under Lusieri's direction, but owing to Elgin's imprisonment in France from 1803

nature of the contents remained unknown to the public. Lord Elgin having become a prisoner in France in 1803, the cases which were addressed to him could not be unpacked until he arrived back in London to claim them after his release three years later.

Prior to his seizure by the French, his ambassadorial term coming to a close, Lord Elgin made a trip to Rome in April, 1803. His company of artists, including Lusieri, Feodor, and Balestra had preceded him there.[81] Ostensibly he went for the Easter festival, but his real purpose was to see Canova, to show him the drawings of the Parthenon sculptures made by the Calmuck, and to ask him, as Lusieri had suggested, to restore them. Canova's refusal made history and his words are thus recorded by Elgin:

> The decision of that eminent artist was conclusive. He declared that however greatly it was to be lamented that these statues should have suffered so much from time and barbarism yet it was undeniable that they had never been retouched; that they were the work of the ablest artists the world had ever seen . . . that he should have had the greatest delight and derived the greatest benefit from the opportunity Lord Elgin offered him of having in his possession and contemplating these inestimable marbles, but (his expression was) "it would be sacrilege" in him or any man to presume to touch them with a chisel.[82]

For Elgin, the judgment of Canova had both its positive and negative aspects. On the one hand, it must have been extremely reassuring to have an authority like Canova, who had not previously hesitated to restore important works of classical art, such as the figures

---

to 1806, the Turco-British war of 1807–1809, and the subsequent Napoleonic Wars, it became increasingly difficult to get them transported to England. In a letter of Elgin to Lord Mulgrave of February 16, 1808 (ADD. MS. 40,096, fol. 54, British Museum Library, Department of Manuscripts), subsequently submitted by Lord Mulgrave to Lord Collingwood of the Admiralty, we learn of Elgin's predicament in trying to get the remainder of his collection out of Athens when he asks for the assistance and protection of British naval vessels: "It is possible, tho' I can mention it only as a vague wish, that by my secret communications with the authorities at Athens and a demonstration of force from the Shore, concerted with the Governor of Athens, the Cases in the Town might be brought down to the Port." Obstacles were finally removed in 1812 and 80 more cases of Elgin's acquisitions were sent from Malta to England. Of these a major shipment of 68 cases, containing the remainder of the collection of marbles, arrived in Deptford aboard the *Navigator* on May 25 of that year. (See *Report*, Appendix No. 5, Postscript, London, February 29, 1816, p. xv; also *JHS*, XXXVI, p. 315.)

81. The names of these three members of Elgin's company are specifically mentioned by the foreign gentleman writing from Rome (*Monthly Magazine*, XVI, 104, p. 15).

82. *Memorandum*, 1815, pp. 39–40.

of the children in the Nile group of the Vatican,[83] place so high a stamp of approval on the Parthenon sculptures as to set them, by implication at least, above the level of some of the known masterpieces of later antiquity as well as beyond his own ability to emulate. This constituted, for Elgin, the first official confirmation of their quality from a source other than the members of his own company. Furthermore, it was made essentially on the basis of drawings,[84] for Canova was not to see the originals until he visited London in 1815. In his high regard for the marbles, we perhaps can detect the influence of his countryman Ennio Quirino Visconti, director of the Louvre and eminent classical scholar, who had eulogized the Parthenon sculptures in the commentary he had supplied a few years earlier for the text of the *Museum Worsleyanum*, a private publication of the collection of antiquities in the possession of the English dilettante Sir Richard Worsley. But Visconti's judgments also were made entirely on the basis of renderings of the sculptures—the original drawings of them made by William Pars and the engravings published in the second volume of Stuart and Revett's *Antiquities of Athens*. Except for the section of the east frieze acquired by Fauvel for Choiseul-Gouffier and transferred to the Louvre in 1801,[85] Visconti also re-

83. Michaelis, *Im Neuen Reich*, VII, p. 85.

84. *Farington Diary*, IV, p. 56, entry of December 5, 1806. Flaxman reports Elgin having told him that he showed Canova several articles of Greek sculpture when he asked him to restore the marbles. If so (though there is no way of verifying it), they could have only been small fragments possibly of the Parthenon frieze, for by that time all the larger pediment pieces had been shipped to Malta (see note 80).

85. This frieze section was the only piece of "ex-situ" Parthenon sculpture known to experts in France and available for study before the Elgin Marbles were shown in London, having arrived at the Louvre in 1801 (see E. Michon, "Les Fragments du Parthénon conservées au Musée du Louvre," *Revue archéologique*, Series III, XXIV, 1894, pp. 85–88). Visconti appears not to have immediately recognized its significance. It was first put in storage, but upon questioning by the First Consul on January 8, 1802, according to the Louvre archives, Visconti admitted that it might be from the Parthenon and possibly by the hand of Phidias. The First Consul was astonished that such a precious fragment had not yet been shown and wanted it immediately put on display, but Visconti reported that it was considerably mutilated and would first have to be repaired. Most of the heads had been broken off and lost in shipment. Although Visconti agreed, under pressure, immediately to initiate trial attempts at restoration on casts of the fragment, actual work on the original was not undertaken until 1818–1820 when, at his death, Choiseul-Gouffier's Parthenon metope was purchased by the Louvre, at which time both pieces were restored. (Michon, pp. 88–91.) We may surmise that the news of Canova's refusal to restore the Elgin Marbles in April, 1803, arrived in time to convince Visconti and the officials to abandon, for the time being, restoration of their frieze piece.

mained unacquainted with the originals until he saw them in 1814, one year before Canova. On the other hand, Canova's refusal to restore the marbles upset Elgin's plans to bring before the public a complete representation of Periclean Athens, an intention to which he had already alluded several times in his correspondence. In spite of the fact that he says Canova's judgment was final, it seems that at the time he could not easily reconcile himself to it. At his persistence, Canova said that if he was determined to have them restored he would recommend that it be done by the British sculptor, Flaxman, who, he maintained, could perform the task as well as he.[86]

With his detention in France and the necessity upon his return to England of gathering, unpacking, and finding a suitable residence in London for his collection, it was not until 1807 that Elgin could pursue Canova's suggestion. He then approached Flaxman who with equal prudence would not presume to undertake what Canova had admitted he could not successfully accomplish himself. He thoroughly discouraged Elgin's hopes of seeing the marbles made whole by modern hands. If it were to be done at all, Flaxman said, it should be done in toto, which, he feared, would consume a great length of time and an enormous expense (above £20,000). Even then, when completed, the execution would be far inferior to the original parts in many places and in as much as conjecture would be involved in reconstructing the missing parts, it would become a source of constant dispute among artists and connoisseurs as to whether the restoration was accurate. He corroborated completely Hamilton's earlier opinion, first offered to Elgin in 1802, that the results at best could only lower rather than raise the intrinsic value of the collection.[87] Having thus spoken, Flaxman consented only to the job of repairman, not restorer, of the Elgin Collection. He was assigned to the task of refitting broken limbs or other fragments of the originals to the places from which they had come.

One might have supposed that Flaxman's opinion would once and for all have shattered whatever illusions Elgin still had about restoration. Yet there is evidence that even as late as 1814 when he invited Visconti to visit London, he still clung to the notion. In a letter to Hamilton of August 24 of that year, he writes, "My object (in inviting Visconti) was to obtain from the best judge in Europe (one who having been guardian of the Museum of the Vatican has since had the charge of Bonaparte's) an appreciation of my collection, *advice as to what parts of it are susceptible of restora-*

86. *Farington Diary*, IV, p. 56.
87. *JHS*, XXXVI, p. 297.

tion. . . ." [88] But Visconti's antipathy to the idea, and his assurance of the Periclean authenticity [89] and excellence of the collection as it stood, must have settled the matter for we hear no more of it from Elgin after this.

On his way home from Rome by way of Genoa and Marseilles, Elgin was stopped at Paris late in May of 1803 when a decree was issued by the First Consul making all Englishmen between the ages of 18 and 60 prisoners of war. He was kept in France for the next three years where, by his own admission, he was allowed to live peacefully in a rented house with his family who came over from Scotland to join him.[90] Only twice was he subjected to punitive treatment, once in 1803 when he was confined in the Château Fort at Lourdes in political retaliation for the imprisonment of General Boyer in England, and a second time in 1805, when, as a result of a letter from an English traveler whom Elgin declined to name in his testimony, complaining of the removal by Lusieri of part of the Parthenon frieze,[91] he was taken one morning from bed by a gendarme and locked up for about two weeks at Melun.[92] That some pressure must have been applied by the French during his internment to induce Elgin to sell or turn over his collection to them in return for his freedom is suggested by the following statement from an anonymous letter which appeared in an appendix to his *Memorandum*, edition of 1815: "Powerful indeed must have been the determination in Lord Elgin's mind to preserve his collection for his own country when during above three years of confinement and persecution he would at any time have obtained his liberty and any sum of money he had named for ceding them to the French government. . . ." [93] It was also reported by others who had conversations with him that on several occasions Elgin uttered the statement that Bonaparte would

88. *Ibid.*, p. 318.

89. See *Memorandum*, 1815, Appendix D, p. 81; also see *Letter from the Chevalier Antonio Canova and Two Memoirs Read to the Royal Institute of France on the Sculpture in the Collection of the Earl of Elgin by the Chevalier E. Q. Visconti*, London, 1816, p. 2.

90. *Report*, p. 43. He was first in Paris, then in Barèges in the Pyrenees, then finally settled at Pau (*JHS*, XXXVI, p. 255).

91. Among the Englishmen present in Athens in 1805 were Dodwell (his second trip), William Gell, Sir Charles Monck, Dr. MacMichael (see W. Miller, *The English in Athens before 1821*, London, 1926, p. 21). Lusieri also mentions a Mr. Beken (Bacon?) and a Mr. Mackencie (Mackenzie?) (*JHS*, XXXVI, p. 261). Of all these, the most likely author of the complaining letter of which Elgin speaks is Gell, whom Lusieri mentions as having collaborated with the French in opposing his activities (*ibid.*, p. 262).

92. *Report*, p. 43.

93. *Memorandum*, 1815, Appendix E, p. 93.

have given any price to have his collection.[94] Thus, in his correspondence with Charles Long, member of Parliament, in 1811, concerning the possible sale at that time of his collection to the government, Elgin cited an article from a recent French periodical which, in giving an account of a French translation of Stuart and Revett's *Antiquities of Athens* in progress at the time, called the ornaments belonging to the Parthenon the only undoubted works of Phidias in existence.[95] This demonstrates, he contends, "in what estimation the collection I have brought to England is held in France, and affords a ground of judging far less exceptionably than on any assurances from me, whether, during my detention of three years there, it must not have been constantly in my option to have made the most advantageous terms for ceding them to the French government." [96]

It is open to question, however, just how seriously we should take this remark when we learn in a later report from Elgin himself that on first being arrested and fearing his detention might be protracted, he sent instructions to members of his family at home that in his absence his entire collection was to be made over to the government unconditionally.[97] Apparently he had never had any intention of using his marbles as a political expedient or as a weapon for his personal salvation or profit. But his family, out of doubts or misunderstanding, failed to comply with his request [98] and simply allowed the cases of marbles to accumulate at the customs offices of the various ports at which they arrived. Thus, when the main cargo of fifty cases arrived in January, 1804, containing, among other things, the major pediment figures, the bankers notified the Dowager Lady Elgin, asking where to send them.[99] The cases were first taken to the Duchess of Portland's house in Privy Gardens, and from there to the Duke of Richmond's,[100] but the Elgin family, completely uncertain of what disposition should be made of them, left them unopened. It was only upon his release and return in 1806 that Elgin himself became fully aware of this situation. Misguided though he may have been, Elgin's assumption that the marbles were safely in the hands

94. See *Diary and Correspondence of Charles Abbot, Lord Colchester, Speaker of the House of Commons, 1802–1817*, edited by his son, Charles, Lord Colchester, London, 1861, Vol. II, p. 328.

95. "Beaux Arts," *Moniteur*, April 20, 1810.

96. *Report*, Appendix No. 5, "Copy of a Letter Addressed by Lord Elgin to the Right Honourable Charles Long, May 6, 1811 . . . ," pp. vii–viii.

97. *Ibid.*, Appendix No. 4, "Memorandum as to the Delay in Transferring Lord Elgin's Collection to the Public, February, 1816," p. v.

98. *Ibid.*, Appendix No. 4, *loc. cit.*

99. *JHS*, XXXVI, p. 295.

100. *Ibid.*, pp. 295–296.

of his own government during the years of his French captivity therefore casts in some doubt the sincerity of his contentions about refusing to sell them to the French at a lucrative price. This seeming flaw in his position [101] was, nevertheless, turned to Elgin's advantage. On the one hand, the directive to his family to cede his marbles to the government, whether carried out or not, at least gave evidence of his honorable civic intentions, while his token resistance to French inducements to sell his collection at a supposedly handsome profit, when perhaps it was no longer within his power to do so, could readily be interpreted as courageous and clever diplomatic parrying to hold the enemy at bay. We should not overlook the point that while such professions by Elgin of his immunity to French pressure to acquire his collection were made ostensibly to defend his personal integrity and conduct, they also had the important subsidiary purpose of increasing the British public's estimate of the monetary value of his marbles and of whetting the incentive of government to purchase them.[102]

From the confusion of his own family, as well as from other evidence, it seems that back in 1803 little was known or understood by Elgin's countrymen of the plans he had in mind for the use of his collection. Opinion on the propriety of his conduct in taking the marbles or the merit of the pieces he had acquired was divided, particularly among the Dilettanti, and although some were decidedly enthusiastic and in favor even of supporting him with a grant of funds, a larger number were suspicious of his motives and began turning public sentiment against him. Sometime early in 1803 Thomas Harrison, the Scottish architect who had originally proposed the idea behind Elgin's operations, received a letter from Elgin [103] requesting

101. It should be noted that Appendix No. 4 of the *Report* in which Elgin attributes the delay in the transferral of his collection to the public to his family's misunderstanding of the directive he had sent them when he was interned in France is dated February, 1816, while Appendix No. 5 of the *Report* in which he speaks of his subsequent resistance to French pressure to get him to sell his collection was written five years earlier, in May, 1811. The inverted order of these events in the *Report* makes it more difficult for the reader to see the inherent contradiction.

102. Thus, the purpose of the 1811 edition of the *Memorandum* is attacked by one commentator as a device to rally public support for the purchase by government: " . . . a suspicion arises that though the professed purpose for publishing this *Memorandum* be to promote a subscription to have engravings and casts made of the various articles brought from Greece . . . the latent purpose is to excite a popular feeling in favour of Lord Elgin's claim to remuneration." (*Extract of a Review of Lord Elgin's Memorandum*, reprinted from the *British Review and London Critical Journal*, 1811, p. 42.)

103. *JHS*, XXXVI, p. 294.

information which would be of use to Lusieri in his further pursuits
in Greece. This letter Harrison communicated to the notable
collector-antiquarian Charles Townley who was a prominent member of the Society of Dilettanti and a close friend of Richard Payne
Knight, leader of the group. Townley's reply to Harrison [104] and
the subsequent turn of events expose the split reaction at this time in
Britain to Elgin's activities, which already augured the trouble that
awaited his return. Townley, whose own taste was essentially beau-
idealist, having been formed by his extensive Greco-Roman collection which was the largest and best in England, nevertheless was
favorable to Elgin's enterprises. "I have lost no opportunity," he
says, "of informing persons of taste and judgment in the Fine Arts of
the interesting operations which Lord Elgin is now so eagerly carrying on. His Lordship's zeal is most highly approved and admired and
every hope and wish is entertained for his final success. But our Government is universally blamed for not contributing their political influence as well as pecuniary aid towards these operations, for the
advancement of the Fine Arts in this country." [105] This last remark
Lord Elgin later used as evidence to support his contention that he
received no financial assistance from the state for his antiquarian pursuits.[106] From the next sentence, however, we become aware that
Harrison himself must by now have grown alarmed at the unan-
ticipated scope of endeavor that his modest suggestions to Elgin in
1799 had led to and no longer supported his patron's scheme. "You
appear to decline Lord Elgin's invitation," says Townley, "to supply
Signor Lusieri with more documents and information relative to his
further pursuits and researches in Greece." Harrison's change of
heart,[107] however, in no way dampened Townley's own enthusiasm

104. See *Report*, Appendix No. 7, "Copy of a Letter from Charles
Townley Esq. to T. Harrison, on the subject of Lord Elgin's Marbles,
London, February 8, 1803," pp. xxii–xxiii. The letter begins: "I feel myself
exceedingly obliged to you and most highly gratified by your kind communication to me of Lord Elgin's most laudable exertions toward collecting
either original Marbles or Casts of the most valuable monuments of sculpture
and architecture in Greece. . . ."
105. *Report*, p. xxiii.
106. *Ibid.*, Appendix No. 3, "Memorandum as to Lord Elgin's Exclusive
Right of Property in the Collection of Marbles, February, 1816," item No. 8,
p. iv.
107. Harrison, sensitive to the criticism of Elgin brewing in England by
that time, and anxious to escape further involvement himself, apparently
did not have the courage to respond directly to Elgin's letter and instead
turned it over to Townley, to whom he expressed his own reservations.
With Elgin himself Harrison did not resume communication until March
31, 1814, when he confesses apologetically: " . . . Our correspondence has
indeed been long interrupted and I am ashamed to acknowledge the cause

for Elgin's activities and he ends his reply on this optimistic note: "But it is in contemplation with a few members of the Dilettanti Society to whom I have communicated Lord Elgin's letter to make a handsome remittance to Signor Lusieri and engage him to make some researches and execute some plans and drawings of monuments which shall be indicated to him." Townley's letter is deceptive, however, for ensuing events were to show that he over-estimated the Dilettanti's approval of Elgin. Somewhere along the line his promise of financial assistance to Lusieri died. The last that was heard of the matter which was laid before the Society on Sunday, February 13, 1803, was a minute in its records to the effect that the letters be referred for consideration to the Committee of Publications.[108] No further action was ever taken by the Dilettanti in support of Elgin and it has generally been supposed that the antagonistic influence of the erudite Payne Knight, whose judgment in such matters dominated the opinion of the membership, was already making itself felt.[109] Townley died two years later, before Elgin's return from France and without ever seeing the original marbles, but even had he lived, it is doubtful that he would have opposed Knight's recalcitrant position in spite of his initial enthusiasm.

Apart from the coolness of the Dilettanti, it was around this time also that strong criticism of Elgin's enterprises first began to appear in the London periodicals. The letter of an anonymous gentleman from Rome, published in August, 1803,[110] follows the cue of Dod-

---

rests entirely with me. Your Lordship will, however, find from the inclosed copy of a letter from the late Mr. Charles Townley . . . that your Lordship's very interesting letter from Constantinople was received and how much your proceedings were approved of by him and other men of taste and judgment. It appeared to be so serious an undertaking for your Lordship that I have frequently accused myself for the part I took in advising it and had hoped before now to have seen the Marbles, along with Mr. Townley's, in the British Museum. I was in London three years since and made several visits to your Collection and heard with pleasure from Mr. West and other painters as well as sculptors their approbation of it. In the course of my faint attempts to imitate the purity of Greek art . . . I have often thought of your Lordship. I must not neglect to make my acknowledgements for the honourable mention of my name in the narrative of your Lordship's proceedings. . . ." (original, Elgin Papers, Broomhall, Vol. IV). In all this Harrison seems to have played the role of a fair-weather friend to Elgin, withdrawing his support when Elgin was first under attack in 1803 and renewing it only after the marbles had been widely acclaimed and were close to government purchase.

108. See L. Cust, *History of the Society of Dilettanti,* London, 1898, p. 130.

109. *JHS,* XXXVI, p. 295.

110. *Monthly Magazine,* XVI, 104, part II, pp. 15 ff. (See note 74.)

well and Clarke who had already expressed their objections, at least vocally if not yet in print, to the operations of Elgin's workmen which they witnessed in Athens in 1801 and 02. The writer [111] here deplores the removal of the Parthenon sculptures as the

> . . . last gleaning of what had been spared by the successive spoilers of the ornaments of Greece. Not only have all the removable works been carried away, but many things which had been hitherto considered as immovable [112] have been torn away from the places where they had remained unmolested for thousands of years. Thus, for instance the metopes of the Temple of Minerva . . . have all been broken out of the wall and the round carved works of the tympans have likewise been carried away.[113]

Furthermore, unaware of Elgin's expressed intention to nationalize his collection, the author impugns his motives, accuses him of vanity, and creates the impression, against which Elgin, a prisoner in France, was powerless to defend himself,[114] that his main purpose was to form the most exclusive private collection of antiquities in all of England. "Lord Elgin was induced to this undertaking," he claims, "that he might have the glory of enriching his country with the spoils of ancient Greece and that he might possess a cabinet surpassing others in the rarity of the articles it contains." [115] Lamenting the fact that such collections are open only to connoisseurs and not to the general public,[116] he raises the same insinuation against Elgin

111. This may have been Lord Aberdeen, who was in Athens in 1803 and could have been in Rome at the time of Elgin's visit. Clarke cited Aberdeen's opposition to Elgin's activities in the published account of his travels (see text, p. 149). Since he was himself a rival nobleman-antiquarian, with intense Hellenic interests, who, upon his return to Britain, became known as "Athenian Aberdeen," it is perhaps understandable that he would have preferred to remain anonymous at this time, lest suspicion be cast on his own motives.

112. We are here reminded of the statement of Père Robert de Dreux, a 17th-century missionary and commentator on the Parthenon, who attributed the Greek authenticity of the metopes to the supposition that they were so embedded in the architecture as to be immovable without injuring or destroying the structure. (See J. M. Paton, *Chapters on Medieval and Renaissance Visitors to Greek Lands*, Princeton, 1951, p. 13.)

113. *Monthly Magazine, ibid.*, p. 16.

114. "Les absents ont toujours tort," comments Hamilton to Haydon in a letter of December 25, 1840, referring to Elgin's misfortune to have been away while he was being attacked. (See B. R. Haydon, *Lectures on Painting and Design*, London, 1844, Vol. II, Appendix, p. 288.)

115. *Monthly Magazine, ibid.*, p. 16.

116. The author complains that England lacks the public institutions of Paris or a free museum open all year round. The British Museum cannot be seen without much difficulty, he tells us, and even the "golden catapult of Philip of Macedon cannot always force open the doors of private collections." (*Ibid.*, p. 15.)

when he says "may he be incited by a nobler ambition to render these treasures generally useful by a free access to them, so that the traveller who has in vain looked for them in Greece might at last find them in England!" [117] Obviously the author does not expect Elgin to show such civic spirit, at least not without some prodding on his part. This skepticism he retains even after the conversations he mentions having held with Elgin's artists in Rome [118] in which the educational goals and public accessibility envisioned for the collection by Elgin must have been disclosed to him. Nor were these fears entirely without foundation. As things turned out, in spite of Elgin's wishes to the contrary, the marbles did, in fact, remain a private collection for ten years after his return to England. Their availability for inspection in the earlier years of this period only to those with the special permission of Elgin himself, the failure of Elgin to approach the government over the matter of purchase until 1810, the collapse of the first purchase negotiations in 1811, and the constant rumors circulating about that he was on the verge of selling the collection to a foreign nation [119] made the early admonitions raised by this writer in 1803 seem almost prophetic. These circumstances tended in the minds of some to taint the marbles themselves with a political and moral stigma that prejudiced aesthetic appreciation of them as works of art.

During the years of his imprisonment in France more fuel was lent to the anti-Elgin fire not only by the jealous French but by other English travelers who came to Greece. Sir William Drummond who succeeded Elgin as Ambassador to the Porte was decidedly opposed to Elgin's antiquarian pursuits [120] and gave Lusieri, who was now managing all activities at Athens in Elgin's behalf practically by

117. *Ibid.*, p. 16.

118. Whether the writer actually met with Elgin himself or, as appears more likely, only with members of his company, is not certain. He never mentions speaking directly to Elgin. Furthermore, he says, "Lord Elgin has brought along with him all the drawings and plans which were executed upon the spot; but only a few persons of the highest rank (as for instance, Lord Bristol and the Prince of Mecklenburgh-Stroelitz) have been favored with a sight of them" (*loc. cit.*) From this, it would appear that the writer himself was not so favored, which may perhaps account for his pique.

119. It was hinted in 1810–11 that French attempts were being made to induce Elgin to sell his collection in Paris so that it might be added to the Musée Napoléon along with the rest of Napoleon's booty. (See Michaelis, *Ancient Marbles*, p. 141.) The collapse of purchase negotiations with Parliament in 1811 served further to encourage ambitions of potential foreign buyers.

120. *JHS*, XXXVI, p. 257. Elgin also claimed that William Drummond had "behaved in a manner too scandalous to be brought forward in a Court of Justice" in a private transaction involving his family. (See Abbot, *Diary*, II, p. 327.)

himself, no support. Predatory collectors, secretly plotting to bypass the defenseless artist's jurisdiction, tried unsuccessfully to purchase the Parthenon frieze directly from the Turkish officials for a tempting sum,[121] while envious archaeologists sought to pre-empt the excavation privileges of Elgin's company in the hope of finding for themselves other buried treasures of the Parthenon. Thus, in 1805 Dodwell returned to Athens again and registered his objections once more to Lusieri's operations, this time even more vociferously because he could not obtain the same privileges to dig on the Acropolis as had been extended to Elgin's workmen.[122] Even more troublesome was the classical archaeologist William Gell (1777–1836) who was also there at the time and whose failure to obtain a firman for excavation led him spitefully to use French influence [123] as well as Ambassador Drummond's coolness to Elgin to prevail upon the Voivode to forbid all further excavations on the site of the fortress.[124] By the time Elgin returned to England the hostility and bitterness of such frustrated competitors had gone a long way in arousing public resentment against him.

While such antagonistic feelings toward Elgin were in the mak-

121. On Sept. 26, 1803, Lusieri wrote to Elgin of this attempt to take advantage of his absence: ". . . I have run a very great risk in these last days. Two very rich English gentlemen were on the point of offering as much as 50,000 piastres to obtain the frieze. Happily I was told of it and I made them see it was impossible, that it was necessary to have *firmans,* but that in any case I would not let your Excellency be second to anybody . . ." (*JHS,* XXXVI, p. 257).

122. Letter of Lusieri to Elgin, July 4, 1805. In addition to Dodwell, Lusieri mentions at least three other Englishmen (Monck, Gell, and Bacon) who were trying unsuccessfully to get digging firmans: "They conduct themselves in such a way as to disgust everybody . . . have wanted to undertake diggings without firmans, without asking permission of the Voivode, or the landowner, and without making any return. The Voivode has been so much disgusted that he has stopped them from going on, letting all know that he would not allow anyone whatever to dig except me" (*ibid.,* p. 261).

123. Fauvel had returned to Athens as Under-Commissary in January of 1803. Their mutual hostility toward Elgin's operations drew Gell and Fauvel together. Gell often copied from Fauvel's drawings and models of the Parthenon and other Acropolis structures. His original sketchbooks in the British Museum, Department of Prints and Drawings (Nos. 8 and 13, in particular) show various views of the Parthenon, some containing details of the sculptures "in-situ" * * * , others of individual frieze or pediment pieces. A number of these are labeled as having been taken from Fauvel's models. (See L. Binyon, *Catalogue of Drawings by British Artists . . . in the British Museum,* London, 1898–1907, Vol. II, pp. 198–201, Gell's Sketchbook No. 8, Drawings L. B. 4, 6, 7, 9.)

124. Letters of Lusieri to Elgin October 5 and October 8, 1805 (*JHS,* XXXVI, p. 262).

ing and while the marbles lay unpacked in London, Elgin and Hunt, interned in France, remained more or less unaware of the state of British opinion and continued optimistically planning for the future of the collection. Hunt, in a letter written from Pau on February 20, 1805, to Mrs. Hamilton Nisbet, Lady Elgin's mother, reviews the accomplishments of the Elgin mission to date, prefacing it with the following disclosure of what Elgin had in mind for the marbles immediately upon his return to England: "The project that has been suggested to his Lordship of forming his collection of original marbles as well as the models, casts, drawings, and plans into a public exhibition at London has made me endeavor to recollect the principal objects it contains." [125] Judging from this, Elgin's plan to open the marbles to the public, to which he had been referring in his correspondence since 1801, remained unaffected by the French interlude. In fact, it now seemed more definite than ever and had some indication of it, such as that given by Hunt above, appeared in the London press at the time it might have served as an effective rebuttal to the mounting criticism of his conduct or suspicion of his motives. Hunt's letter goes on to discuss in some detail, the metopes, frieze, and pediment sculptures of the Parthenon, and is interesting because it contains some of the first indications on record of the effects which close observation of the marbles, "ex-situ" as it were, was beginning to have. We have already mentioned Hunt's reaction to the sheerness and anatomical suggestiveness of the drapery treatment in some of the female figures of the west pediment, something he had not expected to find so highly developed in the Phidian period. In this letter, he seems also to be the first to mention the fact that "the metopes are in such high relief as to be absolutely groupes of statues and are in general finished with as much attention behind as before [126] in order that they might strike the eye of the spectator with effect, in whatever direction he approached the Acropolis. . . ." [127] Fauvel, who had once climbed up to the level of the tympana, was the first to note that the backs of the pediment figures were as finished as the front surfaces. Hunt's discovery that the same

125. *Letters, Countess of Elgin*, p. 328.
126. Stuart does not mention this fact in the *Antiquities of Athens*, II, where there is practically no technical discussion of the metopes although there are six detailed engravings of them. To what extent Pars or Chandler were aware of it is difficult to say. Pars could certainly have seen the finished undersides, if not the backs of the metope figures from his position on the architrave. Furthermore, the extent of the cast shadows in some of his original drawings of the metopes * * * suggests many forms almost completely in the round.
127. *Letters, Countess of Elgin*, p. 331.

was by and large true of the metopes [128] led to the subsequent realization that both the pediment figures and the metope plaques were first carved in the workshops and then set in place on the temple.[129] Deploring their state of mutilation he nevertheless agrees with Hamilton and accepts Canova's judgment that they should remain unrestored: "Even in that condition they are much superior to anything that modern restoration could effect, were the attempt even made by the hand of Canova." [130]

More significant than this is the awakening sensitivity which Hunt shows to particulars of anatomy or action and to aspects of common rather than ideal nature, anticipating Haydon, Hazlitt, and other romantic critics. On the figure of the prostrate Lapith in Metope XXVIII [see fig. 56] he comments: "The relaxed muscles of one of the Lapithae who is lying dead and trampled on by a Centaur is among the finest productions of art." [131] On the Selene horse-head of the East pediment [see fig. 45] he is not only more eloquent, but also more specific than any earlier commentator. He finds it "surpasses anything of the kind . . . in the truth and spirit of the execution. The nostrils are distended, the ears erect, the veins swollen, I had almost said throbbing. His mouth is open and he seems to neigh with the conscious pride of belonging to the Ruler of the Waves." [132] Only in the last phrase, when he sees the horse's open mouth proudly neighing in conscious awareness of its nobility and divinity,[133] does Hunt still seem to retain vestiges of a neoclassical concept of expression which seeks general meanings of a higher order in the concrete details of lower nature. But in the rest of his observations, in his delight with all the empirical signs and assorted

128. The metopes are in various degrees of high relief. In parts they are completely in the round, while elsewhere there is a decided flattening of the surfaces. The initial plane was the background of the plaque, the figures being independently carved and superimposed thereon. (See A. H. Smith, *Sculptures of the Parthenon*, p. 29.)

129. With reference to the pediment sculptures Visconti makes this point clear when he says they were finished on all sides so that they could be submitted to public inspection before being placed up in the pediment (*Letter from . . . Canova . . .* , p. 9). The metopes were also carved and completed on the ground before being hoisted up and slipped into place between the triglyphs. (See W. B. Dinsmoor, *op. cit.*, p. 177.)

130. *Letters, Countess of Elgin*, p. 331.

131. *Loc. cit.*

132. *Ibid.*, p. 334.

133. It is interesting to contrast Hunt's interpretation of the Selene horse-head which sees it neighing with fiery spirit and divine pride with more recent views which see its drooping head and open mouth as symptoms of fatigue or exhaustion. (See P. E. Corbett, *The Sculpture of the Parthenon*, London, 1959, pp. 28–29.)

revelations of life and emotion in the horse's head, which he records
as they strike him in a rush of random sensations, he shows more
romantic sensibility. In the frieze too what intrigues him most are the
references to Athenian genre or contemporary incident rather than
its mythological content or idealized graces. He characterizes its
subject as "representing the whole of the solemn procession during
the Panathenaic festivals," but sees its function primarily as a diver-
sionary attempt to occupy the attention of those who were waiting
in the vestibule and ambulatory of the temple until the sacred rites
commenced.[134] Not its symbolic, but its pragmatic purpose concerns
him, and not its gods, but its mortals interest him. More completely
than Stuart in the *Antiquities of Athens* or Visconti in the *Museum
Worsleyanum*, he enumerates its varied citizenry, including the horsemen, charioteers, oxen-leaders, canephorae, skiaphorae, priests, magis-
trates, and warriors, but of the seated deities over the east entrance
with whom the procession terminates there is no mention. He is drawn
also to the theory of some antiquaries who, he says, have examined
the frieze closely and believe that among its figures it contains por-
traits of leading Athenian personalities, particularly Pericles, Phidias,
Socrates, and the young Alcibiades.[135] No doubt much of this may be
simply due to the change from a far to a near view of the originals,
but in his fascination with realistic rather than beau-idealistic nature,
with fact more than with myth, with intimate details rather than grand
ensembles, and with immediate human situations rather than abstract
humanistic virtues Hunt shows the swing from a neoclassical to a
romantic orientation that had already overtaken British taste before
the Elgin Marbles arrived in London and which was to have a profound effect on their critical interpretation.

When it came to the content and iconography of the pediment
sculptures, however, Hunt's understanding was in no way enlight-
ened by a closer observation of the originals and remained circumscribed by the established confusions of 17th- and 18th-century
speculation. Following Spon and Wheler, rather than Stuart and
Revett, he still took the west façade to be the main entrance and its
theme to be "the mythological history of Minerva's birth from the
brain of Jove." [136] Unaware as yet of "Carrey's" drawings (although
they had by then been rediscovered) he follows Stuart's reconstruction (but not his theme) in imagining Jupiter to be seated in the
center of the pediment,[137] while the central standing male figure

134. *Letters, Countess of Elgin*, p. 332.
135. *Loc. cit.*
136. *Ibid.*, p. 333.
137. *The Antiquities of Athens*, II, Ch. I, Pl. III * * *.

with striding legs, which was described by Spon and Wheler as Jupiter, and which in reality was Poseidon, Hunt thought to be Vulcan coming prominently forward from Jupiter's left with axe in hand.[138] Further following Spon, he mistook the figure of Athena for a "Victory" holding the horses of the chariot which introduced the new goddess to Olympus, recounting the discovery by excavation at the west end of the temple beneath the house of one of the Turkish Janisseries of a finely draped female torso which he assumed to be part of the said Victory figure [139] [see p. 141]. Also mentioned as the fruits of this digging are the Torso of Jupiter and part of the so-called Vulcan, which in reality were the fragment of Poseidon and the torso of Hermes. On the matter of the disputed "Hadrian-Sabina" group, he takes a position similar to Fauvel's, accepting the Phidian authorship of all the statues except for the Roman addition of these two, which he thus explains: "When Athens lost her freedom she showed her adulation and servility to the Roman power by adding the statues of Hadrian and Sabina to the groupe by Phidias." [140] Unaware that they still remained on the Parthenon, Hunt was under the mistaken impression that these two statues had been removed and shipped to England along with the rest.[141] As for the east front, his remark that "in digging beneath this pediment some beautiful pieces of sculpture have been procured" [142] is puzzling in view of the fact

138. *Letters, Countess of Elgin*, p. 333.

139. *Ibid.*, pp. 333–334. Hunt's confusion is actually between the Athena and the so-called *Iris*, the two female figures which flank the central Poseidon in "Carrey's" west pediment drawing * * * . The error is perfectly understandable in view of the similarity in the stance and disposition of the drapery of these two figures, especially around the legs, according to "Carrey's" sketch. Had Hunt known the "Carrey" drawing he might have avoided this mistake as well as the false insertion of a seated Jupiter in the center for which there is obviously no room. Interesting also is his explanation of the missing helmet and aegis of the supposed Athena which he concocts with more imagination, if not more insight, than Spon and Wheler. The latter had assumed her in the guise of the goddess of Learning rather than War (G. Wheler, *Journey into Greece*, London, 1682, p. 360), but Hunt offers this instead: "Unlike all other statutes of Minerva, she was here represented with the captivating graces of Venus. . . . The elegant, the amiable people of Athens delighted to see the warlike Pallas with the cestus of Venus" (*Letters, Countess of Elgin*, p. 333).

140. *Loc. cit.*

141. Hunt says, "I believe his Lordship has also had the Hadrian and Sabrina taken down and sent to England" (*ibid.*, p. 334). This misconception is puzzling in view of the fact that Hunt could have verified it with Elgin, unless we are to assume that Elgin, whose communication with Lusieri during his French internment was very scanty (*JHS*, XXXVI, p. 256), was under the same mistaken illusion.

142. *Letters, Countess of Elgin*, p. 334.

that all existing records and drawings of this side from "Carrey's" time up through Elgin's seem to indicate that the statues which Elgin took from here were all still "in-situ." [143] Besides, Hunt himself alludes to practically all of them when he speaks of "two or three colossal groupes each containing two female figures" having been lowered from the pediment, as well as the Selene horse-head and the figure of the Dionysus [see fig. 47], all of which, misreading the theme as the contest of Minerva and Neptune, he erroneously identifies as sea-deities.[144] Apart from such iconographic blunders, his uncertainty about the actual number, location, or origin of the pieces acquired [145] indicates that his memory of the operations at Athens,[146]

143. Feodor the Calmuck, Elgin's artist, does not appear to have made a representation of the east pediment sculptures as he found them but instead made a restored version of the entire pediment supplying the missing figures. Speaking of this restoration Lusieri says in a letter to Elgin of November 16–28, 1802 (*JHS*, XXXVI, p. 238), that Feodor made use of the position of the figures that were extant and that are now in "your" possession. In view of the fact that this drawing contains every one of the east pediment figures in the Elgin Collection and that they appear in exactly the same position as they did in "Carrey's" drawing, we must assume that none of them had to be excavated from the ground and that no additional ones were found. Hunt has either confused the two pediments in his mind or is under the erroneous impression that some of the east pediment figures had fallen and been re-discovered by digging. That this was not the case is also corroborated in the journals of Benjamin Haydon who in September of 1809 records Elgin's account to him of how his workmen first dug at the west end and found fragments of the Jupiter and Minerva and then thinking they would be equally successful at the other end, procured the house of the Turk that lived there and dug under it, but found nothing. (See *The Diary of Benjamin Robert Haydon*, edited by Willard B. Pope, Cambridge, Mass., 1960–63, Vol. I, p. 87.) Further corroboration that the east pediment pieces acquired by Elgin were all found in the tympanum comes from a sketch by William Gell, made in 1805, of the Parthenon from the southeast, but most likely copied from an earlier one of Fauvel made not long before Elgin's arrival (original in the British Museum, Department of Prints and Drawings, Gell Sketchbook No. 13, Drawing No. 53.3.57.109; L. B. 76). It shows all the east pediment sculptures "in-situ."

144. *Letters, Countess of Elgin*, p. 334.

145. Once the marbles had been removed and shipped confusion or uncertainty over the original position of some of the pediment pieces led Visconti to mis-assign the figure which Hunt had called a Victory and which had been found in the excavations under the west façade to the east pediment instead (*Letter from . . . Canova . . .* , p. 45, No. 9). The error was not corrected until 1909 (see Smith, *Sculptures of the Parthenon*, pp. 11–12). Visconti was under the mistaken impression that the figure was found thrown down on the floor of the pediment which was why it did not appear in "Carrey's" east pediment representation.

146. Hunt says in closing his letter, "I have thus exhausted the list of Lord Elgin's successful labours on the Parthenon, or at least of such parts of them as my memory unaided by notes can now recall . . ." (*Letters, Countess of Elgin*, p. 336).

now almost three years behind him, was faulty. Hunt's mistakes would have had little significance were it not for the fact that his résumé of the Elgin Marbles later served as the basis, almost without modification, of the published *Memorandum* of Elgin's activities in Greece, which in its three editions between the years 1810 to 1815 [147] stood as the official account of the operations and represented not only the views of Hunt and Hamilton, but of Elgin and the rest of the company as well.

Even after Elgin's release from France and return to England Lusieri continued his antiquarian pursuits in Elgin's behalf until his own death in Athens on March 1, 1821.[148] But with Elgin's arrival in England in 1806, the focus of attention, so far as the marbles were concerned, shifted to London. It was there that the drama of the struggle surrounding their reception unfolded with increasing intensity and international interest during the next decade. Entering a situation already prejudiced against him even before the marbles were exposed to view, Elgin himself had little awareness of the controversial embroilment in which both the reputation of the sculptures as works of art and his own reputation as either their destroyer or saviour were soon to become involved.

147. The first edition, published in Edinburgh, appeared in 1810, the second in London in 1811, the third (called Second Edition, Corrected) in London in 1815. A. H. Smith was of the opinion that Elgin himself, not Hamilton as has generally been supposed, was the author of the *Memorandum*. He cites a letter by Hamilton to Elgin of December 15, 1810, containing the remark, "When I ventured to speak to Admiral Durham of a few Expressions in your Memorandum . . ." (*JHS*, XXXVI, p. 308). But in view of the possibility that the phrase "your Memorandum" may simply be a shorter way of saying "Memorandum of your pursuits," this does not seem to be conclusive enough proof, although it should certainly not be ruled out as a possibility.

148. *JHS*, XXXVI, p. 288.

THE ARCHITECTURE OF THE PARTHENON

WILLIAM BELL DINSMOOR
[The Design and Building Techniques of the Parthenon—1951] *

> Descriptions of the architecture of the Parthenon that are based on solid archeological facts and a minimum of fantasy are hard to find. None surpasses in clarity and precision that by William Bell Dinsmoor. Dinsmoor's first-hand study of the Parthenon covers many years spent in Athens. Tool marks, weathering, and many other symptoms and clues that can only be read by means of a close and methodical scrutiny of the ancient stones are all taken into consideration in his analysis of the structure. (There is a diagram of the Doric order on p. 322 of this volume [text fig. 67], which the reader may especially wish to consult in conjunction with this section.)

It is at Athens that we may best study the works of the culminating period [of Greek architecture]. For the prohibition of religious building had been annulled by the act of Pericles in 449 B.C. And so it is on the Acropolis that we find the masterpiece of all these works, the Parthenon. It was officially the temple of Athena Polias, but was distinguished from the other temple of this cult by the name Hecatompedon (or "Hundred-foot Temple") inherited from its predecessors, the name Parthenon being extended a century later from the west room to the whole. The work of Ictinus and Callicrates in partnership, and described in a lost book by Ictinus and a certain Carpion, it was executed in a perod of nine years, from 447 to 438 B.C., and after its dedication at the Panathenaic festival in the

* From William Bell Dinsmoor, *The Architecture of Ancient Greece: An Account of Its Historic Development,* 3rd rev. ed. (London, 1951). By arrangement with W. W. Norton & Company, Inc.

latter year the labour of the sculptors was continued until the eve of the Peloponnesian War in 432 B.C.[1] The site was the lofty platform already prepared on the south side of the Acropolis for the Older Parthenon, a site which not only made it the principal crowning feature of the Acropolis as seen from the south and west [fig. 2], but on the Acropolis itself rendered it the most imposing structure there [fig. 4] so that it was worthy of the various subtleties both in line and in proportion that it was to receive at the hands of Ictinus and Callicrates, and of its enrichment by Phidias with the most beautiful sculpture that the world has seen.[2]

The plan [text fig. 7] is more sumptuous than that of any other Doric temple erected on the Greek mainland, recalling temple 'GT' at Selinus with its octastyle façades and seventeen columns on the flanks; the size, however, is considerably smaller than in its great Sicilian prototype. The new plan did not agree with that of the older platform [text fig. 2] which was left unoccupied for a length of 14 feet at the east end, and likewise for 5½ feet at the south; on the other hand, the new building overlapped the old platform by 13 feet at the north, requiring additional foundations of this width along the north flank. The total dimensions of the bottom step are 110 feet 6¾ inches by 237 feet 3⅜ inches, being 24 feet and 6¾ inches wider than in the Older Parthenon, and 8 feet 8½ inches longer. The purpose of the great increase in width was to allow for a colossal cult statue, as at Olympia, but without crowding it tightly between the

1. The authorship and date of the temple are given by several passages in ancient literature, combined with the fragments of the marble inscriptions containing expense accounts of the temple and of the gold-and-ivory statue.

2. The Parthenon remained almost intact for more than 2100 years, apart from the loss of its original roof, the alteration of its interior colonnades, the construction of an apse in the pronaos and the piercing of three doorways in the middle cross-wall, during its transformation into a Byzantine church. Between 1208 and 1458 it served as the cathedral church of the "Frankish" dukes, and a marble campanile was built in the opisthodomus beside the west entrance. After 1458 it became a Turkish mosque, the campanile being continued upward as a minaret. In this condition it remained until a shell from a Venetian battery, on September 26, 1687, exploded a powder magazine temporarily established by the Turks in their mosque, causing the destruction of fourteen of the forty-six columns of the peristyle and of practically all of the inner building with the exception of the opisthodomus. Considerable destruction of the south entablature resulted from Lord Elgin's removal of some of the sculptures in 1801–1803, and slight additional damage was incurred during the sieges of 1822–1823 and 1826–1827. But in 1835–1844 the temple was cleared of modern accretions (with the exception of the minaret) and portions of the columns and walls were unskilfully restored. As the result of an earthquake in 1894 a few scientific repairs were undertaken in 1898–1903, and finally, in 1921–1929, the entire north flank was rebuilt by piecing together the scattered fragments.

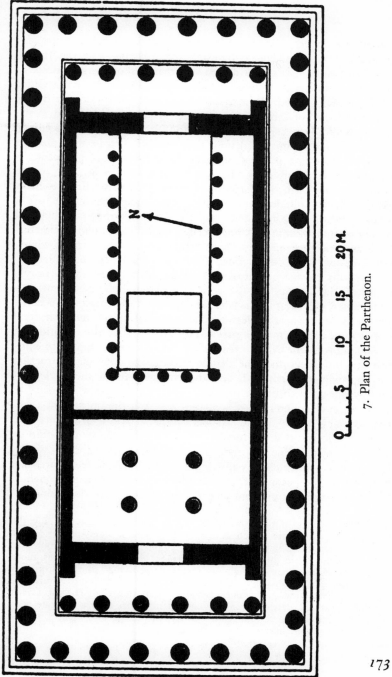

0   5   10   15   20 M.

7. Plan of the Parthenon.

173

internal colonnades: the exact dimensions of the stylobate were determined by the elements composing the peristyle. For the fundamental principle of the new design was that it should incorporate as
much as possible of the second-hand material, destined for the Older
Parthenon, lying about the Acropolis; even though the lowest drums
of many of the columns, having been set in place and exposed to the
burning scaffolding, had become unfit for further use, there were still
several hundred unfinished drums in fit condition to be incorporated
in the peristyle and porches of the present Parthenon, permitting a
considerable economy at a time when transportation was one of the
most important items in the cost of stone. Hence the basic element
was the normal column diameter of 6 feet 3 inches, equivalent to 5⅝
Greek (Doric) feet, inherited from the Older Parthenon. The axial
spacing of the columns was now related to the old column diameters
as 9:4 and thus became 13⅛ Doric feet, except at the corners where,
with excessive angle contraction, it became 11⁵⁄₁₆ Doric feet. The reason for this excessive contraction of 24 inches was the octastyle
nature of the façade; for the relative spacings and heights of columns, while varying to some degree in individual temples in accordance with scale, nevertheless tended to yield fairly uniform total
proportions for normal hexastyle façades, so that the addition of
two columns to the width created a violent contrast. It was to miti-
gate this difference in some degree that the amount of contraction
was approximately doubled; and the enlargement of the angle column by one-fortieth of the diameter, for optical reasons, still further
reduced the clear interval to 25 inches less than the normal intervals.
The resulting width of the stylobate became 94½ Doric feet; and,
following the law that the number of columns on the flank should be
one more than double the number on the façades, that is, seventeen,
the length was made nine axial spacings or 118⅛ Doric feet more than
the width and so became 212⅝ Doric feet, thus being proportioned to
the width exactly as 9:4, just as the axial spacing is to the diameter.[3]

3. The stylobate dimensions, while generally recognised as forming the
ratio 4:9, are often interpreted as 100 by 225 "Greek" feet—but of a foot
unit (12⅛ inches) which no Greek ever employed. The Doric foot unit
actually employed in the Parthenon was 326.85 mm. or 12.868 inches, more
than in the Erechtheum but almost identical with that in the Propylaea
* * * . It seems necessary here to insert a word of warning against the
validity of the numerous modern attempts to derive the plans of Greek
temples, and of the Parthenon in particular, from more or less intricate geometrical diagrams such as interrelated concentric circles and squares, penta-
gons or pentagrams, hexagons or hexagrams, octagons, decagons, "whirling
squares," or the "golden section."

The total height of the order, that is, of the column and entablature together, was made 3⅕ times the axial spacing or 7⅕ lower diameters, that is, exactly 42 Doric feet, and again forms the proportion of 4:9 with the width of the stylobate. This consistency in proportions is most unusual and suggests the care with which the entire design was studied.

The jointing of the steps and stylobate was based on the principle that there should be three blocks to each axial spacing, every third joint coinciding with a column axis. The columns are barely less than 5½ diameters in height. The profile of the capitals exemplifies the most perfected stage of the Doric style, the echinus very stiff and yet forming a continuous hyperbolic curve. The abacus was originally planned to have a spread of 6 feet 6⅞ inches, as executed on the west and south sides; but this dimension, apparently regarded as too small, was subsequently enlarged to 6 feet 7⅜ inches in the west half and to 6 feet 8½ inches in the east half of the north flank, and finally to 6 feet 9 inches on the east façade; the angle capitals in each case showing enlargements proportionate to that of the column diameter, there is a contrast, for instance, between the southeast angle capital and that adjoining it on the south flank amounting to 3⅜ inches. Apart from these unforeseen irregularities it is interesting to note, in the metopes of the façades, a repetition of the perspective illusion given in the colonnade by the angle contraction; for in the Parthenon instead of the usual enlarged metopes adjoining the angle triglyphs, we find a careful gradation from excessively wide metopes at the centre to narrow metopes toward the corners, with a maximum difference of 4⅛ inches in width, and with the result that no triglyph on a façade is exactly centred above the corresponding column. The fascias above the triglyphs and metopes have a crowning beaded astragal as exceptional decoration. The face of the tympanum is recessed 8 inches behind the architrave-triglyph plane, to give a greater depth for pediment sculpture. The sima of the pediment shows, not the cyma recta profile employed at Bassae, nor the type inherited from Corinthian terracottas as at Olympia, but rather a derivative of the latter under Ionic influence, the ovolo dominating with offset fascias below and above, which became peculiarly characteristic of the Periclean designers. On the flanks the sima is replaced by antefixes, located above each mutule so that there are four to each column spacing; but since there were six rows of tiles to each column spacing the antefixes were alternately true and false, the latter corresponding to two lines of cover-tiles. The acroteria were colossal openwork designs in marble, about 9 feet high, consisting of stems and tendrils, springing from nests of acanthus leaves, forming scrolls and finally ending in great palmettes.[4]

The plan of the building within the peristyle included hexastyle porticoes at both ends (rather than tetrastyle as in its predecessor), raised on two steps, of which the lower is accurately located concentrically within the stylobate, while the upper step—and with it the entire inner building—is thrust diagonally toward the northeast so that the width of the tread varies on all four sides. The lateral displacement may have been a result of a clerical error; but the eastward thrust certainly resulted from adjustments required by a peculiar difference in the columns themselves. For the west or opisthodomus columns inherited the diameter of 5 feet 7½ inches, equivalent to 5¼ Greek (Doric) feet, employed for the porch columns of the Older Parthenon; but since the next hexastyle opisthodomus utilised the material from six of the original eight columns, it was decided that the remaining drums left for the pronaos were so few as to justify a new design, in which the diameter was reduced to 5 feet 4⅞ inches. The porch column height being uniformly 32 feet 11⅞ inches, the pronaos columns exhibit the unusually slender proportions of 6¹⁄₁₀ diameters. On the hexastyle porticoes rested the usual Doric architrave with regulae and guttae, spaced as if they were intended to come below triglyphs;[5] but the regulae appear here merely as the conventional crowning feature of the Doric architrave, carrying up the lines of the columns, while on the flanks of the cella building, where they would have had no such function, they were replaced by a simple band of the height of regula and taenia combined. For above the architrave, instead of the usual trigylphs, was a continuous Ionic frieze such as Ictinus employed inside the cella at Bassae, though above Ionic columns; another precedent was the Peisistratid temple on the Acropolis, where a sculptured frieze was used across the ends of the cella building, likewise above Ionic columns; and while the Parthenon was in course of erection the same treatment was applied to the ends of the cella building in the Hephaesteum, but above Doric columns. The use of a continuous sculptured frieze round the entire inner building of the Parthenon, with a length of 523 feet 7¼ inches (top of background), marks a distinct innovation. Above this frieze

4. In the British Museum are representative pieces of the architecture of the Parthenon, a Doric capital and a top drum from the north peristyle, parts of the frieze crowning mouldings, an antefix, and a fragment of an acroterion.

5. It has sometimes been suggested that the regulae imply that a triglyph frieze was once planned here and was replaced by the Ionic frieze; but this is extremely improbable.

was a very decorative interior cornice (repeated on the inner face of the main entablature), forming the transition to the marble ceiling.

The plan of the cella building contains two distinct chambers, the cella proper behind the pronaos, and a rear chamber entered from the opisthodomus [text figs. 1, 7]. The term Parthenon given to the whole building is a later title, as noted above, and was confined at first to the rear chamber, officially known as the Parthenon (chamber of the Virgin); the cella was known as the Naos Hecatompedos (cella of 100 feet), this being, however, a name inherited from the archaic poros Hecatompedon so that we are not justified in dividing the length by 100 and adopting the quotient as the foot unit.[6] In the cella there were formerly ten Doric columns on either side and five columns across the rear, counting those at the corners twice.[7] They carried an architrave with superposed Doric columns above, as in the temples at Aegina and Paestum already mentioned; the primary object of these columns would seem to have been the support of the beams of the ceiling and roof, as there is no evidence for galleries. The columns returning across the rear constitute a development of the plan employed at Bassae (and again with a central column on axis), in this case forming a true ambulatory with the aisle carried round the interior of the cella, with bronze barriers fixed between the columns, so as to allow privileged travellers like Pausanias to walk round the chryselephantine statue of Athena and see it on all sides; a similar arrangement existed in the temple of Zeus at Olympia, except that there were no columns at the west end, a space merely being left at the back of the pedestal to permit one to pass round. The portion of the floor enclosed by the colonnades is sunk 1½ inches, as at Bassae, so that the columns seem to rest on a low stylobate; the sinking of the floor does not, however, indicate that the area was hypaethral [open to the sky, not roofed]. Enough light would have been admitted through the great eastern doorway, 13¾ feet wide, between pivots, at the bottom and 32 feet high (an

6. Such attempts have frequently been made, but always with erroneous results; the internal length of the cella was actually 91½ Greek (Doric) feet. It would be 100½ Doric feet if the cross-walls at both ends were included; but a literal application of the name does not seem to be indicated.

7. Most authorities prefer to restore L-shaped piers at the two inner corners; but such would seem too sophisticated for the period, and, furthermore, circular traces were noted by Cockerell and Woods before 1820. The Greek columns were replaced in Roman times, probably after a fire, by second-hand Doric columns of a much later style, of which a few fragments and many of their architraves and triglyph frieze blocks still remain. Recent attempts to prove that these Roman colonnades were Corinthian, and that they supported arches rather than architraves, are quite unfounded.

area of 440 square feet). In the middle, located with reference
to the columns, was the site of the chryselephantine statue, a
large rectangle wherein the marble pavement is economically replaced by poros limestone blocks, surrounded by the engraved outline of the lower step of the pedestal, 26 feet 4½ inches wide and 13
feet 5¼ inches deep. The roof over the nave (with a clear span of 33¾
feet between the architraves) must have been supported on braced
beams (from which the ceiling might in part have been suspended).
The ceiling of the Parthenon chamber, on the other hand, was carried by four Ionic columns; the reason for the employment of this
order was the desire to avoid the superposed storeys of columns,
which in such a shallow room would have seemed rather absurd,
and yet at the same time to occupy less floor space than would have
been required for Doric columns tall enough to reach the ceiling.[8] It
was a principle derived from the temple at Bassae, and soon afterward imitated in the Propylaea.

The temple is so well preserved, in its essential parts, that it is
possible even to analyse mathematically those subtle refinements both
in design and construction which make it the most remarkable building in the world.[9] Referring to these refinements, it has been said:
"The whole building is constructed, so to speak, on a subjective
rather than an objective basis; it is intended not to be mathematically
accurate, but to be adapted to the eye of the spectator. To the eye
a curve is a more pleasing form than a straight line, and the deviations
from rigid correctness serve to give a character of purpose, almost of
life, to the solid marble construction."[10] Some of the irregularities,
however, seem to be due rather to alteration of the design during
erection rather than to a desire for spontaneous freedom; and the
discrepancies in the spacing of the columns may be traced to a misunderstanding by the workmen who centred them on joints of the
stylobate rather than on engraved diameters such as were employed
elsewhere. The delicate curves and inclinations of the horizontal and
vertical lines include the rising curves given to the stylobate and

8. While there are several more or less faithful modern replicas of the
exterior of the Parthenon, the only reproduction of the interior at full size
is that which I designed in 1927 for the Parthenon at Nashville, Tennessee.

9. These refinements were first noticed by Allason and Cockerell (1814),
Donaldson (1820), and Hoffer and Pennethorne (1836–1837), and in 1846
were measured by Penrose, who published his well-known work in 1851
(with a second edition in 1888). Later still, all this evidence was analysed and
summarised by Goodyear (1912), whose tendency, however, was to lay
too much emphasis on what were really accidental variations or workmen's
errors.

10. Percy Gardner, *Grammar of Greek Art* (1905), p. 39.

entablature in order to impart a feeling of life and to prevent the appearance of sagging, the convex curve to which the entasis of the columns was worked in order to correct the optical illusion of concavity which might have resulted if the sides had been straight, and the slight inward inclinations of the axes of the columns so as to give the whole building an appearance of greater strength; all entailed a mathematical precision in the setting out of the work and in its execution which is probably unparalleled in the world. We are justified in regarding these as optical refinements; for, in spite of certain modern experiments made with the purpose of demonstrating that the optical illusions, which these refinements were supposed to correct, might not actually have occurred, we have nevertheless definite evidence that the ancient Greeks believed that such illusions required correctives and, in consequence, must admit that such was the primary purpose of their employment.

Of one group of refinements, consisting of variations from normal dimensions, we have already noted several instances. Such is the contraction of the angle intervals of peristyles, occasioned primarily by the difficulty in the triglyph frieze, but accepted also as an optical refinement because it gave at the end of the colonnade a sense of stability and rest, and at the same time, by emphasising the perspective effect of the narrowing of the more distant intervals, it might seem to increase the length of a colonnade. That this perspective illusion was appreciated is shown, for instance, by the Parthenon, where the contraction was doubled to exaggerate the effect; though here again was a second motive, the improvement of the general proportions. A second refinement of this nature is the repetition of the perspective illusion in the triglyph frieze; this is found, however, only on the façades of the Parthenon, where we noted that the maximum variation is 4⅛ inches. A third variety is the thickening of the angle columns of a peristyle as mentioned by Vitruvius, "because they are sharply outlined by the unobstructed air round them, and seem to the beholder more slender than they are." Hence this refinement was not applied to the end columns of such prostyle colonnades (as in the porches of the Parthenon and the Propylaea) as were generally seen against solid walls or other obstacles. It was desirable, furthermore, only after the archaic distinction between the sizes of the front and flank columns had been abandoned, and was apparently first used at Aegina and in the Older Parthenon. Vitruvius says that the enlargement should be one-fiftieth of the diameter, which agrees with the Periclean Doric examples (one-fortieth in both Parthenons, one fiftieth in the Hephaesteum).

The second group of refinements consists in the inclination of lines or planes which are supposedly vertical. The most important is the effect of upward tapering, and hence of greater stability, imparted to the whole building by the inward inclination of the column axes, a refinement described by Vitruvius. In the Parthenon the inward inclination of the columns [text fig. 12] is 2⅜ inches; it may be calculated that the axes of the columns on both flanks, if prolonged, would meet in a line more than 1½ miles above the pavement; the axes on the two façades being inclined at the same rate, it is apparent that the axes of the angle columns, being inclined both ways on a diagonal line, have a greater inclination in the proportion of the diagonal to the sides of a square. In the Propylaea the inclinations are relatively greater, 3⅜ inches with smaller columns, so that the axes of the flank columns would meet five-eighths of a mile above the stylobate. Such inclinations had appeared earlier than the Periclean period in the Older Parthenon and at Croton in Italy. In some Peloponnesian temples, as Aegina, Olympia, Tegea, and Nemea, only the flank colonnades inclined, confining the effect to the façades (as Vitruvius recommended). Walls likewise sometimes incline inward, either because they taper, as at Bassae (the inner faces being vertical), or in sympathy with the inclinations of the columns, as in the Parthenon and Propylaea; but cross-walls containing doorways are always strictly vertical. In porticoes in-antis the antae sometimes lean backward following the line of diminution of the columns between them, as at Bassae; but in Doric prostyle porticoes the antae lean forward toward the columns, as in the Propylaea and the inner porches of the Parthenon (in the latter to the extent of 4¼ inches). Of a similar nature are the inclinations of door and window jambs, resulting in the upward diminution of such openings. The sides of the abacus of a capital in some buildings have slight inclinations, in the Parthenon following the inclined axis of the column, though in other cases, as in the Propylaea, the faces lean outward on all sides, sometimes contrary to the inclination of the axis. Similar inclinations, either backward or forward, occur also in most members of the entablature and pediment; these would seem to be due to the position from which the building was seen, and to its illumination by the sun's rays, or to the desire to correct certain optical illusions or the effect of foreshortening, or even to agree or contrast with other inclinations.

The third group of refinements, the most interesting of all, includes the deviations from apparently straight lines, forming curves, of which we may first consider the horizontal curves.[11] The upward

11. First noticed by Hoffer and Pennethorne. The fact of their existence was warmly disputed by Bötticher and Durm, with the argument that they resulted from settlement at the corners of temples. But there can be no doubt

curvature of the stylobate was intended partly to impart a feeling of life to the whole, and even more to prevent any effect of sagging that might otherwise have resulted from the long row of vertical columns bearing down upon the horizontal line of the platform, as mentioned by Vitruvius; but its origin may be traced to the utilitarian function of shedding rain.[12] As a refinement it had already appeared at Corinth, in the Peisistratid temple of Athena, and in the Older Parthenon, but it seems to have been omitted at Bassae, as well as in some of the smaller Periclean temples, and also in the Propylaea platform where the interruption of the stylobate by the central roadway would have neutralised its effect. The upward curvature of the stylobate [cf. text fig. 8] in the Parthenon amounts to 2⅜ inches on the façades and to 4⁵⁄₁₆ inches on the flanks; the radius of the latter curve, an arc of an enormous circle, is about 3½ miles. In the Hephaesteum the rise amounts to ¾ inch on the façades and 1¼ inches on the flanks. Even more delicate had been the upward curvature planned for the flanks of the Older Parthenon, with a rise of 2⅜ inches and a radius of about 7½ miles. But it is not to be supposed that the architect ever troubled to calculate the radius or to establish the form of an arc of such a theoretical circle. His system consisted rather in deciding first the maximum increment of curvature desired, and then any convenient arbitrary number of equal intervals between the corner and middle of the building (the beginning and apex of the proposed curve); the maximum increment of curvature was next divided by the square of the above-mentioned number of intervals, thus determining the size of the fractional parts of the height, so that the curve could be set out either in diagrammatic form as a parabola with the equally spaced ordinates descending on either side of the apex as successive square numbers of the fractional parts [text fig. 9], or on the actual temple as a colossal arc by replacing the ordinates with the corresponding levelling blocks (the *scamilli impares* of Vitruvius).[13]

---

of their intentional character; apart from the fact that the corners would be the least likely to settle (particularly in the same manner in so many temples), we have such instances as the west end of the temple at Corinth and the northeast quarter of the Parthenon with the solid rock rising almost to the bottom step without any leeway for settlement, also the intensified curve on the south flank of the Parthenon actually countersunk in the top of the older platform, and the measured variations in the Doric column heights of the Propylaea intended to permit their capitals to fit the upward curvature of the architrave even though the bottoms (by exception) rest on a horizontal platform.

12. Thus in the Croesus temple at Ephesus the pavement slopes up toward the cella, giving somewhat the effect of a deck roof.

13. For instance, in a length of 228 feet might have been twelve intervals

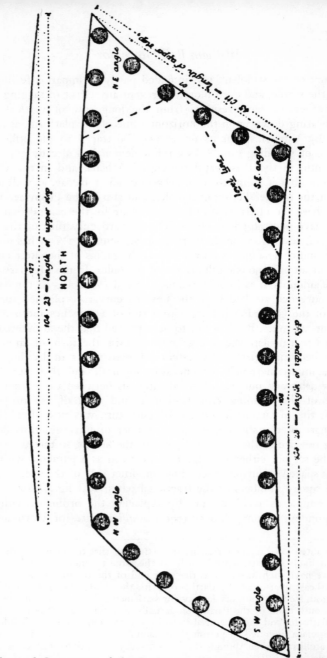

8. Upward Curvature of the Stylobate (Hephaesteum), exaggerated.

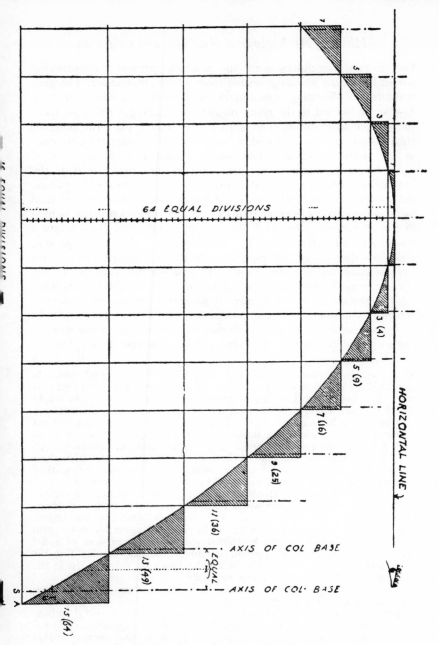

9. Diagram for Construction of Stylobate Curvature.

For at this tremendous scale the resulting parabolic construction would have been indistinguishable from a true circular arc. The general effect of the rising curves upon the platform as a whole [text fig. 8] may be likened to the result obtained by cutting a rectangle from the surface of a melon. The steps of the temple platform being of equal height from end to end, it was necessary to start the curvature as low as the foundation. The columns, likewise, were normally of equal height throughout, so that the curvature determined at the bottom was transmitted to the entablature;[14] but in the Propylaea, the stylobate being level, the central columns were made higher than those at the corners in order to obtain an upward curvature of ¾ inch in the architrave soffit. And through the entablature the curvature was carried up to the top of the cornice or bottom of the tympanum; and since the tympanum triangle retained the ordinates proper to a straight-sided triangle, the sloping tympanum top and the raking cornice were likewise constructed in the form of oblique curves.[15]

The vertical curves, generally confined to columns, are most conveniently expressed by the maximum amount of the entasis, that is, of the deviation of the convex outline of the arris from the straight line or chord connecting the bottom and top of the arris.[16] Thus in

---

of 19 feet, six on either side of the centre. Then, if the desired curvature were, say, 4½ inches, it would be divided by the square of six, into thirty-six parts of ⅛ inch each. The first ordinate on either side of the apex would descend ⅛ inch lower than the apex, the second ½ (4⁄8) inch, the third 1⅛ (9⁄8) inch, and the fourth 2 (16⁄8) inches, the fifth 3⅛ (25⁄8) inches, and the corner 4½ (36⁄8) inches. The differences between the successive ordinates were the successive odd numbers, 1, 3, 5, 7, 9, 11 parts (*ad infinitum*); [*cf.* text fig. 9]. Thus the wooden levelling blocks by means of which these rising curves were executed became *scamilli impares* in two senses: they were not only unequal but they differed by odd (not even) numbers.

14. Vitruvius seems to have assumed, and probably rightly, that the entablature curve followed and was a consequence of that of the stylobate. Penrose on the other hand argued, with less probability, that the reverse was the case; that Ictinus, in order "to obviate a disagreeable effect produced by the contrast of the horizontal with the inclined lines of a flat pediment," which gave an apparent dip to the former, decided that the horizontal lines must rise towards the middle, requiring a similar rise in the stylobate in order that the columns might be of equal height.

15. Curves in plan, convex or concave to the exterior, have sometimes been mentioned in connection with the Parthenon and the temples at Paestum and Segesta. But these are either imaginary or of doubtful authenticity, those in the upper parts of peristyles being due to accidental deformation of the colonnades. It is to be noted, furthermore, that concave curves in plan at high levels would serve only to neutralise the upward curve transmitted by the columns.

16. First noticed by Allason and Cockerell, and afterwards measured and verified by Penrose. Delagardette had observed it as early as 1793 at Paestum, but had considered it to be merely Roman recutting.

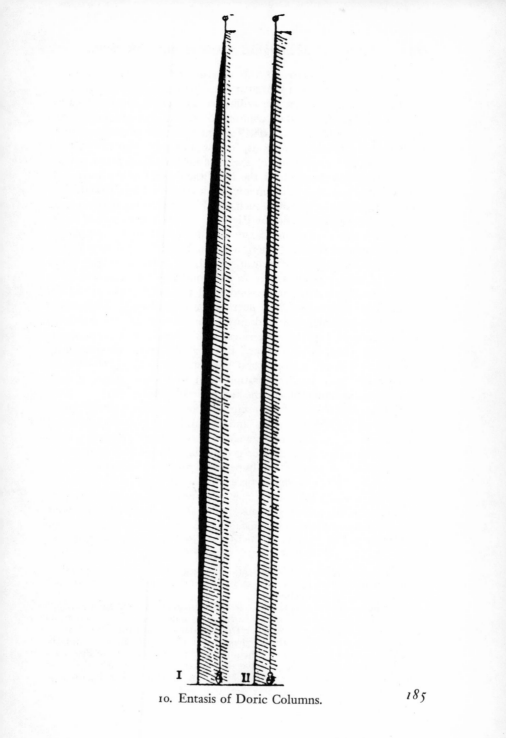

10. Entasis of Doric Columns.

the Parthenon the entasis of the tapering column shaft [text fig. 10, II] is probably likewise a circular arc,[17] with a maximum increment of about 11/16 inch, so that the radius would have been nearly half a mile. In the slightly smaller columns of the main porticoes of the Propylaea it is stronger, ¾ inch. The entasis varies in different temples and is not found in some, as, for instance, the temple of Athena Nike and in the east portico of the Erechtheum. The entasis is most delicate in the north porch of the Erechtheum and in the Ionic columns of the Propylaea (the amount of deviation from a straight line in both cases being less than ¼ inch), and is most pronounced in early examples such as the Basilica at Paestum (where the deviation is 2⅛ inches [text fig. 10, I]), or in late examples, such as the temple of Zeus Olympius at Athens (where it is 1⅞ inches).[18] No such entasis was applied, during the Periclean period, to walls or antae, except that the slender makeshift pier in the southwest wing of the Propylaea is slightly thicker at the middle of the height than at bottom or top. The entasis had "the purpose of correcting a disagreeable optical illusion, which is found to give an attenuated appearance to columns formed with straight sides, and to cause their outlines to seem concave instead of straight." But it also gave to the column an appearance of elastic strength and vitality; and it was probably this quality that caused its exaggeration even to a cigar shape in later times, when the moderation of the best period had been lost.

With regard to the shorter curves, not properly optical refinements, employed in mouldings and in profiles where perfection of contour was of prime importance, the Periclean architects seem usually to have preferred regular geometrical curves such as true arcs of circles and portions of the hyperbola, parabola, and ellipse, especially for convex mouldings where contour is more important than in concave mouldings. Among the most beautiful examples of such curves are the hyperbolic echinus of the Doric capital, the parabolic soffits of Ionic or raking Doric cornices, and various forms of the hawksbeak and cyma reversa. In the case of the fluting of the col-

17. Penrose argued that it was rather a section of hyperbola; and others have attempted to prove that it was an even more complicated curve such as the conchoid of Nicomedes.

18. The comparative entasis given approximately by Penrose (*Athenian Architecture*, p. 40) is 12 for the Corinthian temple of Zeus Olympus, 11 for the larger and 9 for the smaller Doric order of the Propylaea, 8 and 6 for the Doric peristyles of the Parthenon and Hephaesteum, and 4 for the Ionic north columns of the Erechtheum; the Ionic columns of the Propylaea (in which Penrose did not perceive the entasis) would fit into the series with the index number 2 (the height of the column being regarded as uniform).

umns in the Parthenon an approximate curve struck from three centres, and known as a false ellipse, was adopted; the central portion of the curve had a radius equal to the width of the flute, and the radii of the portions on either side diminished with the decreasing depth of the flutes in the upper portions of the shaft, the principal object throughout being to accentuate the arris. In the Propylaea, as also in most of the earlier Doric examples in south Italy and Sicily, the curves were segments of circles.

The Parthenon being a completed work, much of the evidence for the method of its construction is derived from other Greek Doric buildings which for various reasons have never been finished, such as the archaic Olympieum at Athens and the older temple at Sunium, the temple 'GT' at Selinus and that at Segesta mentioned in an earlier chapter, also the Older Parthenon, the temples of Nemesis at Rhamnus, Demeter at Eleusis, Apollo Ismenius at Thebes, Zeus at Stratos and Poseidon at Molycrion in Aetolia, of Apollo at Delos, the so-called stoa (telesterion) at Thoricus and the stoa of Philip V at Delos, and, to a lesser degree, the Olympieum at Acragas, the temple at Bassae, and the Propylaea of the Athenian Acropolis, and also from some Ionic temples such as those at Didyma, Samos, and Sardis. From Segesta and Thoricus it may be inferred that the peristyle of a temple was generally the first part erected * * *. Similar evidence is derived from the temple at Aegina (where three of the peristyle columns were omitted until the last moment so that material for the cella could be brought in), from the Older Parthenon (where the cella walls never rose higher than the moulded base though the columns were in process of erection to complete height), from the present Parthenon (where the entire cella building was shifted after its lower step had been built in accordance with the peristyle), and from the Hephaesteum (the inner foundation trenches being cut through the fill thrown up inside the outer foundations). As for the point at which the work was begun, it was sometimes the main façade (as in temple 'GT' at Selinus and the temple of Athena at Priene), but frequently the less important rear (as in the archaic temple of Apollo at Delphi and the Parthenon), thus giving the main front the advantage of any last-moment improvements. The foundations of temples of the fifth century were usually of various qualities of poros limestone, carefully coursed and bonded as ashlar masonry, forming concentric hollow rectangles supporting walls and columns but leaving the intervening spaces for mere earth fill, though there was usually a stone grid or a continuous course of underpinning to support the pavement. The Parthenon itself appears to be an exception in this respect, since the foundation erected for the Older Parthenon, doubtless because of its unstable location on the steep declivity of the Acropolis and the extreme depth required on the south flank, was made a solid mass of ashlar masonry. In many of the unfinished buildings the columns are still unfluted, and the treads and risers of the steps retain their rough unworked surfaces; often they retain also the ancones or ears, projecting bosses by which the stones were hoisted and lowered into their positions.[19] The gradual rise of the stylobate was constructed, according to Vitruvius, by means of the *scamilli impares*; his remarks on this subject are not clear, but it evident that he referred to the formation of the curve, on the top course of the foundations, by means of levelling cubes of various heights, so arranged that when their tops lay in a horizontal plane, their bottoms described the proper curve and indicated to what depth the course below them had to be dressed [text fig. 9]. It is clear that, because of the absence of variation in the steps, the exact curvature had to be worked out on the top of the foundation, in the case of the Parthenon the thin marble levelling course on the north and west, the top course of the old basement of poros stone on the south and east. The work was made easier by the fact that the old basement had already been constructed on a curve—though to a lesser degree—through its four topmost courses in order to impart a similar refinement to the Older Parthenon.[20]

The column drums as delivered from the quarry to the temple site were in the form of roughly dressed disks, coarsely worked with the point and mallet, not only on the cylindrical exterior but also on the top and bottom beds. From four points on the circumference protruded large bosses, as much as 8 to 10 inches wide and 6 to 8 inches in projection, suggesting that they were hewn out of the corners of the square block within which the circular drum was inscribed. Transportation from the Pentelic quarries must have been effected by wheeled carts, drawn by thirty or forty yoke of oxen, mentioned in the Eleusinian inscriptions and responsible for the ruts still remaining in the quarries and on the roads. Only exceptionally huge drums, such as those of Selinus, were transported by the remarkable method of rolling along the ground in the manner described by Vitruvius.[21] The drums were prepared on the ground by

19. It is impossible to assume, as is sometimes done, that the bosses were used also to work the stones backwards and forwards in order to grind the joints (see below, with regard to the centring pins).

20. To increase the amount of curvature in the present Parthenon, the crown of the curve was retained at its previous level, but the ends were countersunk into the old foundation, thus furnishing one of the proofs of the intentional character of the curvature.

21. The frequently mentioned theory that all column drums, including

dressing the lower bed within an exact circle about 1½ inches outside the proposed final diameter, this circle being marked at the bottom of the face by a drafted margin about 1½ inches high; the rest of the circumference of the drum was then dressed back to the surface indicated by the drafted margin, at first by cutting vertical channels midway between the bosses, then by supplementary channels enframing the bosses, and finally by dressing off the twelve intervening areas with a fine stippled surface from which only the four bosses protruded. On the lowest drum of a Doric column the flutes were finished for 2 or 3 inches in height, the rest being left in its rough cylindrical mantle. Then, with the addition of the special lower bed dressing described below, the drum was ready for hoisting and placing; the corresponding upper bed dressing was not executed until the next drum was ready to be set. Where the stylobate received the lowest drum of the column the surface was sunk to its proper depth [text fig. 11], and on this were traced the diameters marking the axis of the column and in many cases also a circle forming its circumference; the area within the latter was worked lightly over to give some hold to the lower surface of the drum. The bottom surface of the lowest drum of a marble Doric column of the Periclean age was not fastened to the stylobate;[22] but at the upper joints the arrangement was different. There a square sinking was made in the centre of the upper and lower surface of each drum [text fig. 11], about 4 to 6 inches square and 3 to 4 inches deep, in which plugs (empolia) of cypress wood were fixed; at the exact centre of the drum a round hole about 2 inches in diameter was bored in each plug, so that a circular wooden pin, inserted in the hole in the plug at the top of a drum, would fit the corresponding hole at the bottom of the drum above,[23] forming a simple method of centring the drums accurately one upon another.[24] Between the centre and the circum-

---

those of the Parthenon, were transported by rolling along the ground, and that the empolion cuttings in their top and bottom beds were used primarily as hub cuttings for the attachment to the oxen, is sufficiently controverted by the presence of the four bosses (effectively preventing rolling) and by the absence of empolion cuttings on unfinished drums which had completed their journey to the Acropolis.

22. In later work in marble, as well as in soft limestone materials in all periods, the same centring device was often employed also under the bottom drums of Doric columns.

23. In rare instances all the parts, empolia and pins, were made of bronze, as in the Tholos at Delphi and Philon's porch at Eleusis. In the Tholos the pins are slightly conical with the butt ends fixed in the tops of the lower beds.

24. In earlier editions of this work it was assumed that the wooden pins were really pivots on which the drums were worked round so as to

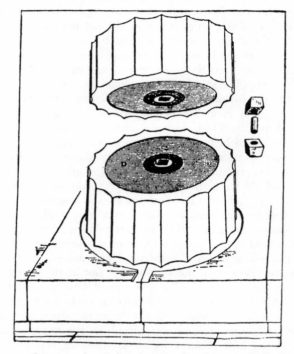

11. Construction of columns showing centering
pin.

ference several concentric circles appear on the bed of the drum, the
outermost ring being smoothly polished to form a joint that was
practically invisible, while the next zone was slightly roughened in
order to give the drums better hold upon each other; a third zone
was slightly depressed, with the object of reducing the amount of

grind the blocks closely together, a theory evolved by Penrose, against
which there are numerous grave objections. Among these are the occur-
rences of the same device on semi-columns engaged to wall blocks which
obviously could not be rotated, and on column drums of later date into
which additional pairs of metal dowels were affixed near the circumference
before setting (thus effectually preventing rotation), and even the negative
fact that it is absent from the bottoms of Doric columns (which could be
centred on the stylobate by comparing the arrises and fluting with the
engraved diameters and circles) as contrasted with its presence on the bottoms of Ionic bases which with their undercut torus mouldings could not
otherwise have been readily set in their exact positions.

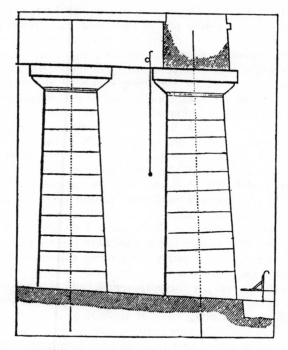

12. Inclination of Doric columns, exaggerated.

surface that was actually in contact; and generally there was an innermost zone, rising again to the level of the joint, immediately round the wooden plug mentioned above. There are from ten to twelve of these drums in each column of the Parthenon. None of the drum joints was truly horizontal, all being perpendicular to the inclined axis of the column [text fig. 12]. But on the lowest drum, in consequence of the curve of the stylobate, the side toward the corner of the building had to be carried down a fraction lower than on the side toward the central axis of the building, and likewise, both on account of the curvature and because of the inward inclination of the column axis, the outer face had to be carried down considerably lower than the back (toward the cella wall).[25] Similar difficulties

25. Penrose and other authorities have applied to the variations of height on the different sides of the lowest drums, due to their adjustment both to the curved stylobate and to the inclination of the columns, the term *scamilli impares* used by Vitruvius; but the latter was referring only to the stylobate construction.

were experienced with the uppermost drums, because of the necessity of presenting for the bed of the capital a plane parallel to the
soffit of the architrave. The necking of the capital was also fluted to
correspond to the bottom of the shaft, and the echinus was perfectly finished; [26] but on the abacus were sometimes (as at Segesta) left unworked corners to protect them. These processes, in
which the painstaking care bestowed upon the erection of the columns was complicated by the rising curves of the stylobate and
entablature and by the inward inclinations of the column axes, all entailed a mathematical precision which is almost incredible.

The walls were likewise built up with their faces completely enveloped in the unfinished protective surface, in the case of marble
about ⅜ inch outside the proposed final wall planes,[27] or more in
other sorts of stone; the lifting bosses still remained on the blocks.
The vertical joints were hollowed with the exception of a polished
band 2½ or 3 inches wide at the two vertical edges, and across the
top (but not across the bottom) the so-called anathyrosis, in order
to secure closer contact; and all the joints, both horizontal and vertical, were left with a slight bevel intended to prevent chipping when
the blocks were placed together. At internal corners, either vertical
or horizontal (as when a wall recedes from a step or a belt course
protrudes from a wall), a finished marginal band of about two inches
was sunk to the final surface. In all horizontal joints of this character, and likewise in other cases of projecting or receding surfaces
where the edges of beds were likely to chip or spall, a relieving margin about ½₂ inch deep protected the edge from close contact. For
hoisting and placing, lifting tongs worked with pulleys and derricks
usually gripped bosses left on the exposed faces of the blocks, which
could thus be set directly on their final beds and almost in their exact
positions, requiring no blocking up or other adjustment beyond a
lateral shift of a few inches by means of crowbars. For some special
work the tongs grasped the joint surfaces of the blocks by means of
special tong holes; and the last-laid intermediate block of a course
had the tong holes cut in its top so that it could descend accurately
into its position between the vertical joints of its neighbours and at
the same time leave the tongs free for removal [text fig. 13 c, d].
This preoccupation with the removal of the lifting appliance under-
lies all the varied inventions employed both earlier and later: loops

26. There is no basis for the statement that it was turned in a lathe.
27. An exception must be made for the "prefabricated" marble wall
blocks of the Hephaesteum, which never had protective surfaces and were
therefore provided with relieving margins at the bottom, leaving slightly
open joints.

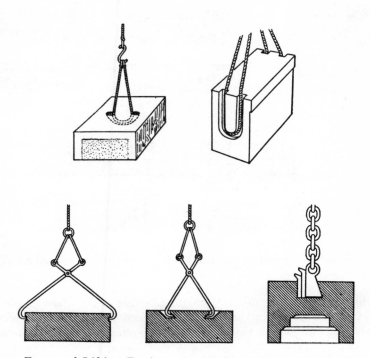

13. Forms of Lifting Devices: (a, b) Rope loops; (c, d) tongs; (e) lewis.

of rope passed through tunnels in the tops of blocks (as in the Heraeum at Olympia) or through U-shaped channels in both end joints (as in the Olympieum at Acragas and the temple at Aegina), or lewis irons fitting corresponding wedge-shaped holes in the tops of blocks (tapering on one end only in the best Greek periods, on both ends in late Hellenistic and Roman times). All the blocks were laid dry, without mortar; for a bonding material was used iron, dowels to fasten the blocks to those below them, and clamps of double-T form to connect blocks in the same course, all sealed in molten lead [text fig. 14 d]. Special forms of dowels and clamps were employed in unusual positions, even in the work on a single building such as the Parthenon. And in earlier or later buildings we again encounter variant forms of dowels and clamps characteristic of different periods or localities. Thus the archaic dovetail clamp,

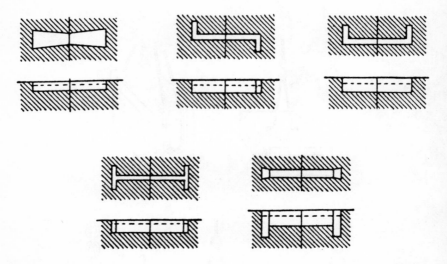

14. Forms of clamps: (a) Dovetail; (b, c) double- Γ ; (d) double-T;
(e) hook.

which in Egypt was of wood, might be either of pure lead (poured
molten into the cavity) or of lead reinforced with an iron bar with
the ends bent down; the double-T clamp was preceded, and sometimes accompanied, by the double-Γ form, usually with the ends of
the bar bent in opposite directions, right and left, rarely in the same
direction; and latest of all came the simple bar with both ends bent
down to form the Hellenistic and Roman hook clamp.

The members of the entablatures and ceilings appear to have been
set in place practically finished.[28] The unworked surfaces with a few
exceptions were confined to the platform and columns and walls,
these being the portions most liable to injury during the process of
erection. On the completion of the temple the faces of the walls were
dressed and rubbed so that the bevels at the joints, and almost the
joints themselves, disappeared; and the treads and risers of the steps
were worked down to their smooth surfaces. Exceptionally careful
was the treatment of the columns, of which the cylindrical stippled
mantle passed through three additional stages after the columns had
been erected and the bosses hewn off [text fig. 15]. First, the entire

28. In later work narrow protective strips were sometimes left at the
vertical joints to prevent chipping or spalling.

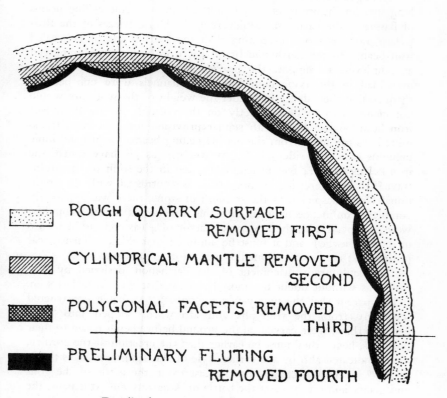

ROUGH QUARRY SURFACE
REMOVED FIRST

CYLINDRICAL MANTLE REMOVED
SECOND

POLYGONAL FACETS REMOVED
THIRD

PRELIMINARY FLUTING
REMOVED FOURTH

15. Detail of processes of fluting Doric columns.

shaft was recut in the form of a polygon of forty sides, twenty of them wider and marking the positions of the flutes, while the twenty narrower facets were to become the sharp arrises. Next, the twenty wider facets were hollowed to form the preliminary fluting, the narrower facets remaining like the fillets of an Ionic column. Finally, all the surfaces were cut back about ⅜ inch more to the positions of the finished flutes already worked on the bottom drums and the capitals, the fillets then being transformed into the almost razor-edged Doric arrises (actually ¼₃₂ to ¹⁄₁₆ inch wide). All these processes may be seen in temple 'GT' at Selinus and are mentioned in the expense accounts of the Erechtheum. And through them all it was necessary to preserve the delicate entasis which gives such beauty to the outline of the shaft.

Among exceptional structural processes required by the use of long spans or heavy masses, such as the hollow marble ceiling beams of Bassae or the balanced cantilevers in the Doric friezes of the Propylaea, none is more interesting than the sparing use of concealed iron beams. In the Parthenon broad flat iron beams were employed as cantilevers to support the heaviest pediment statues; they were imbedded in the tympanum wall and channels were cut beneath them so that their deflection under the weight of the sculpture would not cause them to bear directly on the cornice. In the Propylaea iron beams 6 feet long, with similar provision for deflection, transmitted 6⅔-ton loads from the marble ceiling beams toward the Ionic columns on either side * * * . At Acragas, as we have noted, the iron beams were 14 feet in length, located in the soffit of the architrave.[29] It is interesting to note that, as contrasted with the traditional Greek suspicion of the strength of stone, there was apparently complete confidence in iron; thus the iron beams in the Propylaea were employed with the low safety factor of 4 (as contrasted with 6 in modern usage), and it must be admitted that this confidence was justified in that they functioned properly for 2,120 years.

The sculptured enrichment of the Parthenon, designed by Phidias, was without doubt the most beautiful that the world has seen. It is apparent that the ninety-two metopes * * *, being constructed separately from the triglyphs and afterwards slipped into place between them, were carved on the ground before being raised to their positions; hence they must be earlier than the erection of the cornice, a fact indicated also by the earlier style of the sculptured slabs themselves.[30] Their subjects are, on the east front, the battle of the gods and giants, and on the west the battle of Amazons and Athenians; the long south flank was occupied by the contest of the Centaurs with the Lapiths and on the north flank was the fall of Troy. The sculpture is in such high relief that, in contrast to the metopes of temple 'C' at Selinus, it protrudes far beyond the triglyphs and even overhangs the architrave taenia below. On the other hand, the continuous Panathenaic frieze in low relief on the external walls of the cella formed an integral part of the structure, and was carved *in situ*; a remarkable feature of it is the location of such sculpture in a position where it

29. Much less scientific was one iron beam imbedded in a lintel soffit of the Erechtheum, in that the marble lintel itself had to crack (which it did) before the iron beam could begin to function.

30. The earlier style is probably due, not so much to the very slight difference in date, as to the fact that Phidias at this stage had not yet had time to mould the individual styles of the artisans of the old school to his own.

could hardly be appreciated [fig. 16]. Nothing was said by Pausanias about this frieze, 523 feet 7¼ inches in length, representing the procession which took place every four years during the Panathenaic festival; it starts from the southwest angle, running east and north, and meeting over the pronaos, where the procession, headed on either side by the maidens selected to work the sacred robe and here represented as bearing religious offerings, arrives before the Athenian officials and the assembled gods who are grouped in the centre, seated, while behind them the old peplos is being folded up to be stored away. The figures decorating the pediments, the latest of the marble sculptures of the temple, are known to have been executed on the ground before being set in place. The only literary notice that we possess of the subject of the pedimental sculptures is from Pausanias, who says, "the whole subject of what is called the pediment over the entrance (i.e., the east pediment) is the circumstances of the birth of Athena, and that at the back is the contest of Poseidon with Athena for the land." [31] Attention may be drawn also to the superb lion heads carved as false spouts at the four corners of the temple, not exactly at right angles to the cornice but peering obliquely toward the façades.[32] Finally, a few words should be said about the the chryselephantine statue of Athena, Phidias's masterpiece. This was constructed on a wooden core, having ivory for the face, arms, and feet, and gold for the drapery and accessories, the thin gold plates weighing about 2,500 pounds. The engraved outline of the pedestal on the pavement, and the rectangular hole for the central mast, define its exact position. The total height of the statue and its sculptured pedestal was twenty-six cubits (39 Doric feet, and so 41 feet 10 inches); and from the description of it given by Pausanias, and from the numerous smaller marble copies (such as the Varvakeion statuette at Athens) and the representations on marble or gold reliefs or on gems and coins, we obtain a fair idea of its appearance. The column inserted to support the right arm, with a capital that seems to be Corinthian, if not part of the original design, is at least as early as the beginning of the fourth century.

Last of all, a few words must be said with regard to the painting, primarily the architectural polychromy * * * . In general, the most

31. Drawings made in 1674 for the French ambassador De Nointel, and sometimes attributed to Jacques Carrey, give the positions of the lost central figures of the west pediment; but in the east pediment the central group was already missing before this time and can be only conjecturally restored.

32. The best preserved of the sculptures of the Parthenon are in the British Museum, including eighteen of the pediment figures, fifteen of the south metopes, and 247 feet of the Ionic frieze, besides numerous fragments. One metope and one long piece of the frieze are in the Louvre.

important structural members were free of colour, being left in the natural white of the marble just as, in poros buildings, these portions were covered with white marble stucco.[33] Thus the Doric peristyle contained no colour below the capitals; the deep incision under the necking was painted blue, the annulets at the base of the echinus blue and red. The triglyphs were blue (as Vitruvius also reports) and thus formed the key to the colouring of the entablature; for the regulae and mutules recalling the triglyphs at the top of the architrave and on the soffit of the cornice were likewise blue, and the alternating members, as far as necessary (the taenia of the architrave, the viae between the mutules and the fascia below them and the scotia above), were all in red. In the Parthenon, moreover, the taenia of the architrave had a gold maeander on the red ground and the regulae similarly a gold anthemion on the blue ground. The guttae were apparently dazzling white (at Bassae they were separately inserted bits of marble), often with circles painted on the bottoms. The metopes were always white (except insofar as figure sculpture in relief demanded coloured details); and in poros buildings the metopes were often specially inserted marble slabs for this reason. An uninterrupted frieze such as that of the Panathenaic procession or the Nike temple parapet, however, had in addition to the coloured details of the sculpture a blue painted background, an effect gained in the Erechtheum frieze by an Eleusinian stone background, giving the cameo effect of Wedgwood's jasper ware. Likewise an interior cornice might have elaborately painted maeander or anthemion designs on the main face of the cornice, as well as decorated bed and crowning mouldings. Such mouldings received painted patterns according with their profiles: the hawksbeak had squarish conventional leaves, alternating blue above with red below and *vice versa*, with rims and midribs in gold, green, or white; similar colours were used for the egg-and-dart on the ovolo and the heart-and-dart on the Lesbian cyma (or cyma reversa), red and blue predominating with a sparing use of gold, green, or white where the alternation would otherwise have been confused. The ceiling coffers had successive tiers of egg-and-dart patterns, and the slightly vaulted top panels sometimes contained eight-pointed stars on the blue ground (as in the Hephaesteum, temple of Ares, and east portico of the Propylaea), but in the Parthenon

33. The excessive application of polychromy in architectural restorations made during the nineteenth century has led to some misconceptions of its purpose and, consequently, of Greek taste. Some have not hesitated to cover entire columns with yellow or saffron (based apparently on traces of chemical change or oxidation of the iron content in the marble), the echinus with a huge egg-and-dart, the abacus with a maeander, the architrave and cornice faces with elaborate floral patterns, etc.

(and also in the west portico of the Propylaea) had elaborate floral patterns. Likewise the square area of cornice soffit at each corner of the temple received a floral pattern (carved in relief in the case of Segesta), and sometimes the viae were similarly painted with palmette compositions. The ovolo sima in the Parthenon received a delicate anthemion, though in the Propylaea it had a huge egg-and-dart. And the alternate red and blue of the petals and scrolls of the antefixes repeated the hieratic finial scheme of the archaic grave stelae. These colours are now preserved only in the most sheltered areas, and elsewhere are distinguishable only by the relative warmth or coolness in the tones of the marble, by discoloration or disintegration of surfaces in accordance with the chemical effects of pigments and their varying degrees of protection, and in some cases by the engraved outlines of the ornament.[34] As for representational painting, mural decoration on a large scale, we know this chiefly from literary sources, such as the decoration of the pronaos walls of the temple of Athena Areia at Plataea by Polygnotus, or those of a temple of Athena at Elis by Panaenus, or also from the preparations for such painting as in the case of the stippled surfaces and waterproofed joints of the porch and cella walls of the Hephaesteum. Sometimes, moreover, additional decoration was applied in later times as, in the Parthenon itself, the series of bronze shields (some dedicated by Alexander the Great) fastened to the architrave, and Nero's great inscription in bronze letters on the architrave of the east façade.

A. MAVRIKIOS
Aesthetic Analysis Concerning the Curvature of the Parthenon—[1965] *

In the following study, Mavrikios draws a parallel between classical Greek sculpture and the Parthenon. His purpose in making this comparison is to explain in a new light the aesthetic function of the horizontal curvature of the Parthenon. Rejecting the old cliché that the upward curvature of stylobate and architrave corrects for an illusion of sagging, producing a feeling of lightness, Mavrikios argues

34. The discoloration, or the effect of relief caused by the disintegration of surfaces in the interstices of the patterns, may be so pronounced as to bring out the patterns clearly by photography, just as paper casts (squeezes) of moulding may reveal the engraved outlines of patterns.

* A. Mavrikios, "Aesthetic Analysis Concerning the Curvature of the Parthenon," *AJA*, LXIX (1965), pp. 264–268. Reprinted by permission of the Archaeological Institute of America and the editors of the *American Journal of Archaeology*.

that on the contrary, the curvature results in an emphatic and carefully calculated expression of structural weight and an awareness of the pull of gravity. The curvature helps us to visualize the manner in which the weight of the entablature is transmitted to the ground, investing the entire structural composition with a greater sense of the dynamic interrelation of its parts. This dynamic flow is not upward moving, but downward moving, and hence it is expressive of a feeling of ultimate repose, which is the hallmark of classical art. Mavrikios' interpretation of the curvature provides us with a useful starting point for a modern review of the aesthetic problem of classical art, freed from the terminology inherited from the nineteenth century.

When Phidias made defined and carefully studied use of curves in the Parthenon he had some serious intention in mind, since the choice,[1] tracing and construction of the curvature require, in addition to sensibility, additional labor and trouble which is avoided when building on an entirely level base.[2] Our opinion is that this intention has not been sufficiently studied. Can we respond deeply to the beauty of the Parthenon and teach others to respond to this beauty while we remain ignorant of some of its basic aspects or have an erroneous conception of them?

With this question in mind, let us proceed to an investigation of the curvature—not the curves [3]—of the Parthenon, in the hope that new points of view and new factors will lead us to positive conclusions, and that we may become aware of what it is that "charms" us in this building, of the effect which "perhaps escapes analysis." [4]

1. It would seem to be due to choice that the curvature begins from the lowest underground levels of the stereobate. They would have been given the appropriate curvature during their construction.

2. According to W. B. Dinsmoor, *The Architecture of Ancient Greece* 155–156, the delicate subtleties of upward curvature are lacking at Bassae.

3. The whole temple is curved, since both the crepis and the entablature are curved masses. It even stands on the curved surface of the stereobate. In addition, the cutting of curved steps in the rock on the west side of the temple shows that the surrounding area was also curved up to a certain distance. It is for these reasons that we must speak of the curvature and not of the curves.

The first to observe the curvature of the Parthenon was Pennethorne in 1837. In 1838 Hoffer and Schauber published details of these curves in the *Wiener Bauzeitung*. According to Penrose, the curvature of the crepis and the entablature on the short sides is 0.065 m. and on the long sides 0.123 m. The measurements made by N. Balanos and published in 1940 show slight differences.

Penrose, and Stevens agree that the curves of the stylobate are parabolae. Karatheodori claims that they are arcs of circles, those on the east and west sides having a radius of 1850 m., while those on the other sides have a radius three times this size, i.e. 5550 m.

4. Choisy writes with reference to the effect of the curvature on the

We must therefore broaden our inquiry and take into account:
a) the sense of plasticity in construction among the ancient Greeks;
b) the role of Phidias in the creation of the Parthenon; c) the analysis not only of the formal data but also of certain statical factors which are inherent in the curvature and which react upon the appearance and style of the temple.

The Sense of Plasticity in Construction Among the Ancient Greeks

Generally speaking, the classical Greeks raised to a new level of refinement the study of the aesthetic effect, derived from the balance of action and reaction between the "borne" and the "bearing" elements, as well as from the interaction of space and solid elements. "Measure," and above all "quality," influenced the development of Greek art. We must therefore begin by examining this theme, and in particular the first of its aspects: the aesthetic effect originating from the relationship between "bearing" and being "borne." And we will start our investigation with sculpture.

Neither the Egyptians nor the Assyrians nor any other peoples made standing or sitting statues in the same way as did the Greeks. For the Greeks the earth on which the figures stand, or the seat on which they sit, does not appear as an obstacle, hostile to their weight, but appears as though "given" for them finally to come to rest on and be held on as they *move* downward.

From this springs the sense of a strange plastic balance, such as we experience when we see a drop of water that has come to rest on the edge of a cornice, and which, while it appears secure, stable and not likely to fall, at the same time gives us the feeling that a certain weight, a certain tension is drawing it downward.

This sense becomes strong especially at the beginning of the fifth century, when sculptors composed and moved the limbs of the figures more freely, thus attaining the classical posture of repose. In this posture almost all the weight of the body is on one foot, and the pelvis is raised correspondingly, while the other foot is on its toes slightly to the rear. It is in this movement, which is opposed to every idea of elevation (from the point of view of the mass), that the construction and plastic appearance of classical sculpture finds its fulfillment.

Parthenon: "The building avoids the ordinary appearance of construction with straight lines and achieves an unsuspected new character which, while perhaps it escapes analysis, yet charms us even if we are ignorant of its true meaning and cause."

The kouros rises up and, although stiff, seems ready to leave the earth on which it stands, as though to throw itself into action, to move, that is, in an external fashion. The classical statue, on the contrary, has no tendency to raise itself: standing or sitting it "places" and "spreads" its weight emphatically on the ground. It does not base itself lifelessly or "statically," but there is a certain "generative" quality in its emplacement which creates the sense of a living bond between the standing figure and the earth or the seated figure and the seat. Thus the statue is linked with its base, and is in repose, at the same time finding an atmosphere suitable for meditation—for internal movement. Elevation is interwoven, one might say synchronized, with a certain lightness, with a certain "depositioning" (ἀπόθεσις) rather than "positioning" (ἐναπόθεσις). This does not contribute toward the creation of an atmosphere of repose, of a dignified mastery of the surrounding space. What the latter requires is rather a "measured" weight, given with a certain definite quality, in the sense that we explain below.

In physics weight may have a particular meaning, but this is not true in art. Here it depends each time upon how it is interpreted. The impression of weight is not always in proportion to the mass of the material. A slender human body may give a feeling of weight greater than that produced by a thicker body. In addition, the same body may on different occasions give a different feeling of weight from the point of view of "quality." The sense of weight which is communicated in these cases depends upon the "movement" of the body —from the particular articulation, balance and "poise" of its "borne" and "bearing" members. Thus the appearance of the weight is determined not only by the quantity of the material, but often by the creative spirit alone. It is for this reason that the question of weight is not to be regarded as of an inferior, trivial or merely materialistic interest. In the hands of a worthy sculptor it may, according to whether or not he gives it a suitable quality, become a means of expression of a spiritual significance.[5] Indeed, one may say that the "springing" of a spiritual quality from a weight that has been interpreted and suggested with the appropriate articulation, balance, and shape of its members—and not from an excess of material—is one of the main distinguishing marks of the plastic construction of Greek classical sculpture and, in extension, of the advanced Doric temples. Each action and reaction, as between body and pelvis in the statue, between architrave and column in the building, is emphasized and,

5. In later periods other great sculptors—Michaelangelo, Rodin—have also relied (and sometimes to an exaggerated extent) upon the aesthetic potentialities of weight in giving form to their plastic conceptions.

with the appropriate articulation, balance, and shape of the members —never sharply and harshly—is brought into powerful juxtaposition, provoking in this way a restrained sense of plastic vigor and controlled dynamism. If we stand before the Parthenon we will experience the same sensation that we experience before its sublime statues, with their calm movement, plastic posture, boundless spirituality and proud dignity.

Let us now examine certain formal elements inherent in the Doric order which support our contention, since it is clear that with the help of these elements the "aesthetic" weight necessary for the appearance and plastic construction of this order is created. We begin our investigation from above and work downward, starting with the cornice.

The mutules with the "water-drops" (guttae) in the form of truncated cones emphasize the downward tendency. Next come the triglyphs and then the regulae with the guttae, these being among the chief elements emphasizing a similar movement. Moreover, as the regulae with the guttae are placed in prolongation of the triglyphs and beneath the taenia which bounds the upper part of the architrave, they stress and interpret the transmission and conveyance of the weight to the architrave. The weight, while it seems to be held by the taenia-topped architrave, at the same time passes through the taenia and continues moving downward, accentuating this movement toward the earth [text figs. 16, 17]. In order to understand how strongly the influence of the triglyphs and regulae stresses this downward movement, we have only to imagine the presence of similar elements on the Ionic entablature. The effect would be disastrous, for these elements come into conflict with the basic aesthetic function of the Ionic order—elevation and lightness.

We now come to the Doric column with entasis. The Doric column receives and "carries"[6] the load with the abacus, concentrates it plastically with the echinus, and "ties" it together with the annulets, the column-neck and the necking-grooves, in order to transmit it from there to the shaft of the column.

The shaft of the Doric column does not reach upward: it simply rises up. It "rises up" above all because of its "diminution" (tapering), and in a subsidiary way because of its fluting. It seems to reach plastically, for it has entasis; yet at the same time it seems to convey and distribute the load downward, first of all due to this entasis, as we shall explain, and then due to the free prolongation of the flute

6. "Carries" because the abacus protrudes beyond the architrave. If it did not protrude or if it were further in, it would simply give the impression of supporting.

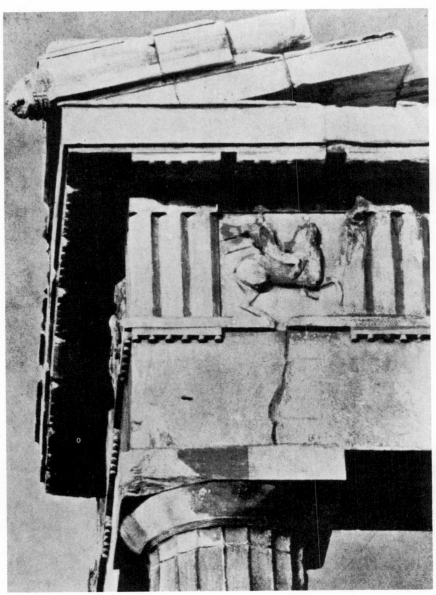

16.

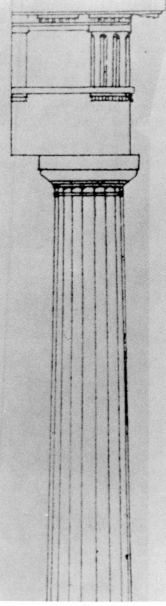

17.

down to the stylobate. Nothing intervenes, until the stylobate is reached, to hinder a free, uninterrupted movement downward. And this is the only direction that the movement can take: above, it encounters the capital, while the sideways tensions are held in check, or "bound," by the "shallow" concavity of the flutes. Another factor contributing to this downward movement is that below the point at which the entasis achieves its greatest development the flutes begin to diverge from their asymptote at an increasingly rapid rate and tend toward the vertical.[7]

Thus the aesthetic function of the Doric column is expressed in the dialectic of two opposing conceptions: a rising up in order to receive and to carry the load, and at the same time a movement downward in order to transmit and convey it to the crepis and from there to the earth.[8] This function may easily be perceived by the careful and sensitive observer.

To clarify this observation a pictorial interpretation of the aesthetic function of the Doric column is added. [Text fig. 18] shows schematically: a) the Doric column with tapering only; b) the same with tapering and entasis. What is the difference in their expression? We will represent the aesthetic "movement" of the column with arrows and we will see whether it corresponds in each case to its form.

In [text fig. 19c] the correspondence between the arrow and the form of the column is obvious. The arrow points upward, in the same way that the column does, as it tapers regularly and gradually.

In [text fig. 19d], where a column with both entasis and tapering is shown, the relationship between the arrow and the form is not satisfactory: something is wrong. There is not the complete correspondence between the arrow and the form that there is in [text fig. 19c]. In [text fig. 19e], on the other hand, there is correspondence between the arrow and the form; what was not right in [text fig. 19d] has been corrected, for the entasis contains a "dynamism" which moves aesthetically both upward (to the architrave) and downward (to the crepis).

So far then we have seen that in the entablature and in the col-

7. The shaft of the column of the Parthenon, according to Penrose, has sides that are segments of the hyperbola. The fact that at that time conic sections as mathematical formulae were unknown does not exclude the possibility that they could have been cut by instinct from aesthetic necessity.
8. The crepis of the Doric temple.was not a pedestal (podium); it did not therefore break in between the building and the earth, but formed a base for the columns. It is for this reason too that the distance of the columns from the edge of the stylobate is so small that the vertical face of the latter almost coincides with their prolongation.

18 a, b.

umns there are factors and solutions which show a tendency—even if unconscious—here to emphasize, there to interpret, and elsewhere to create successively the aesthetic impression of a movement from above downward. This movement is not arrested at the crepis, but is received there, in order to be conveyed plastically and spreadingly to the earth, in the same way as in the emplacement of classical statues. And it must be stressed that how the statue stands, how it is placed, is of prime importance to the sculptor; it is one of the basic factors which he has to consider, for in the final analysis it is this which contributes decisively in determining the aesthetic effect.

We must therefore acknowledge the fact that where Greek architecture is concerned the buildings do not rise out of the earth, as is the case in Egyptian architecture, but stand on the earth. This fact is

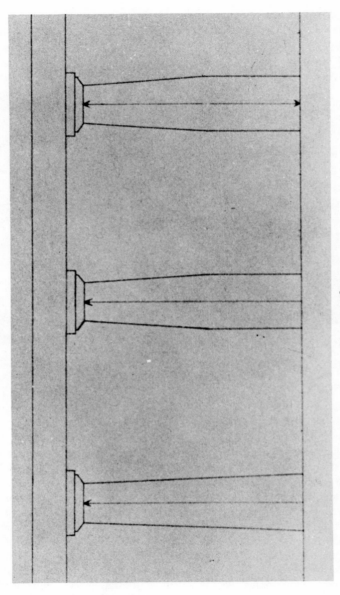

19 c, d, e.

of particular importance in the Doric order, where, in all we have yet seen, nothing contributes to the upward movement (from the point of view of the mass). Thus we come to the Parthenon, where the genius of Phidias who, we believe, was its main creator,[9] was decisive. The same sense impelled and directed the sculptor and the architect in the conception and execution of the building and of its sculptures. It is for this reason, apart from others, that the emplacement of the building as a whole and the emplacement of its sculptures—of those pieces, naturally, that are in a position of repose—have the same quality. There is a certain spread, a certain plastic bond created between earth and statue—the same spread and the same plastic bond exist between the earth and the building. But how is this expression achieved in the case of the temple? External factors which would contribute toward it do not exist. What organic form provided the solution? Is it perhaps the appropriate curvature of the whole temple which is the decisive factor? We believe that it is, as we shall shortly explain, since Phidias saw the building first as a living mass, and only after that saw its members as living masses. But before proceeding to develop this theme we must consider the views of others, in particular the two chief theories which have been advanced concerning the "curves" of the crepis and the entablature. One is the theory of visual correction and the second that of the elevation of the temple. According to the first theory the "curves" were employed only because by their means the impression of the straight line could be achieved—as Vitruvius maintains.[10] This theory has not however convinced many scholars, for the creators' ideal was not to achieve an absolute straight line, but some effect which meant a departure from this, and which derived from the curved form. Moreover, neither the crepis nor the entablature nor the whole temple has ceased to appear curved.

The second theory is based upon the idea of empathy. It starts, however, from a mistaken position, and thus leads to the conclusion that the "curves" were designed to overcome the impression of weight, and to convey the sense of an upward movement. This theory does not convince us. In fact we are diametrically opposed to it, since we believe it leads to an entirely destructive interpretation of the temple's appearance, for the reasons we give below.

A solid volume, as in [text fig. 20], gives the impression of an

---

9. Apart from texts, the comparison of the Parthenon with the temple of Apollo Epikourios at Bassae, of which the architect was Ictinos, has led us to this conclusion. See A. Mavrikios, *Sculpture in Architecture, The Sculpture of the Parthenon* (Athens 1960).

10. See A. Choisy, *Histoire de l'architecture*, Vol. 1, 323.

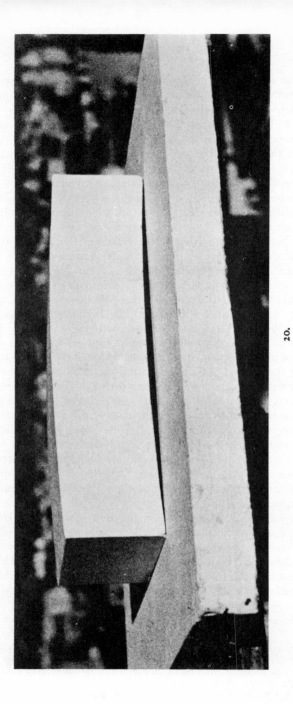

20.

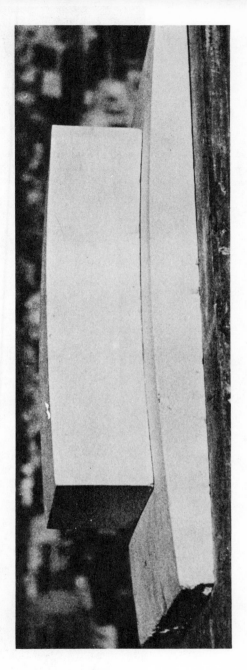

21.

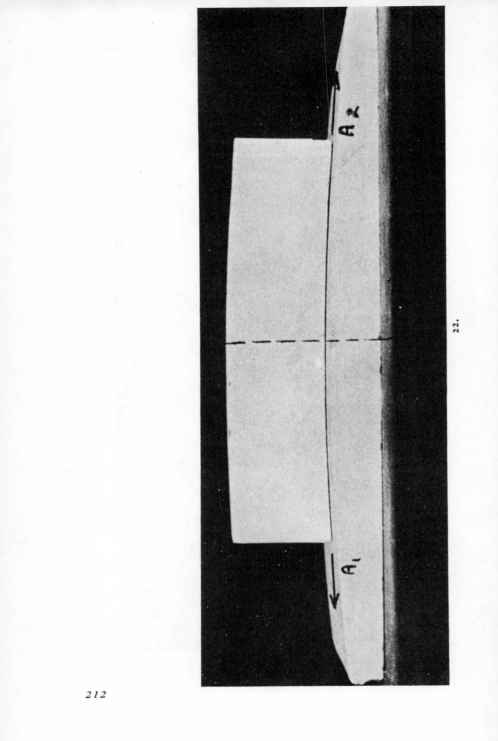

22.

212

23. Northeast view of crepis (platform) of the Parthenon with curvature.

upward movement when it rests on its two extremities, and this because it seems to "displace" its mass from the neutral horizontal surface on which it is supported, assuming the form of a bow. If, however, it rests on the whole underneath surface and this surface is curved [text figs. 21 and 22], it does not seem to rise upward—on the contrary it seems to "impose" its weight on this surface, in a movement that descends from its higher to its lower levels.[11] The surface of the emplacement does not in this case remain merely neutral, but links itself plastically with the mass of the solid volume. This effect is made still stronger in the Parthenon by the triple repetition of the curved emplacement—the three steps which stand out as a whole from the stereobate. If for instance we stand at the northeast corner of the temple, where the curvature of the steps stretches before us [text fig. 23], we feel that there is a movement of the mass away

11. We can sense this better if we imagine ourselves lying back downward on a curved surface.

from the center of the crepis northward and eastward, from the higher to the lower levels—a movement, therefore, opposite to that which would produce a sense of elevation. We have the same feeling when we stand among the columns. It is easy to understand how this phenomenon results from the fact that forces of "slip" are active, as well as vertical forces. A_1 and A_2 [text fig. 22], parallels to the tangents of the curve, are even from the static point of view so small that they need be of no concern. They are, moreover, equal and opposing in relation to the vertical axis of symmetry, and thus create between them a balance which increases the sense of dynamism and yet at the same time of repose. One could of course maintain that this takes place only in the case of a solid volume like that in our example. If, however, we glance at [text fig. 24], which shows a parapet resembling a colonnade, we are given the same impression. It could also

24. Bridge parapet seeming to spread plastically over its curved pavement.

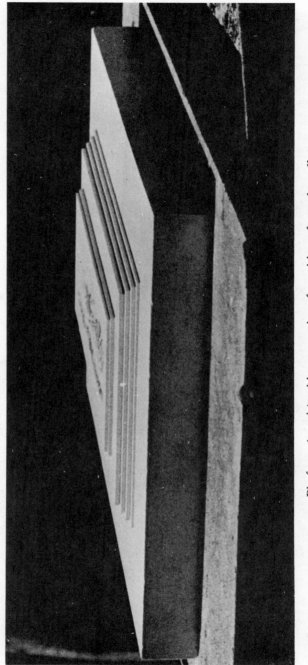

25. Platform (crepis) with preparations for raising of temple walls.

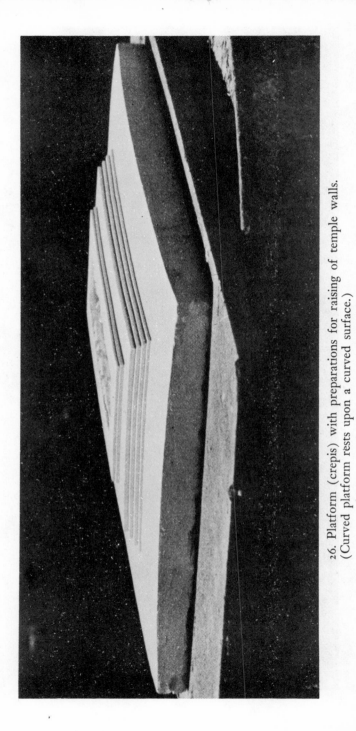

26. Platform (crepis) with preparations for raising of temple walls.
(Curved platform rests upon a curved surface.)

be maintained that, in the case of the Parthenon, which is a peripteral temple, other conditions with other consequences are created.

To clarify matters we have therefore prepared a number of plastic models, the inspection of which will confirm our views [text figs. 25–33].

27. General plastic rendering of short façade of the Parthenon.

28. Short façade of the Parthenon (model).

These rough models of the Parthenon are constructed on the scale 1:200. The curvature, however, was intentionally made on a larger scale, so that the effects are clearer. It should also be added

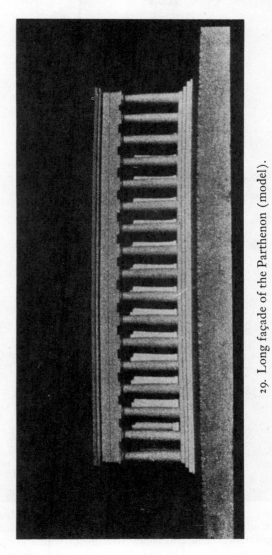

29. Long façade of the Parthenon (model).

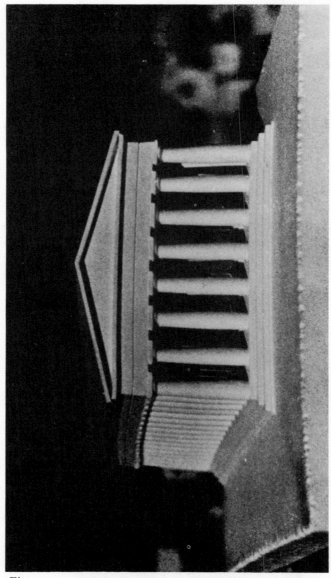

30–31. Figs. 30–33 were taken with different lighting but from the most important angle, i.e., a three-quarter view. The magnificence of the plastic emplacement and controlled dynamism which are a result of the curvature are evident. The mass moves toward the four corners

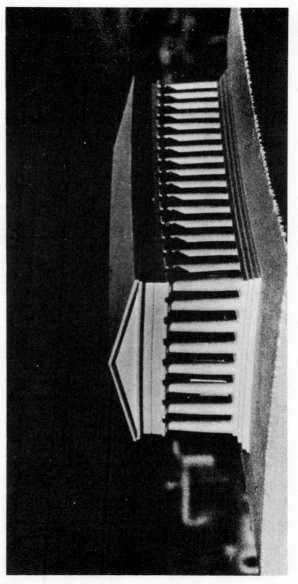

of the building, emphasizing its main boundaries. That this emphasis was intentional is proved by the fact that the thickening of the four corner columns is beyond that demanded for visual correction. Decreasing the gap between these columns and their neighbors also contributes to this emphasis.

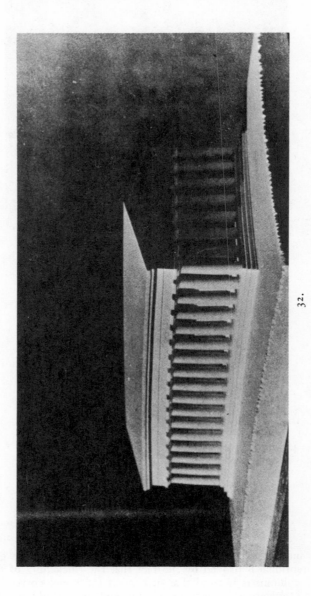

32.

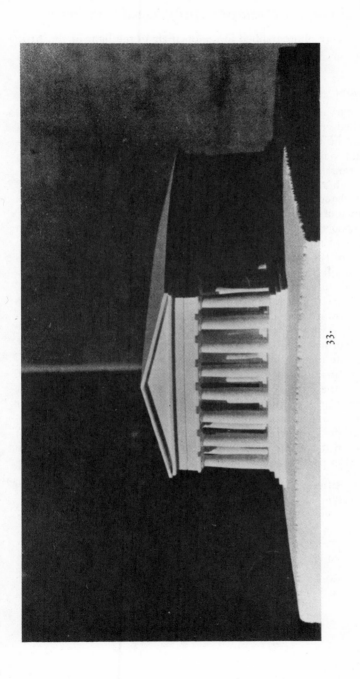

33.

that they were photographed in the open air in the light of the Attic sky.

Conclusions

The curvature of the Parthenon arose out of aesthetic necessity, and refined entasis was given to the columns out of the same necessity (i.e., the formal transmission of the load). The insertion of columns and walls [12] with entasis between an entablature and a crepis the horizontals of which were "rigid" and "hard" would be something which a sensitive sculptor could not allow. All must be molded and articulated to achieve an internal plastic unity, which serves the appearance of the whole temple.

In giving the building curves the artist did not seek to confer on it an upward movement, as has been maintained, for this is foreign to the spirit of the order. On the contrary he sought to achieve an emplacement of the building which was both vigorous and creatively related to the earth, and in which there was a certain "generative" quality: the ground raising the temple slightly in the middle moves its mass toward the corners, thus giving it plasticity, spread, dynamism, and at the same time emphasizing its main boundaries, i.e. the four corners.

Thus the temple, imposing and peaceful, dominates its surrounding space, as the statue of the armed Athena, imposing and peaceful, dominated the internal space. The delicate plastic sense of the Greeks, and particularly of the Athenians, as they externalized it in their sculpture, found its most lofty architectural expression and interpretation in the proportions, appropriate articulation, and balance of members in the whole, and in the general refinements which Phidias employed in the Parthenon.

12. N. Balanos, *The Reconstruction of the Monuments of the Acropolis* (Athens 1940).

THE SCULPTURES OF THE PARTHENON

EVELYN B. HARRISON
Athena and Athens in the East Pediment of the Parthenon—[1967] *

While the Carrey drawings provide us with at least some idea of the composition of the lost west pediment of the Parthenon, the central figures of the east pediment, which had already disappeared before Carrey's day, remain completely unknown to us. The tantalizing problem of creating a workable reconstruction of the missing sculptural composition, once the central motif over the main entrance to the temple, has tempted many scholars. The most recent reconstruction of the eastern pediment, and by far the most convincing, is the work of Evelyn B. Harrison in the following article. Evelyn Harrison is professor of fine arts at New York University, Institute of Fine Arts.

"All the figures in the gable over the entrance to the temple called the Parthenon relate to the birth of Athena." [1] These words, which are all that Pausanias has to say about the east pediment, seem disappointingly few, but they are priceless. Without them it is doubtful whether anyone in modern times would have been able even to guess the subject of the composition, much less to discuss the identity of the single figures that have come down to us. The whole center is lost, and the surviving statues, splendid as they are, preserve for us merely the fringes of a representation which by its position was second only to the cult-statue in importance for the temple.

In no other Greek temple was the sculptural decoration so directly related to the resident divinity as in the Parthenon. The met-

* Evelyn B. Harrison, "Athena and Athens in the East Pediment of the Parthenon," *AJA*, LXXI (1967), pp. 27–58. Reprinted by permission of the Archaeological Institute of America.
1. Pausanias 1.24.5.

opes of the Doric frieze, the most extensive and the most discon-
nected element in this decoration, repeated for the most part mythological themes that were employed with a more concentrated
symbolism in the cult statue itself. All these myths illustrated in one
way or another the triumph of civilization over the uncivilized or
the barbarian. Any Athenian, accustomed to see the Centauromachy, the Amazonomachy and the Taking of Troy in monuments
that celebrated the victory of Athens over the Persians at Marathon,[2]
would naturally have thought of Athens as the protagonist in this
struggle. The struggle of Athens was linked to Athena's own by joining to these myths the battle of the Gods and Giants in the east
metopes of the temple and on the inside of the shield of the statue.

The Panathenaic frieze shows the people of Athens worshipping
Athena and the West Pediment shows Athena winning dominion
over Attica in the presence of the ancestors of the Athenians. In the
East Pediment, then, we are prepared to see not simply the birth of
a great Olympian goddess but the birth of a great Olympian goddess
who is the special patron of Athens. C. J. Herington has shown that
Athenian poets from Solon to Aeschylus had stressed the position of
their city goddess as the own daughter of Zeus.[3] As Zeus was the
most powerful of the gods and Athena his favorite daughter, so the
city which Athena championed was favored above all others. Considering that this special relationship of Athena to Zeus was probably
the one most important reason for choosing the *birth* of Athena
rather than any other of her myths for the front gable of the temple,
one can hardly be indifferent to the question of how it was depicted.

There is thus a great deal of justification for the fact that scholars
have been trying for over a hundred years to reconstruct the lost
center of the pediment, even though no solution has ever been found
which will satisfy every criticism. A certain polarity has been introduced into the reconstructions and criticisms by the Madrid Puteal,
a Neo-Attic round base on which the birth of Athena is portrayed
[text fig. 34]. This was first presented in 1880 by R. Schneider as a
reflection of the central group of the East Pediment,[4] and its claims
to be such have been strong enough to persuade a number of archaeologists since then to base their reconstructions on it in one way or

2. Centauromachy on shield of Athena Promachos (Pausanias 1.28.2),
Amazonomachy and Iliupersis in the Painted Stoa together with the Battle
of Marathon (Pausanias 1.15.2–3).
3. *Greece and Rome*, Supplement to Vol. 10 (1963) 61–73.
4. Robert Schneider, *Die Geburt der Athena* (*Abhandlungen des
Archäologisch-epigraphischen Seminares der Universität Wien* I, 1880).

34. Drawing after the Madrid Puteal. Neo-Attic circular base. Madrid. Archaeological Museum.

another. Those who propose reconstructions at variance with the Puteal feel obliged to explain their rejection of it.[5]

Another line of division is drawn by the question whether the center of the pediment was occupied by a single figure, either Zeus or Athena, or was shared between the two. The adherents of these two positions do not necessarily coincide with the pro- and anti-Puteal groups. Reconstructions based on the Madrid relief have wavered between a symmetrical composition, with the throne of Zeus at the center, and an alternately balanced (*kontra-postisch*) arrangement, with Zeus to the left of center and Athena to the right, using the flying Nike of the Puteal to mark the axis.[6]

Since the evidence, such as it is, for solving the second problem is to be found on the Parthenon itself rather than in any hypothetical copies of it, this seems the logical question with which to begin. Though the central statues and the tympanon blocks behind them are alike missing, the horizontal cornice which formed the floor of the pediment survives and preserves a variety of traces from the setting, fastening and weathering of the sculptures.[7] Sunken beddings for the plinths of the statues such as we have in the Hephaisteion were not used in the Parthenon except in the case of a single statue, east G. If they had been we should not have to wonder whether the center was occupied by one statue or two. In the Hephaisteion it is clear that there was a single large axial figure in the east pediment but not in the west.[8]

5. Frank Brommer, *AthMitt* 73 (1958) 112–116, summarizes the arguments against the Puteal. He lists there and somewhat more fully in *Die Skulpturen der Parthenongiebel* (Mainz 1963) 108–109, no. 16 (hereafter Brommer, *Skulpturen*), the scholars who have taken positions for and against the Puteal.

6. For a list of reconstructions since Michaelis, see Brommer, *Skulpturen* 122–125.

7. These are recorded in accurate measured drawings by Sauer, *AntDenk* I, pl. 58 B, and Carpenter, *Hesperia* 2 (1933) pl. 2 and p. 19, fig. 2 (blocks 17 and 18) and p. 26, fig. 5 (blocks 8 and 9). Jeppesen, *AstaA* 24 (1953) 106–107, adds useful comments based on first-hand observation. A detailed drawing of the cutting for G in blocks 7–8 is given by Brommer, *AthMitt* 73 (1958) Beilage 76, 2 and *Skulpturen* 12, fig. 1. Photographs of the tops of the cornice blocks 7–22 (labeled 8–23) taken from directly above each block, are given by Balanos, *Les Monuments de l'Acropole* (Paris 1938) pls. 110–115, together with drawings recording the principal cuttings but not minor surface traces. Brommer, *Skulpturen* pls. 11–19, gives a very useful series of detailed oblique views extending from block 5 to block 22. I have not had the opportunity to examine the floor of the East Pediment of the Parthenon, but from studying the floor of the west pediment of the Hephaisteion I have acquired a considerable respect for Sauer's accuracy and thoroughness. Jeppesen affirms the accuracy of Carpenter's record.

8. Drawings of the cuttings: Sauer, *Das sogenannte Theseion und sein*

The interpretation of the floor-marks in the Parthenon is thus a rather subtle technical matter and one which still presents some unsolved questions of ancient procedure in general as well as of interpreting single phenomena. It is, however, the kind of field in which progress is to be expected, since our technical knowledge has increased, and reexamination of the floor by trained observers under different conditions has yielded new bits of evidence from time to time. The original survey of both pediment floors by Sauer, published in 1891, remains fundamental, and later observations supplement rather than supersede it. The most important are by Carpenter, Jeppesen, and Brommer.

Sauer's conclusion was that the center of the East Pediment had been shared by two statues. The most prominent marks on cornice block 13 [text figs. 35–37], which is the central one in the pediment though not centered on its axis, are two big cuttings for iron bars which converge toward the front to within 0.325 m. of each other. Between them a long, narrow rectangle marked by a weathered outline, running almost but not quite perpendicular to the tympanon, extends outward from the line of the tympanon to just beyond the line of the ends of the bar-cuttings. Sauer regarded this as a setting-table (Randbank) for a statue located to the left of center, and concluded that this statue was wider and heavier than that which was carried by the bar to the right of center in block 13. Accordingly he deduced a seated Zeus to the left of center, a standing Athena to the right. Sauer took this to confirm Schneider's theory that the Puteal with its profile Zeus was an accurate reflection of the pediment.[9]

This was criticized by Six in 1894 on the grounds that figures so placed would not be tall enough to fill the pedimental field and that the Hephaistos and Athena of the Puteal seem composed as corresponding figures flanking the Zeus. Six therefore designed a centrally seated Zeus, disproportionately large, but did not refute Sauer's technical arguments.[10] This was done in 1896 by Furtwängler, who, desirous of an axial figure independent of the Puteal, took the trouble to consult Bulle and Dörpfeld about the arrangements in the center of the pediment.[11] Dörpfeld was of the opinion that the two bars

---

plastischer Schmuck (Leipzig 1899). Photographs: Thompson, *Hesperia* 18 (1949) pls. 56 (east) and 57 (west).

9. *AthMitt* 16 (1891) 85–87.

10. *Jdl* 9 (1894) 83–87.

11. Furtwängler, *Intermezzi* (Leipzig and Berlin 1896) 22–23. Furtwängler was later persuaded by Sauer to change his mind (*Aegina* 330), but that does not diminish the value of Bulle's and Dörpfeld's original opinions.

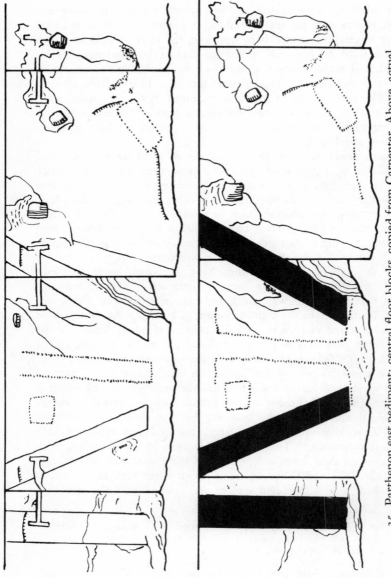
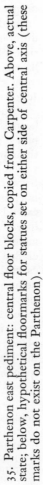

35. Parthenon east pediment: central floor blocks, copied from Carpenter. Above, actual state; below, hypothetical floormarks for statues set on either side of central axis (these marks do not exist on the Parthenon).

36. Parthenon east pediment, floor blocks 13 and 14 (courtesy of Frank Brommer).

37. Parthenon east pediment, floor blocks 12 and 13 (courtesy of Frank Brommer).

supported a single weight centered between them.[12] He explained the choice of two diagonally placed bars here by the desire to avoid the danger of splitting off the corners of the two tympanon blocks which meet in a joint at the center. Bulle agreed that the rectangular mark between the bars was not a Randbank.[13] These two thus became the first of a series of architecturally competent scholars who have declared themselves in favor of a single central figure.[14] In more recent times the Sauer-Six situation has been reversed. Those who have themselves made a special study of the traces on the horizontal cornice have favored a single central figure, while those who for aesthetic or iconographical reasons prefer to split the axial honors either simply follow Sauer or pass over in silence the evidence of the pedimental floor.[15]

Carpenter has given the most detailed explanation, showing clearly that the central rectangular mark does not have the characteristics of a setting-table and indeed that it would have been impossible to use a setting-table for placing a statue that rested on iron bars. He plausibly suggests that the mark was left by weathering around a piece of wood that had been placed here in order to facilitate in some way the resting of the statue on the two iron bars that carried the major portion of its weight.[16] Jeppesen agrees that the two converging bars supported a single burden.

12. *Intermezzi* 23, "Er ist der Meinung, dass die beiden schrägen Barren von Block 13 an Stelle von einem breiten Barren angeordnet sind, der gerade in der Axe liegen würde, 'da er aber hier an die Fuge der Tympanonblöcke gestossen hätte, wobei die Ecken der Steine leicht hätten abbrechen können,' habe man statt des einen geraden zwei schräge konvergierende Barren gewählt, deren Enden von der Tympanonfuge entfernt waren" ["He is of the opinion that the two diagonal bars of block 13 were used (rather than one broad bar lying just on axis, 'since this would have put stress on the joints of the tympanum blocks, so that the corners of the stones could easily have broken away'); thus two diagonally converging bars were chosen rather than one; their ends being at a distance from the tympanum joints"].

13. *Loc. cit.* (supra n. 12).

14. Carpenter, *Hesperia* 2 (1933) 31–39; *AJA* 66 (1962) 265–268; Thompson, *Hesperia* 9 (1950) 120; Jeppesen, *ActaA* 24 (1953) 123–124; 34 (1963) 86.

15. Berger, *Parthenon Ostgiebel* (Bonn 1959), presents a reconstruction of the whole pediment with scarcely a mention of the pediment floor. If one tries to relate his reconstruction to the cornice, however, it becomes apparent that he is generally following Sauer's recommendations. Pfuhl, *JdI* 61 (1926) 169–173, explicitly follows Sauer.

16. *AJA* 66 (1962) 265–267. One should perhaps mention that when he says the strip could not have been metal because it would have left a stain, he must be thinking only of bronze or iron. Lead would not stain, and since lead was very plentiful in classical Athens and is very extensively used

I believe, then, that we can take the answer to this question as settled. The center of the pediment was occupied by a single massive statue which can only have been the seated figure of Zeus.[17] This in itself ought not to make anyone unhappy. Knowing the West Pediment with its concentric waves of transmitted excitement, we sense something similar in the well-preserved corner figures of the eastern gable. The birth of Athena at the center of the pediment must have been felt as an explosion of power, and the center of that explosion, the source of that power, must have resided in the head of Zeus, whence we all know the goddess was sprung. This predisposes us to feel that the Puteal, in which the outward-rushing forms of Athena and Hephaistos have a genuinely explosive force, gives some authentic reflection of the pediment.

What happens if, with this as our basic assumption, we take the Puteal literally can best be seen in Carpenter's reconstruction [text fig. 38].[18] He restores a central group that echoes the relief as closely as is possible for three-dimensional sculptures that conform to the pedimental space. The result is disappointing in two ways. The legs of the profile Zeus extend so far to the right that Athena is pushed away from the center and diminished in height to a degree that hardly befits the heroine of the drama, and the uncompromising vertical of the throne-back so shuts off Hephaistos from the central figure that his diagonal movement loses most of its radial force. The back of the throne becomes even more disturbing when we translate it in our imagination from the depthless elevation of a drawn reconstruction to the three-dimensional reality of the Parthenon. Anyone viewing the pediment from the southeast will have found this flat, inanimate object interposing itself between him and the god. In the surviving sculptures of the Parthenon, on the contrary, we see a remarkable attention paid to the fact that the pediments were to be seen from a variety of angles. Not only are the fig-

---

in modern times for jacking up plinths that are not quite level, the possibility of its use on the Parthenon should not be excluded.

17. Those who have argued for placing Athena in the center, e.g., Furt-wängler, *Intermezzi* 25–26, have maintained that Athena, as the principal goddess of the temple and the city, cannot yield first place to any other figure. The "Solonian" concept discussed by Herington (see supra) seems the best answer to this objection. Cf. also Cook, *Zeus* III 737: "On the other hand religious thought was beginning to outgrow its primitive phases and had by now reached a stage in which Zeus, as power supreme, could not conceivably be superseded by any other deity." This conception of Zeus as a supreme power made it logical that he be shown as strikingly larger in scale than any other figure in the pediment.

18. *Hesperia* 2 (1933) pl. 2.

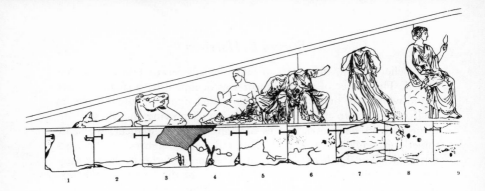

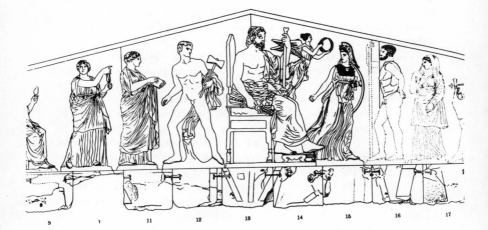

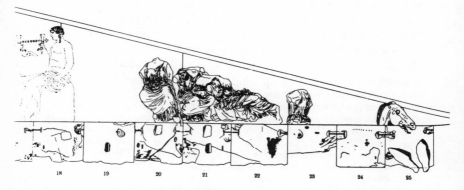

38. Parthenon east pediment, restored by Carpenter.

234

ures themselves for the most part fully worked out in depth (in contrast to those of the Temple of Zeus at Olympia) but many of them are set diagonally within the pediment and some project beyond the front line of the cornice.[19] It is also worth noting that in what we have preserved of the Parthenon pediments an extensive display of woodwork is nowhere to be seen. The inanimate part of the chariot groups in the West Pediment is kept to a minimum, and in the East, the chests on which the two goddesses sit, though surely meant as attributes, are yet strangely unobtrusive.

Schrader proposed to solve the problem of the throne-back by simply removing it, leaving the profile Zeus on a backless throne.[20] This is not an unheard-of situation for the king of the gods but perhaps not quite in keeping with the opulent spirit of the Parthenon pediments. Schrader also tried to pull both Athena and Hephaistos a little closer to the central figure, but his effort was effective rather as a criticism than as a solution. There remains the problem of the importance of Athena and of her special relation to Zeus.

Once we begin to think seriously of the problem of their communication, we can call to mind a whole series of representations in post-Parthenon art which group a seated male figure with a standing female. We have Zeus encouraging Hellas on the Dareios Vase in Naples [text fig. 39],[21] Demos crowned by Democracy on a stele from the Agora [text fig. 40],[22] Zeus with Hera on a Kerch pelike in Leningrad [text fig. 41],[23] and finally, the noblest of all, Corinth crowned by Leukas on the well-known mirror-cover in the Louvre [text fig. 42].[24] In each of these the male sits with his legs to the left and turns his head toward the female who stands to the right of him. The scheme favors their communication in two ways: first, they are actually closer together because his legs are not in the way, and second, the deliberate turn of his head signals the relationship.

Such a turning pose seems eminently suitable for the central figure in a pediment provided that it will satisfy the special conditions imposed by the surviving traces on the Parthenon. Upon investigation it appears to satisfy them admirably [text fig. 43]. The head of Zeus and the center of gravity of the figure still come at the exact center of the pediment above the converging bars on block 13. The feet on their footstool rest near the edge of the cornice on block 12,

19. On this see especially Brommer, *AthMitt* 73 (1958) 109–110.
20. *JOAI* 32 (1940) 191–199.
21. Furtwängler-Reichhold, *Griechische Vasenmalerei* pl. 88.
22. *Hesperia* 21 (1952) 355–357, pl. 90; Thompson, *The Athenian Agora, A Guide* (Athens 1962) 123–124, pl. 8.
23. For literature see Schefold, *Untersuchungen zu den Kertscher Vasen* (1934) 40–42, no. 368.
24. Pfuhl, *Malerei und Zeichnung der Griechen* fig. 624.

39. Zeus and Hellas, detail of Dareios krater [*ca.* 350 B.C.]. Naples,
National Museum.

40. Demos and Democracy. 336 B.C. Athens, Agora Museum.

41. Eleusinian pelike from Kerch [*ca*. 350 B.C.]. Leningrad, Hermitage.

42. Corinth and Leukas. Mirror cover [*ca.* 350 B.C.]. Paris, Louvre.

explaining the need for the iron bar near the right edge of that block.[25] Since there was no joint in the tympanon near by, there was

25. Cf. Jeppesen, *ActaA* 34 (1963) 86, "Diese Barre kann ja nicht eine einzelne Figur von der auf dieser Stelle zu erwartenden Breite getragen haben, sondern wäre eher auf irgendeinen Zusatz zu der Mittelfigur zu beziehen. Carpenter will damit das linke Bein seines Hephästos unterstützen, eine technisch wenig überzeugende Lösung, die uns nicht befriedigen kann" ["This bar cannot have supported a single figure of the width one would expect in this position, but would rather concern some supplement to the central figure. Carpenter would use it to support the left leg of his Hephaestus, a technically unconvincing solution which cannot satisfy us."] Carpenter, *Hesperia* 2 (1933) 35, while rejecting the idea that the bar in block 12 belonged to the Zeus (since his Zeus was in right profile), still

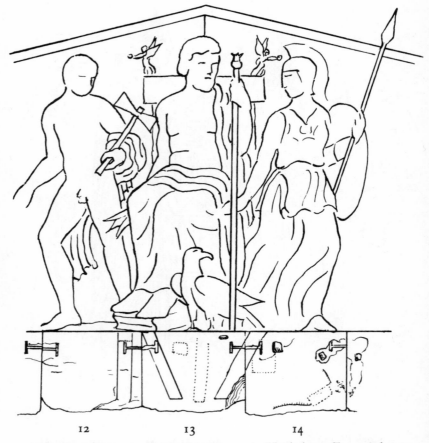

12   13   14

43. Parthenon, east pediment blocks 12–14, Hephaistos, Zeus, Athena.
Floor after Carpenter and Jeppesen. Scale approx. 1:40.

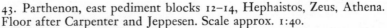

said, "To be sure, the straight floor-bar in block 12 would pass logically and
neatly under the footstool or feet of the great statue; but it is doubtful
whether the weight of this part of the statue would be enough to demand
such a precaution." From the point of view of the statue, it would seem
preferable to give this projecting part the same kind of support as the rest,
even if it was less heavy. Otherwise, the uneven displacement caused by an
earthquake or other shock might easily split it off. So far as the cornice is
concerned, it may well have been a rule to support with an iron bar any
part of a heavy statue that encroached on a block that was already loaded
to near capacity with its own statue. This must have been the case with
block 12.

no need to set this bar diagonally. Finally, the scepter held out in the god's left hand would come naturally to rest in the small but deep (0.042 m.) socket, recorded by Sauer but since split away, in front of the right-hand bar on block 13. Sauer had assigned this hole to the spear of Athena.[26] This corner of the block was already split away in the 1930's when Balanos and Carpenter made their records. Carpenter neither mentions the hole nor uses it in his reconstruction, but there is no reason to doubt its existence.[27] It was quite possibly the cause of the corner's splitting off.

Though the figure of Zeus, and especially his throne, with the back placed frontally and the seat diagonally, will have been conceived in a manner closer to high relief than to sculpture in the round, the main forms of head, body and drapery will have been seen as solid sculpture to be enjoyed from many angles.[28] The inconsistency between the lower and upper parts of the throne will undoubtedly have been mitigated by hiding much of the woodwork with falling drapery. The eagle which various scholars have set beside the throne may very well have been there and helped in this task of distraction.

Brommer raises the possibility of a diagonally seated Zeus though without declaring himself definitely in favor of it, and he mentions in this connection a series of representations of the birth of Athena on Etruscan mirrors.[29] These show Athena springing directly from Zeus' head in the archaic manner, but Zeus himself is a classical figure. Since these mirrors are virtually the only representations of the birth of Athena apart from the Puteal that date from after the Parthenon, it is by no means out of the question that they are influenced by it. One of them illustrates the manner in which the thunderbolt

---

26. *AthMitt* 16 (1891) 87. Pfuhl, *Jdl* 41 (1926) 169 also mentions the hole and follows Sauer's interpretation.

27. The hole still appears in Carpenter's drawing, directly based on Sauer, in *AJA* 29 (1925) pl. 3, but no use is made of it.

28. Pfuhl, *Malerei und Zeichnung* 588, comments that the framing of the east pediment with rising sun and setting moon "fast unplastisch malerisch behandelt ist" ["is treated almost unplastically, but pictorially"]. We shall see other examples of relief-like treatment in this pediment. Studniczka has shown in a surprising sketch-plan how far from rectangular are the chests used for seats by E and F (*Jdl* 19 [1904] p. 6, fig. 2: "Es gehört zu dem unleugbaren Reliefcharakter selbst dieser Giebelgruppen, dass sich die 'Wirkungsform' von der 'Existenzform' oft weit entfernen muss" ["It is characteristic of the undeniable relieflike quality of this pedimental group that the 'effective form' must often be distinguished from the 'existential (actual) form'"].

29. *Skulpturen* 147. The Etruscan mirrors with the birth of Athena are listed by Brommer *RGZM* 8 (1961) 79.

44. Birth of Athena. Etruscan Mirror. Berlin.

45. Birth of Athena. Etruscan Mirror. Bologna.

may have been held in the lowered right hand [text fig. 44].[30] It is not difficult to regard this Zeus and the one of the Puteal as two different elevations of the same figure, especially since another of the mirrors [text fig. 45] shows a figure closer to that of the Puteal but seen in three-quarters view from the left.[31] Though the mirrors omit sometimes the scepter, sometimes the thunderbolt and sometimes both, it is unlikely that either was omitted from the Parthenon.

If Zeus be placed as we have suggested, the block to the right of him, block 14, is entirely at the disposal of Athena. She will have moved diagonally outward in a position which can be read directly from the pediment floor. Two large dowels at the back of the plinth insured the statue against tipping forward.[32] The stride will not have been so wide as is shown in the Puteal and the impression of her rushing away from her father will not have been so strong. The diagonally placed rectangular weather mark near the right front corner of the block does not seem logically placed for a setting-table. It may again, as Carpenter has suggested for the square outline in block 13, be the trace of a thin plaque of some kind introduced under the plinth of the statue during the process of setting.[33] It is quite possible that the advanced left foot of Athena projected somewhat beyond the resting surface of the plinth as in one of the fragments from the west pediment of the Hephaisteion.[34] The weathering line parallel to the front of the cornice, presumably marking the front edge of the plinth, does not argue against a diagonal pose for the figure. A fifth century statue from the Athenian Agora of Aphrodite in a diagonal walking pose has a plinth that runs parallel to the front of the statue, thus projecting some distance forward of the trailing foot.[35] This would contribute not a little to the stability of the figure.

30. Berlin, 2979. Gerhard, *Etruskische Spiegel* pl. 284, I; Cook, *Zeus* III 677, fig. 488.
31. Bologna. Gerhard, *Etruskische Spiegel* pl. 66; *JHS* 49 (1949) p. 9, fig. 10; Cook, *Zeus* II 709, pl. 29.
32. Sauer called both of these dowel-holes (*AthMitt* 16 [1891] 69, 86; *AntDenk* I, text to pl. 58 B) and attributed them to Athena. Pfhul, *Jdl* 41 (1926) 169, follows him. Carpenter considered the cutting nearest to the tympanon "too heavy for a statue dowel" (though the hole is only 2 cm. wider than the other dowel-hole; Balanos, *Les Monuments de l'Acropole* pl. 112, gives 0.08 m. × 0.08 m. for one and 0.10 m. × 0.10 m. for the other). Carpenter suggested that it fastened an invisible pedestal to support the flying Nike (*Hesperia* 2 [1933] 41).
33. *Ibid.* 37. The most practical material for this purpose would be lead. See supra, note 16.
34. *Hesperia* 18 (1949) 235, fig. 2; pl. 52, 5.
35. *Hesperia* 29 (1960) pl. 82. Hafner, *Geschichte der griechischen Kunst* (Zurich 1961) fig. 259. This statue, to be dated around 420, is clearly descended from the Parthenon pediments and seems to show the later style

Jeppesen noted a setting-table (visible only at sunrise or sunset, he says, but one can perhaps make out part of it in Brommer's photograph, [text fig. 36]) in the south half of block 14 near the rear dowel hole.[36] This would be in just the right place for the Athena as we have set her. Altogether, the evidence for the position and extent of this statue seems as clear as anything we have in the lost part of the East Pediment and, once assembled, is a stronger argument against the profile Zeus than any aesthetic or iconographical objections. One small final point seems to clinch the matter. Carpenter observed that a small patch of encrusted patina near the north joint of block 14 was stained a copper green.[37] Since this is the only bit of bronze-stain that he was able to identify anywhere in the East Pediment, though minor bronze attributes and attachments must have existed in a number of places, it would seem logical to assume that any stain strong enough to survive the heavy weathering in this central part of the gable must have originated in a major attribute. Carpenter suggested that the sandals of Zeus, overhanging the footstool, were "adorned with gilded bronze ornaments of some sort." We now see a much more persuasive source in the great gilded bronze shield of Athena.

The Puteal does not show a spear in Athena's hand, but one would like to think that she carried one. In the Homeric Hymn which seems so close to this pediment she rushes in front of her father, brandishing a sharp spear.[38] Several scholars have proposed a reconstruction, based on Roman coins of Athens with an Athena very like that of the Puteal, which gives her a spear in her left hand along with the shield.[39] This seems the most satisfactory. The outstretched right arm of the Puteal looks like a balancing rather than a spear-brandishing gesture. The goddess is not preparing to rush off into battle. She is about to pause and strip the divine armor from her immortal shoulders while Zeus rejoices in his newborn daughter.

The close relationship that we have established between Athena and her father leaves no room for a flying Nike between them. This seems to confirm the suspicion voiced from time to time that the Nike of the Puteal is a space-filler introduced by the Neo-Attic artist, and indeed the extreme difficulty of supporting a flying figure of this

---

of Agorakritos. The idea of using such a diagonal walking pose in a single statue may well have been inspired, like so much else in late fifth-century art, by the Parthenon pediments.
36. *ActaA* 24 (1953) 107.
37. *Hesperia* 2 (1933) 38.
38. Homeric Hymn XXVIII, 9.
39. Cook, *Zeus* III 694–696.

size in the pediment makes us glad to let her go. Still she may not be altogether without a basis in the Parthenon. It would have been entirely in the spirit of Periklean art to have golden Nikai as akroteria on the throne of Zeus. These would have made a splendid frame for his head and a decorative filling for the spaces between it and the heads of the adjoining figures. That the head of Zeus was a magnificent creation we can hardly doubt. We know enough about Pheidias to feel sure that if anyone could endow it with appropriate majesty he could.[40]

Since the Hephaistos on the Puteal is symmetrical to Athena, it is natural to assume that he was so in the pediment. That means that he too will have moved diagonally outward, with a stride not too wide to be accommodated in a single block. The left foot, close to the tympanon, must have rested on or at least over the rear portion of the iron bar in block 12. Since the statue was entirely undoweled, there may have been no objection to having one corner rest on the bar, but it is also possible that the underside of the plinth was cut out to clear the bar.[41] In order to provide the needed stability for the undoweled statue the plinth was probably considerably more extensive than the ground actually occupied by the figure. The swinging himation and the strut that presumably supported it may have been set well back for extra security. The ground is unfortunately wide open for conjecture, since the surface of block 12 is exceptionally weathered and apart from the cutting for the bar no really illuminating traces have been noted by any investigator.

From the aesthetic point of view, the Hephaistos of the Puteal fits in so much better with the Zeus posed as we now have him than with the Zeus in right profile that our confidence in this Hephaistos is actually increased. The singularly unadorned outline of his extended left leg is fully explained when we see that it emerges from behind (or close beside, depending on one's point of view) the richly draped knees of Zeus. The loop of drapery over the left arm of Hephaistos will have provided a spot of color and a welcome bit of linear complexity between the smooth nude torsos of the two male figures.

The style of this drapery is one of the strongest arguments for accepting the Hephaistos of the Puteal as an authentic reflection of

40. Whoever may have executed the marble Zeus for the pediment, it is most likely that Pheidias himself designed it. In some ways it will have been a rehearsal for the great Zeus at Olympia, and the conception of a Zeus that added something to the traditional religion must already have been growing in the mind of Pheidias as he worked on the Parthenon. See supra, note 17.

41. This would have been necessary if the section were as Jeppesen shows (*ActaA* 24 [1953] 110, fig. 5).

the Parthenon figure. Carpenter has mentioned some parallels in relief.[42] In the round, the similar disposition of the drapery wrapped
around the left arm and swinging between the legs in one of the
Dioscuri of Monte Cavallo is worth noting,[43] and we shall see that the
drapery of the other Dioscurus may also be connected with the Parthenon.[44] The statue of Aphrodite mentioned supra (note 35) shows
very much the same rhythm in the himation which is wrapped
around the left arm and swings down between the legs in front. The
rich patterns of the crushed folds bent over the arm and the elegant
swinging curves in this fifth-century original enable us to visualize
something of what has been lost in the Roman reflections of the Parthenon Hephaistos.

If we accept the Hephaistos of the Puteal, it is time to consider
again the suggestion made by Homer Thompson that the torsos of
the Giants from the Odeion in the Athenian Agora are copied from
this Hephaistos.[45] If there was a one-to-one correspondence of dimensions as there is between the torsos of the Tritons and the Poseidon of the West Pediment one could use the Giant to reconstruct the
scale and anatomical details of our Hephaistos. It appears, however,
that the correspondence is not so close. If the Giant were copied at
exactly the same scale from the Hephaistos, his torso should be a
little smaller than that of the Triton, since the head of Poseidon in
the West Pediment was nearer the center of the gable than the head
of Hephaistos can have been in the East. But careful measurements of
the Odeion figures made by John Travlos show that the height of the
two torsos is the same, though that of the Giant is set 10 cm. lower
with respect to the architecture than that of the Triton.[46] It follows

42. Bassae frieze slabs 530, 536, 540 and Nike Temple frieze slab l, figure
4 (*AJA* 29 [1925] 129).
43. This drapery is much coarsened to be sure, so that Furtwängler excluded it from the Parthenon elements in the Dioscuri (*Meisterwerke* 132),
but the repetition of the Puteal scheme here heavily in the round and de-
void of all Neo-Attic elegance strengthens rather than weakens our conviction that it is inspired in both cases from the Parthenon.
44. See infra p. [258].
45. *Hesperia* 19 (1950) 120–121. This idea has so far not been as fully
discussed as it deserves to be, but Jeppesen's recent suggestion that the idea
of Giants and Tritons itself comes from the Parthenon (*ActaA* 34 [1963]
65) should help to reopen the question. Jeppesen is surely right in identi-
fying the rock-torso as the support shown by Carrey under the horses of
Athena, and I am happy to withdraw my suggestion that the torso represents Kranaos (*AJA* 69 [1965] 185), though I am still inclined to favor the
idea that Aktaios and Kranaos as co-judges of the contest were represented
in figures A and A*.
46. The sternal notch of the Triton is 2.16 m. above the top of the base
and that of the Giant 2.065 m. The projection of the lowest torso-muscle
over the left hip at the side is 1.45 m. above the top of the base on the

that if the Giants were copied from the Hephaistos, their scale must have been slightly enlarged, and that means that the copying will have been freer than in the Tritons, so that we have no way of knowing how far the Giants can be used. The fact that no other figure in the Parthenon pediments corresponded to the West Pediment Poseidon either in scale or in the position of the arms (the Hephaistos of the Puteal [text figs. 50–51] has both arms lowered while torso H has both arms raised) will have made it necessary to adapt and perhaps contaminate figures in order to create the Giants.[47] The torso of the Giant is duller to look at than that of the Triton and undoubtedly also duller than that of our lost Hephaistos.[48]

Iconographically our new arrangement of the figures of the Puteal is eminently satisfactory. There results an almost heraldic symmetry of Athena and Hephaistos that carries their relationship beyond the simple role of Hephaistos in the story of the birth. The group of three is curiously reminiscent of the oldest of all pedimental compositions, the Gorgon with her two offspring in the archaic temple in Corfu.[49] Here too the great head at the peak of the gable is felt as the source of a birth that is not literally depicted but known to have taken place. We are moved to protest that Hephaistos is *not* newly born and indeed is not an offspring of Zeus at all, as Hera and Hesiod would eagerly affirm. But in Athens, the birth of Athena makes a new god of Hephaistos, for they share between them the patronage of all things made by hands.[50] How strongly Pheidias felt this aspect of Athena is shown by his choosing the myth of Pandora to adorn the base of the Parthenos. In the pediment the symmetrical placement of the two divinities and the importance it lends to Heph-

Triton and 1.35 on the Giant. This point is measured rather than the lowest boundary of the abdomen because the purely human character and proportions of both figures are already lost by that point.

47. Berger, *Parthenon Ostgiebel* 33–34, discusses the differences in pose that separate the Giants from the Hephaistos of the Puteal and from Torso H, but he does not discuss the possibility of a type created by contaminating the two.

48. A similar discrepancy in aesthetic quality can be seen in the small pediment at Eleusis (contemporary with the Giants and Tritons) between the figures copied closely from the Parthenon and those that were adapted or invented. See J. Travlos, *Deltion* 16 (1960), Chronika, 55–60, and E. Harrison ["U and Her Neighbors in the West Pediment of the Parthenon," in *Essays in the History of Art: Presented to Rudolf Wittkower*, ed. Douglas Fraser et al. (London and New York, 1969), pp. 1 ff.–Ed.].

49. Forthcoming discussion by J. L. Benson in *Festschrift Schefold* [now published: "The Central Group of the Corfu Pediment," *Gestalt und Geschichte: Festschrift Karl Schefold, Antike Kunst*, Beiheft IV (Bern, 1967), pp. 48–60], and E. Kunze, *AthMitt* 78 (1963) 74–89.

50. Cf. Plato, *Laws* 11. 920 D–E; *Critias*, 109 C; *Protagoras*, 321, C.

aistos have thus a specially Athenian relevance. Hephaistos is here not merely as midwife but as working partner to the newborn goddess of work.

Once we accept this more compact and three-dimensional interpretation of the central group of the Puteal we realize that the group no longer conflicts with the position of Wegner's Hera in block 11, where all scholars with the exception of Carpenter and Jeppesen have agreed that she belongs.[51] Berger made this supposed conflict the basis for his reconstruction with its curious counterbalances of moving and stationary figures [text fig. 46].[52] Declaring that there was clearly not room for the three figures of the Puteal in the 3.20 m. of the central three blocks, he split off the Hephaistos from the central group and placed him, reduced in height and widened in stride, beyond Hera in block 10. Zeus and Athena were then spread to fill the central gap. Brommer criticized the inconsistency of thus using the figures of the Puteal while denying their relationship to one another.[53] He accordingly regarded the Hera as an argument against using the Puteal at all as evidence for the reconstruction of the pediment. He took the torso H to be Hephaistos and so placed him to the right of Athena.[54]

So far as one can tell, the stately peplos figure identified by Wegner in two surviving fragments [text figs. 47 and 48] would fit best in block 11, since her restored height is around 2.80 to 2.90 m. [text fig. 62].[55] The edge of a bedding near the front edge of the cornice suggests a position near the front of the shelf. It is hard to tell where the sides of the plinth were. The right edge may have coincided approximately with the boundary between blocks 11 and 12, since the slightly sunken bedding appears to continue this far.[56] The left edge

51. Brommer, who himself places Hera in block 11, says (*Skulpturen* 27) that Berger places her in block 12, but that is not true. In all three of Berger's reconstructions she appears directly above a triglyph, i.e., in block 11. (Perhaps Brommer is here using Balanos' block-numbering instead of Sauer's.) Jeppesen, *ActaA* 34 (1963) figs. 22 b and 23 d, places Hera in block 15, next to Zeus, whom he places in block 16.

52. *Parthenon Ostgiebel.*

53. *AthMitt* 73 (1958) 114.

54. *Skulpturen* 154–155, pl. 151.

55. Berger, *Parthenon Ostgiebel* 13, calculates 2.90 m. Wegner, *AthMitt* 57 (1932) 94 calculated around 2.80 m. Jeppesen, *ActaA* 24 (1953) 115–116, proposed adding 15 cm. to this. Any one of the three heights would still call for a position in block 11 (where the tympanon heights range from 2.78 m. to 3.04 m.) or block 15 (where they are 2.83 m. to 3.06 m.). Jeppesen's 2.95 m. height seems excessive. For purposes of rough calculation we may assume a height of around 2.90 m.

56. See the photographs Balanos, *Les Monuments de l'Acropole* pl. 111, and Brommer, *Skulpturen* pl. 13, 4.

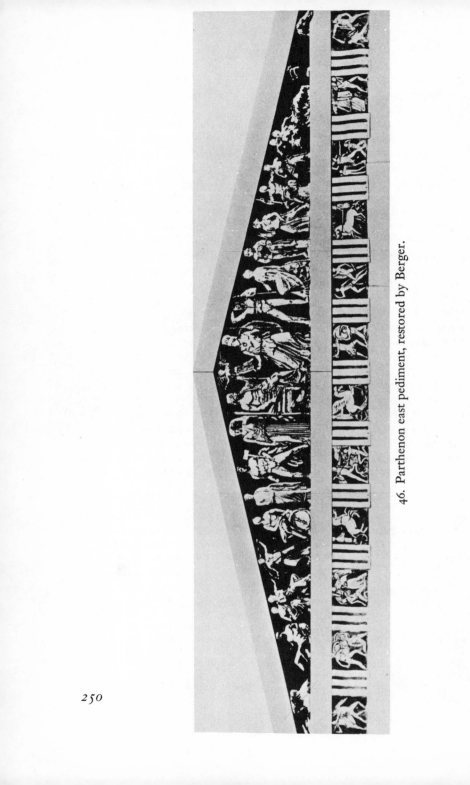

46. Parthenon east pediment, restored by Berger.

250

47. Fragment of Hera. Athens, Acropolis Museum.

48. Fragment of Hera. Athens, Acropolis Museum.

would probably be more likely to fall short of than to overlap the bar cutting which extends 0.20 m. into block 11.[57] The figure thus appears to have been centered a little to the north of the axis of the block, where the tympanon height will have been about 2.93 m. If we calculate the probable width of the statue, we see that if the plinth had been so wide as to overlap the bar cutting, the main mass of the statue still would not have extended so far south, and this would have made the overlapping useless if not dangerous.[58] We may rea-

57. Balanos, pl. 111, drawing.

58. The plinths of the Erechtheion caryatids were 0.671 m. wide and the caryatids including their plinths but not their architectural headgear were 2.16 tall (Stevens, *Erechtheum* pls. 26–27). That would give 0.311 m. of plinth breadth per meter of height. Our statue by these proportions, if the height were 2.90 m., would have a plinth 0.90 m. wide and so overlap the

sonably assume, then, that the plinth was trimmed closer to the
statue, as Wegner and Jeppesen have drawn it. Its width may have
been about 0.80 m.

The stability of the statue is another question. It is noticeable that
in spite of the fact that this was a tall, relatively narrow statue and
set near the front of the cornice it was not doweled to the floor. It
may well be that the Hera was a kind of sculptural "last-laid block,"
having been inserted after the heavier pieces to either side had been
set. Carpenter pointed out that the two cuttings in the back of the
lower part of the figure must have been used in some way for hoisting the statue rather than for fastening it to the tympanon.[59] It seems
possible, however, that this belongs to a resetting at some later date.

A fragment of a veiled head with a complicated assortment of
holes for attaching some kind of ornaments [text fig. 49] was assigned to the Parthenon by Sauer, who saw in it the head of a queenly
woman in festive attire.[60] Its scale as he calculated it fits our Hera [61]
and it has been given to her by various scholars, most recently by
Berger [62] and Brommer.[63] The angle at which the veil crosses the top

---

bar cutting by only 5 cm. But the plinths of the Caryatids extend some distance beyond the drapery on both sides, and so it would seem sensible in
the Parthenon figure to have trimmed the plinth closer in order to avoid
having it overlap the bar.

59. *Hesperia* 2 (1933) 47–50.

60. *Festschrift Overbeck* 74–78; *Der Weber-Laborde'sche Kopf* 30–31.

61. Sauer said, *Weber-Laborde'sche Kopf* 30–31, that the original height
of the head must be at least 0.38 m. If we subtract the plinth height of 0.09
m. from the ca. 2.90 m. of the Hera, we get 2.81 m. for the restored height
of the figure and 0.38 m. goes into this 7.4 times. Compare the table of
head-heights in proportion to total heights given by Sauer, *ibid.*, 106–107.

62. *Parthenon Ostgiebel* 60–70. The attribution of this fragment to the
figure of Helios by Marcadé seems to me untenable, but it has proven tena-
cious enough to deserve serious refutation (for Marcadé's side of the case,
see *BCH* 80 [1956] 161–182; *GBA* 1957, 65–72; *BCH* 81 [1957] 76–84;
MonPiot 50 [1956, appeared 1958] 11–47). Marcadé himself complains
(*BCH* 88 [1964] 623–624) that Brommer has rejected it "sans opposer
d'ailleurs aucune objection dirimante et sans proposer de solution meilleure"
["without ever setting forth any invalidating objection, and without pro-
posing a better solution"]. To me Brommer's general objections that the
head appears female and that the hole at the back is not suitable for attaching a thin piece of drapery seem valid, since they coincide with my own
impressions.

There is another objection which I feel is more conclusive, however,
and which no one seems to have mentioned. The grain of the marble runs
horizontally in the Helios and vertically in the head. It is a general rule,
which one can verify even from casts and photographs, that the grain in
the Parthenon pedimental sculptures runs in the direction of the greatest
dimension of the statue. So reclining figures near the corners have hori-

of the head, falling some distance behind the right ear and slanting sharply forward toward the left side of the head, strongly suggests that the figure's head, turned to her proper left, was meant to be seen nearly if not quite in right profile. This angle results when the lower part of the veil rests firmly enough on the shoulders so that the turn of the head does not carry the veil with it. It is a frequent motif in reliefs and paintings of the later fifth century; the Eurydice of the Orpheus relief may be mentioned as a familiar example.

Both Berger and Brommer, on the other hand, have restored the head in approximately front view, turned, if at all, a little away from the center of the pediment. This throws the veil on the proper right side of the head so far back that we lose it as a framing for the face. Berger thinks it desirable that the junction between the veil and the elaborate crown be concealed from view.[64] Brommer believes,

---

zontal grain, standing and most seated figures vertical grain. In the Helios the horizontal grain is obvious in many places. I have taken pains to verify the vertical grain of the head fragment by examining it in a good light in the Acropolis Museum, but if the issue of the connection with Helios had not been so strongly raised and defended one would have been willing to state this from the photographs alone. Sauer said in his first publication, *Festschrift Overbeck* (Leipzig 1893) 74, "die Structur des pentelischen Marmors lässt für den Kundigen selbst der Lichtdruck erkennen" ["the texture of Pentelic marble can be perceived by an expert even in a photograph"]. His picture, however, shows only the finished surfaces. The broken surfaces are still more eloquent. Marcadé's own photographs, especially the excellent one labeled "Grande cassure latérale" in *MonPiot* 50 (1956) 35, fig. 17 c, show the situation clearly. This "grande cassure" ["large crack"], which runs vertically, is all more or less in one plane and clearly represents a splitting parallel to the direction of the grain. The lower break, whose contours are visible in this picture though its surface is in shadow, is a chunky break of the sort that results when a piece is snapped off across the grain of the marble. Marcadé's description of this fracture is perfectly accurate. Only he does not mention the fact that this sort of concave break which "se creuse franchement vers l'intérieur" ["clearly deepens toward the interior"] is normally a cross-grain break. We see good examples in the Athena and the Poseidon of the West Pediment where the vertical splitting along the grain and the concave horizontal breaks are even more obvious than in Acropolis 2381. (See Brommer, *Skulpturen*, pls. 104–105 for Poseidon, pl. 100 for Athena.) The thigh fragment of Amphitrite from the West Pediment found in the Athenian Agora (*Hesperia* 24 [1955] pl. 38) shows the same phenomena, a more or less flat vertical break and a concave horizontal break.

63. *Skulpturen* p. 92, no. 7 (with references to his arguments against Marcadé's attribution to Helios). Jeppesen uses the fragment in his drawing of Hera, *ActaA* 34 (1963) 77, fig. 23 d, but does not mention it in his text.

64. *Parthenon Ostgiebel* 68: "Auf eine Fortsetzung des kostbaren Schmuckbandes über den Schleier hinaus konnte der Bildhauer jedenfalls nur dann verzichten, wenn das Zusammentreffen von 'Schleier' und

49. Head of Hera. Athens, Acropolis Museum.

following Sauer, that the large cutting in the back of the head is for
a strut anchoring the statue to the tympanon and so would determine
a facing position slightly turned to the proper right.[65] Neither of

---

Schmuckglied auf der rechten Seite des Kopfes dem Blick des Betrachters
verborgen blieb. D. h., unser Kopf müsste mindestens so weit nach seiner
Rechten gedreht gewesen sein, bis er 'en face' erschienen wäre" ["The
sculptor could have avoided extending the precious crown out over the veil
only if the meeting of 'veil' and crown on the right side of the head were
concealed from the viewer. That is, our head must have been turned at
least so far to its right as to appear 'en face' "].

65. *AthMitt* 71 (1956) 50.

these arguments seems very convincing. We are surely meant to think of the band on which the ornaments of the crown were carried as passing under the veil in back,[66] and I see no reason to imagine that the overlapping was awkward. It is rather more likely to have been so on the proper left side, where the veil came so far forward that if the whole head-dress were rendered literally it might have passed over some of the projecting ornaments.[67]

As for the cutting, the head seems an unlikely place for an original anchoring bar because of the strain this would put on the neck.[68] Also, one would expect an original anchor to be horizontal, whereas this hole slopes downward to the outside. Marcadé's suggestion that the large hole is for the tenon of a piece of drapery fastened on [69] is contradicted by clear traces of iron rust below the hole. A tenon such as he postulates would be secured with lead rather than with iron. The hole is too big for an ordinary piecing dowel, however. It may be that it results from a Roman repair. Brommer has commented on a roughly finished spot at the edge of the veil which he felt the Parthenon artists would never have allowed to be visible.[70] This

66. The roughly carved torus to which leaves were probably attached is definitely shown as passing under the veil.

67. The vase-painters are rather cavalier about this problem. Cf. the Hera in the gigantomachy on a cup by Aristophanes (Pfuhl, *Malerei und Zeichnung* fig. 587; Beazley, *Attic Red-Figure Vase-Painters*, 2nd ed., 1318 [hereafter *ARV²*]). This head is also one of the many examples of short curly hair in front of the ears on a long-haired female figure. The short fringed bride's veil worn by this Hera as well as by the very similar Hera in the Karlsruhe Judgment of Paris by a follower of the Meidias Painter (Pfuhl, *op. cit.* fig. 595; *ARV²* 1315) may well have been the kind worn by our statue.

68. All the surviving cuttings for statue-supports in the tympanon of the West Pediment seem to be below head-level.

69. *BCH* 80 (1956) 177, "La cavité comprise à tort par B. Sauer comme un 'Ankerloch' n'est autre chose qu'une mortaise—la mortaise où s'encastrait le tenon d'ajustage de cette pièce rapportée—" ["The hole wrongly understood by B. Sauer as an 'anchoring bar' is none other than a mortaise—the mortaise where the tenon of that corresponding piece was inserted"]. He does not mention the iron stain and was probably not aware of it.

70. *Marburger Winckelmann-Programm* 1956–1958, p. 7, "Unsere Abbildung 14 zeigt am Schleierrand über dem Haar auf der rechten Kopfseite eine ungeglättete Abarbeitung. Da eine solche rauhe Stelle, mindestens an den sichtbaren Partien der Parthenonskulpturen nicht vorkommt, kann man, wenn man den Kopf trotzdem für den Parthenon erhalten will, nur schliessen, dass diese Stelle irgendwie, vielleicht durch eine Hand, verdeckt war" ["Our figure 14 shows a rough area at the edge of the veil over the hair on the right side of the head. Since such a rough spot would not occur at least in the visible parts of the Parthenon sculptures, if one nevertheless retains the head for the Parthenon one can only conclude that this area was somehow concealed, perhaps by a hand"].

looks, in fact, like a subsequent dressing-down of a chipped edge with a dragged toothed implement or rasp. Altogether, one has the impression that at some time in the Roman period this statue was knocked out of position by an earthquake or other disturbance and had to be reerected and propped up, perhaps rather crudely, with an iron support which was anchored in the surviving cutting in the head.[71]

As the Hera by our new arrangement now fits without difficulty into the place in block 11 to which she has naturally gravitated, so block 15 remains available for the male torso H [text figs. 50 and 51], which has most often been placed there.[72] There has been some dispute about the scale of the figure, but Sauer's calculations, based on

50. Torso of Poseidon, front view.   51. Torso of Poseidon, back view.
Athens, Acropolis Museum.   Athens, Acropolis Museum.

71. This prop cannot have been connected with the tympanon. It may either have been a bent bar braced on the floor or a shorter piece connected with a neighboring statue.

72. Sauer, *AthMitt* 16 (1891) 89; *Weber-Laborde'sche Kopf* 29; Furt-wängler, *Intermezzi*, p. 28 and fig. on p. 29; Svoronos, *Journal d'archéologie numismatique* 14 (1912) 281–284 and pl. 19 (reconstructed as Ares); Cook, *Zeus* III pl. 58, 3; Berger, *Parthenon-Ostgiebel* pls. 1, 11 a–b (i.e. in all his drawn reconstructions, though in the text he is hesitant about the scale. See infra).

an accurately measurable anatomical dimension, the distance between the sternal notch and the navel, which he compares with a number of classical standing and moderately active figures, are more persuasive than those of Berger, who compares less satisfactory dimensions with a single *running* figure, West H.[73] Berger keeps Sauer's placement and general pose in any case, so that his worries about the scale seem to have led nowhere. Carpenter, on the other hand, who had given block 15 to Athena, calculated the original height of H as 2.45 m., the extreme lower limit of Sauer's scale of possibilities, and placed it in block 16.[74] Jeppesen squeezes it into block 17.[75]

Sauer's analysis of the movement of the torso and his suggestion for placing it are for the most part convincing. According to him the figure had his weight on the left leg and the right leg extended. Both arms were raised, the right somewhat more so than the left, and the left was flung farther back while the right was more in line with the torso. He suggested a diagonal placement with the left foot well back, the right near the front of the cornice. A dowel in the rear south part of block 15 would have helped prevent the figure, which was overbalanced toward the right, from tilting in that direction.[76]

Sauer felt that a hole centered over the joint between blocks 15 and 16 might also be for a dowel, lighter than the above-mentioned, but Balanos does not include it as a dowel-hole in his drawing,[77] and Carpenter states that it is more likely to be a socket for a staff, spear or trident.[78] This looks plausible in Balanos' photograph. Both Carpenter and Berger identified torso H as Poseidon and both showed his trident anchored in this hole, held by the right hand in front of the figure according to Carpenter and by the left hand behind him in Berger's reconstruction. Furtwängler and A. B. Cook had previously also restored H as Poseidon but without planting his trident in the socket.

A number of others following Sauer have interpreted the figure as Hephaistos. Brommer most recently has used this as one of the arguments against the Puteal.[79] He remarks that the unclad upper torso is more suitable for Hephaistos than for Poseidon, who always appears more formally dressed at the birth of Athena.[80] In this, how-

73. Sauer's calculations, *Weber-Laborde'sche Kopf* 29. Berger's *Parthenon-Ostgiebel* 32.
74. *Hesperia* 2 (1933) 24–25.
75. *ActaA* 34 (1963) 88.
76. *Weber-Laborde'sche Kopf* 58–59, 60–61.
77. *Les Monuments de l'Acropole* pl. 112.
78. *Hesperia* 2 (1933) 23.
79. *AthMitt* 73 (1958) 114.
80. *Skulpturen* 155.

ever, he seems to be misinterpreting the trace of drapery on the back of Poseidon's left shoulder. This, described by Carpenter as "a scarf-like piece of drapery," [81] is in fact anything but scarflike; it is the edge of a full-sized himation that has been draped in the normal manner and is slipping off as the result of some violent action. The splendid figure of a marshal starting back before an on-rushing chariot in block XVIII of the north frieze presents a good analogy both for the draping and for the effects of the strong action on a muscular torso. The reclining hero, A, in the West Pediment also exhibits folds in a comparable position on the left shoulder and once more they belong to a full-sized draped hima-tion. A truly scarflike garment simply does not exist in ancient Greek male dress. When we see what looks like one, it is a shorter himation or chlamys that has been folded up small and slung over the shoulder or wrapped around the arm to get it out of the way. Such a garment will either rest solidly on the shoulder or leave it entirely bare. It will not overlap only the outer edge of the shoulder in back as does the drapery on torso H.

The slipping himation, which we know also from the west pedi-ment at Olympia,[82] has a practical as well as an iconographical use in pedimental sculpture. It gives a solid support for the legs and pro-vides a means whereby some counterbalancing weight can be added to the lower part of the figure. A stump-like strut such as Sauer sug-gested [83] becomes quite unnecessary.

It is interesting to notice that the second of the two horse-tamers of Monte Cavallo [see *supra*, p. 247] has a long himation falling from his raised left arm to the ground and serving as a strut to support the left leg. The right leg is supported by a purely Roman cuirass. There is an obvious contrast between the short end of the himation swinging down in front of the left arm, whose pattern seems gen-uinely Parthenonian,[84] and the long end falling to the ground, whose folds are singularly heavy, stiff and uninspired. One is tempted to see the influence of our pedimental figure in the strong, squarely

81. *AJA* 66 (1962) 268.
82. In the figures of Theseus and Peirithoos. B. B. Shefton, *Hesperia* 31 (1962) 356–360, discusses the iconographical significance of this "himation motive" in the centauromachy at the feast. "It expresses by the very fall of the cloak the suddenness of the uproar at the banquet, where everyone, hosts and guests alike, had been decently dressed and expecting anything but sudden violence." In the marshal of the frieze also it must express sud-denness of action.
83. *Weber-Laborde'sche Kopf* 64.
84. Compare the fragment Smith 7 (British Museum 337), best illustrated by Brommer, *AthMitt* 71 (1956) Beilage 31.

patterned musculature of the torso, and to imagine that the course of the drapery has been altered in its lower part. Probably the himation on the Parthenon figure will have been still caught over the right knee, as in so many fifth century figures, and will have curved down to the ground between the legs [text fig. 52].

Roughnesses in the surface of torso H near the proper left side, on the front as well as on the back, suggest that the upper end of

15   16   17

52. Parthenon, east pediment blocks 15–17. Poseidon and Amphitrite. Floor after Carpenter. Scale approx. 1:40.

the himation may have swung as if windblown close to the body in front even though it did not actually touch. A channel over the lower ribs looks like part of a large drill-hole that was not fully obliterated. Three small drill-holes in the left flank are hard to explain. These look like holes for some fairly light metal attachment rather than simply remains of undercutting that went too deep between the drapery.[85] The placement is about right for a sword-scabbard but neither Hephaistos nor Poseidon wears a sword; there is no hole to attach a baldric on the right shoulder, and it is hard to see how what was attached here can have been visible through the drapery. It is understandable, therefore, that not even Svoronos, who took torso H to be Ares, made any use of these holes in his reconstruction.

It must be confessed that everyone who has drawn a reconstruction of this figure, whether as Hephaistos, Ares, or Poseidon, has made him look rather ridiculous. Svoronos' Ares[86] is certainly the worst, since he has to hold his weapons in a way that makes no sense but it is also interesting to note how few of the fairly numerous company of scholars who have said that the action best suits Hephaistos have actually drawn a Hephaistos for us. Though it is easy to say that a pose with both arms raised suits an axe-swinger, the actual moment of wielding the axe fits neither the story nor the torso. Athena, after all, is already born, and it is true, as Cook says, that none of the vase-paintings that we have shows Hephaistos swinging the axe.[87] So far as the torso itself is concerned, a right-handed axe-wielder who wants to land a single well-placed blow normally has his left shoulder farther forward than the right, since the right hand, which directs the blow, is nearer the head of the axe. The axe-swinging figure 7 in the west frieze of the Hephaisteion[88] which Sauer cites as a parallel

85. In the east frieze of the Hephaisteion, for example, it is not always certain whether a given drill-hole is made for an attachment or is simply the remains of undercutting.

86. *Op. cit.* (supra n. 72). Also in Brommer, *Skulpturen* 123, fig. 13 c.

87. *Zeus* III, 696 n. 5. For the most recent and complete list of vase-paintings representing the Birth of Athena, see Brommer, *RGZM* 8 (1961) 66–83.

88. Koch, *Studien zum Theseustempel in Athen* (Berlin 1955) pl. 37, above. Sauer, *Das sogenannte Theseion und sein plastischer Schmuck* pl. 4. Morgan, *Hesperia* 31 (1962) pl. 80, below. The position with the right hand nearer the head of the axe seems to be normal for the heavy workman's or sacrificial axe, not necessarily so for the lighter Amazonian battle-axe which can also be wielded with one hand. Some canonical right-handed axe-swingers, besides the Hephaisteion figure mentioned above, are: west pediment at Olympia, Theseus in centauromachy; Theseus in centauromachy frieze from Gjölbaschi-Trysa (Eichler, *Die Reliefs des Heroon von Gjöl-baschi-Trysa* [Vienna 1950] pl. 4/5, B 2); Clytemnestra killing Cassandra in

for the movement of our figure differs from it in precisely this respect. Since the left hip is back and the left shoulder forward there is a torsion in the trunk of this figure which torso H does not exhibit. Jeppesen,[89] whose drawings are honest at all costs, has drawn a left-handed Hephaistos, but no one else has faced the problem. If this *is* Hephaistos, then, he is no longer swinging the axe but starting back in surprise after having struck his blow. But the gesture of the left arm in that case has no motivation other than astonishment, and the torso is no better suited to Hephaistos than to Poseidon. So far as the story is concerned, all the gods are supposed to have been astonished at the birth of Athena,[90] but Hephaistos was a workmanlike god who would not be likely to stand in the path of the explosion that he was himself about to touch off. For this reason, the great majority of the vase-paintings show him behind the throne of Zeus. So far as significance is concerned, the relationship of Hephaistos to Athena that has led some scholars to call for Hephaistos "on the side of Athena" is better served by the symmetrical grouping we have postulated than by representing Hephaistos as unsettled by her birth.

In the case of Poseidon, there is at least literary if not pictorial evidence for a deep disturbance caused by the birth of Athena. We read in the Homeric hymn: "great Olympus began to reel horribly at the might of the bright-eyed goddess, and earth round about cried fearfully, and the sea was moved and tossed with dark waves. . . ."[91] Now, Poseidon is the Earth-Shaker and Amphitrite personifies the sea. Given the close relationship that seems to exist, however it is to be explained, between this hymn and the pediment, it is easy to imagine that Poseidon and Amphitrite were represented in greater agitation than any of the other gods attendant on the birth.

---

a cup from Spina by the Marlay Painter, Alfieri-Arias, *Spina* pl. 99, *ARV*² 1280, no. 64; Phlyakes vase in Bari, Birth of Helen (Cook *Zeus* III, fig. 535; Bieber, *History of the Greek and Roman Theater* [2nd ed. Princeton 1961] fig. 492; Pfuhl, *Malerei und Zeichnung* fig. 805); man sacrificing a bull on cup from Boscoreale in the Louvre (Ryberg, *Rites of the State Religion in Roman Art* pl. 50 d); man sacrificing on Antonine relief in Louvre (*ibid.* pl. 56, fig. 87).

89. *ActaA* 34 (1963) 77, fig. 23 d.

90. Homeric Hymn XXVIII, 6: σέβας δ' ἔχε πάντας ὁρῶντας ["and awe siezed the gods as they gazed," trans. Hugh G. Evelyn-White]; Philostratus, *Imagines* 2.27: οἱ μὲν ἐκπληττόμενοι θεοὶ καὶ θεαί ["These wonder-struck beings are gods and godesses," trans. Arthur Fairbanks].

91. Homeric Hymn XXVIII, 9–13. Compare also Pindar, *Olympian* 7.38: Οὐρανὸς δ' ἐφριξέ νιν καὶ Γαῖα μάτηρ ["Heaven and Mother Earth trembled before her (Athena)," trans. Sir John Sandys]. The upheaval of the sea is not mentioned by Pindar, but it follows naturally on that of the earth.

To speak of Amphitrite leads us on to consider the space to the right of Poseidon, which has been filled in various ways by different scholars. Carpenter used each of the two very wide diagonal bar-cuttings in blocks 10–11 and 16 for a pair of unconnected plinths,[92] but most scholars have looked for a single figure or group of exceptional weight for each of these positions. Sauer suggested that the heavy bars carried enthroned figures,[93] and Furtwängler, Schwerzek, Cook, and Jeppesen followed this in their reconstructions. Svoronos and Berger also placed a seated figure to the right of torso H, though they split the opposite bar between two figures.[94] It is clear, however, that reasonable as these seated figures may be as an explanation for the heavy bars, they do no good to the composition. If Carpenter's paratactic standing statues tend, as Picard complained, to interrupt the *sacra conversazione*,[95] these stodgy monoliths stop it dead. The violent movement of Poseidon can only seem absurd when it comes up against such an unmoved mass, especially when, as in several of the restorations, the seated figure is perched on a piece of wooden furniture.

If we take the excitement of torso H at its full value we can hardly doubt that there was lively movement behind as well as in front of the figure. The analogy of the marshal between chariots remains a good one. We sense that Poseidon is not only reacting strongly to the event before him but holding back some untamed force behind him. It must mean something that our best analogies for both the fall of the drapery and the movement of the torso belong to the horse-taming rather than to the tool-wielding world. The figure of Amphitrite could best express the turmoil of the sea if, as in the West Pediment, she had one of the sea-creatures with her. Riding a *ketos* or a hippocamp, she would make a group full of movement and exotic form, amply heavy and broad of plinth to justify the bar-cutting and explain the floor-marks in block 16 and the southern half of 17. Jeppesen has rightly said that the bars in blocks 10–11 and 16 are most comparable to those for the horses in the West Pediment, even though he himself uses them to support two massive thrones.[96]

92. *Hesperia* 2 (1933) 23, 29.
93. *AthMitt* 16 (1891) 87.
94. See Brommer, *Skulpturen* 122–125; Jeppesen, *loc. cit.* (supra n. 89).
95. *RA* 6th Series, 1 (1963) 85. Jeppesen's reconstruction well illustrates the difficulty of placing enthroned figures at this point in the composition. Their scale has to be such that they must either be larger than Athena (which is permissible for Zeus but not for others) or else they must perch like Jeppesen's Poseidon on an elevated seat whose inert mass is out of all proportion to the animate part of the figure.
96. *ActaA* 34 (1963) 85.

It is just at this point that we have to make up our minds whether the East Pediment of the Parthenon belonged to the static world of the Olympia East Pediment and of the Alkmeonid Temple at Delphi or whether, like the West Pediment of the Parthenon, its figures were joined by continuous waves of movement. Picard argues eloquently for the latter: "Là où les statues antiques subsistent, elles se montrent intimement associées par une 'arabesque' mouvementée, dont le fronton Ouest d'Olympie marquait déjà la valeur rhythmique; on la retrouvait au fronton de la Dispute, d'après le dessin de l'Anonyme de Nointel" ["As far as the statues are preserved, they show themselves to be intimately interconnected by an exciting 'arabesque,' the rhythmic value of which had already been demonstrated by the west pediment at Olympia; we find the same thing in the Dispute (in the Parthenon's west pediment) in the drawing of the Nointel Anonymous."] [97] The torso H is the strongest proof we have that he is right. The East Pediment is not a Homeric family council of the Olympians, "great big people perched on chairs." It is a cosmos of deities attendant on a cosmic event that leaves no corner of the world unmoved.

From the compositional point of view it would be good to have Amphitrite riding a real hippocamp with forelegs beating the air [text fig. 52]. If the left hand on Poseidon was not wholly occupied with his trident he may have held the bridle of this creature as the Poseidon copied from the West Pediment on the Kerch hydria in Leningrad holds the bridle of a horse in his left hand. It would be hard to be sure whether any fragments have survived. Jeppesen is probably right in attributing to a Triton under the horses of Poseidon in the West Pediment the fragments of a sea-monster's tail which Brommer wrongly gave to the creature beneath Amphitrite's feet. There remains, however, a horse-like eye, which cannot belong to the dolphin drawn by Carrey.[98] If Brommer is right in saying that all the heads of chariot horses in the pediments are otherwise accounted for, this might belong to a hippocamp. Only if we were sure of the scale could we say whether any of the forehooves rejected by Brommer [99] might also belong.

As for Amphitrite herself, it seems not at all unlikely that fragments have survived, since her husband and perhaps her attendant monster are so represented. To identify any of these positively would be rash, but there is one particularly lovely piece that is strikingly suitable in type and is still homeless in the pediments. When we

97. *Loc. cit.* (supra n. 95).
98. *Skulpturen* 85, no. 196, pl. 118, 2, Acropolis 830.
99. *AthMitt* 69–70 (1954–1955) 51.

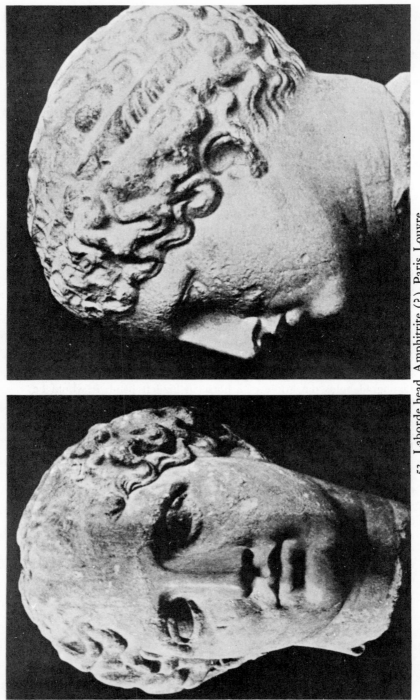

53. Laborde head, Amphitrite (?). Paris, Louvre.

54. Nereid from Epidaurus [380–70 B.C.]. Athens, National Museum.

consider the head of the best preserved riding Nereid from Epidauros [100] [text fig. 54] and the way in which it is set on the neck, we realize that the Weber-Laborde head [fig. 54 and text fig.

100. Crome, *Die Skulpturen des Asklepiostempels von Epidauros* pls. 6–8.

53] is suitable in pose for a riding Amphitrite. We may also compare
the set of the head in the riding Aphrodite of a fourth-century bronze
mirror.[101] The scale of the Laborde head seems to be appropriate,
since the height from chin to crown is 0.33 m., i.e. about one and
one-half times life size.[102]

The coiffure shows a practical elegance that eminently suits the
goddess of the sea in an Olympian context. This is not the sea-wet
streaming hair of the Hellenistic Amphitrite. The sea-winds play
with it but cannot shake it loose. There are attachment holes for
earrings and for some kind of light metal wreath or crown. A tightly
twisted rope of hair wound around the head binds the hair into a
compact mass, but within this mass the strands wave and interweave
with unusual liveliness. We are tempted to recall that Athena's birth-
day was in midsummer, when the strong north wind stirs up the
Aegean in just such lively waves. Buschor, in describing the Laborde
head says, "so steigert dieser Kopf die stillere Art der Artemis des
Ostfrieses zu heftigem Gewoge" ["in this head the quietness of the
Artemis of the east frieze is transformed by a wave of emotion"].[103]
The head of Amphitrite on the Talos vase [104] [text fig. 55], the only
example in vase-painting which has something of the monumentality
of Pheidian sculpture, is strikingly similar in type. Becatti has rightly
compared the heads of Arethusa on the late fifth-century coins of
Syracuse,[105] but none of them is so regal as this. Excitement and
queenly majesty could not be more beautifully combined.

The Laborde head has, of course, been attributed to a great number of figures in both pediments. It would be hard to find another
Parthenonian question on which so little consensus exists. More
scholars have favored an identification with the head of West G than

101. Züchner, *Griechische Klappspiegel* (*Jdl* Ergänzungsheft 14, 1942)
KS 9, pl. 5 and fig. 7.
102. Sauer reckoned the standing height of the figure as between 2.31
and 2.59 m. Neither extreme is likely for the Parthenon. If we take 7.4 times
the head height (0.33 m.), we have a standing height of 2.44 m. In the
akroterion from Epidauros, where the horse, lacking hindlegs, is about on a
level with a hippocamp, the elevation of the mounted figure about makes up
for the loss of height in its half-seated pose. The tympanon height in block
16 goes from about 2.83 m. to about 2.56 m. This would allow extra room
for a plinth, a somewhat more erect head position than the Epidauros
Nereid has, and a somewhat more restive mount. Sauer had placed the head
above the right end of block 17, since he thought a cutting in the back of
the head was made to clear the nose of the cornice (*Weber-Laborde'sche
Kopf* 34–36). Carpenter had placed it in block 11, but was obliged to explain the small scale by a wish to keep the three Fates on a similar scale
(*Hesperia* 2 [1933] 61).
103. *Phidias der Mensch* 111.
104. *ARV²* 1338, 1.
105. *Problemi Fidiaci* 51.

55. Talos krater, detail: Amphitrite [*ca.* 400 B.C.]. Ruvo, Jatta Collection.

any other,[106] but Carrey's drawing shows clearly that G's head is inclined in the opposite direction. One cannot accuse Carrey of mis-

106. See the list of attributions, Brommer, *Skulpturen* 67. [Editor's note: the letters assigned to the figures in the pediments belong either to existing fragments or to figures in the Carrey drawings or to both. The labels may be conveniently studied in the plates in Adolfe Michaelis, *Der Parthenon* (Leipzig, 1871) and in Brommer, *Skulpturen*.]

drawing it, for it is consistent with the whole pose of the figure. Also, the careful carving of the proper left side of the Laborde head would not make sense if it were meant to be seen in right profile.[107]

Becatti attributed the head to the reclining female figure W in the right-hand corner of the West Pediment.[108] This has not been more generally accepted than any other theory, but Becatti makes two statements so positively that if no one takes the trouble to refute them, they may seem like good arguments deliberately ignored. The first is that a head which was brought to Venice by San Gallo, the secretary of Morosini, must have been one of those existing in the pediments when Carrey drew them in 1674. It is "quasi impossible," he says, to think that it might have been a head that had been lost from the pediment earlier. This quasi-impossibility appears to me to be no such thing. There were all kinds of ways in which buried antiquities might come to light on the Acropolis in almost any period, and if Gravier d'Ortières could bring back an archaic kore from the Acropolis to Marseilles,[109] it would be no great trick for one of Morosini's entourage to acquire a Parthenon head that had been buried and somehow rediscovered.[110]

It is admittedly a curious fact that no single fragment from any of the ten heads drawn by Carrey in the West Pediment has ever been identified and joined to its statue. The only piece we have is the back of the head of Athena, which Carrey did *not* see still in the pediment. My guess is that these heads were mostly so badly weathered that the surfaces of faces and hair did not survive the crash to the ground following the explosion and the fall of the raking cornice. In any case, the Laborde head is well enough preserved to make us think it might have fallen off some centuries earlier.[111] The damage

107. Cf. *Hesperia* 29 (1960) 369 n. 4.
108. *Problemi Fidiaci* 48–51.
109. Michon, *CRAI* (1935) 377–378. It is not *proven* that he was the one who brought the kore back, but since she was in the possession of the Gravier family, the presumption is very strong.
110. Sauer, *Weber-Laborde'sche Kopf* 27–28, describes convincingly the conditions under which East Pediment pieces might have survived and been recovered.
111. Of the West Pediment possibilities which Brommer mentions for the Laborde head, *Skulpturen* 67, U and U' must be excluded as too small, T because the head had already lost its features before Carrey's time. F is probably also too small (her head would have come just left of the tympanon joint which is 2.171 m. high, as measured by W. B. Dinsmoor). That leaves only D, which has nothing positive in its favor. I still incline, against Brommer, to believe that the Laborde head was turned slightly to the left (i.e. proper right), whereas one would expect D to turn, if only slightly, toward the child on her left.

to eyebrows, nose, lips and chin appear to be due rather to battering than to heavy weathering.

The second statement of Becatti's which cannot pass unchallenged is that the inclination of the Laborde head precisely suits West W. The figure in the drawing appears to be in a relaxed pose, but if one assumes this pose in a relaxed manner the right shoulder rises higher and the neck is pressed more closely against it than can have been the case with the Laborde head. There is an alertness about the poise of this head despite the bend of the neck that makes it seem unsuited for a reclining figure.

Brommer has said that one might at least eliminate some of the suggested attributions for the Laborde head by checking the grain of the marble.[112] A more or less vertical grain does appear, as he says, to be indicated by the weathering on the proper right side of the face. This is the most usual direction for standing and seated figures.[113] West W, like the other reclining figures, is horizontally layered and has split accordingly. On this count, too, the head is unlikely to have belonged to it.

Buschor assigns both the Laborde head and the Artemis of the East frieze to Alkamenes, saying that in the head the style of the Artemis has been developed into the rich style.[114] This judgment seems to be fully supported by the fragments from the frieze of the Temple of Ares, for which Alkamenes made the cult statue. This frieze was in higher relief than that of the Parthenon and clearly somewhat later in date. The manner of carving the fine folds of the chiton in the Artemis of the Parthenon is obviously ancestral to that which we find in two of the Ares figures,[115] and the richly folded himation of the seated Poseidon on the same Parthenon slab bears a similar relationship to a fragment of a seated male figure from the Temple of Ares.[116] One has the impression that the same hands were employed in both places.

The heads from the Temple of Ares, though they have not the majesty of the Laborde head, have various features in common with it. The tilt of the head on the neck recurs in the fragment S 320 as

112. *Skulpturen 67.*
113. See supra n. 62.
114. *Phidias der Mensch* 111, "Alkamenes, von dem der Weber-Laborde'sche Kopf herrühren wird, hat hier die Stufe des Reichen Stils erreicht, auf der er offenbar noch eine grosse Zukunft entfaltet hat" ["Alkamenes, to whom the Weber-Laborde head is attributed, has here reached the level of the Rich Style, in which he evidently was to develop an important future"].
115. S 676 (*Hesperia* 21 [1952] pl. 22, e), S 18344 S 2024.
116. S 1778.

well as in the veiled head [117] S 1538. S 320 has also the "Venus rings" in the neck which the Laborde head displays but which are not yet present in the Parthenon frieze. The depth of the cranium is matched in the very fragmentary head S 400 and in the now-lost male head S 305. Finally, the decorative richness of the coiffure of the Laborde head finds its counterpart in the rich variety of coiffures and stylizations of hair in the Ares heads.[118]

The Amphitrite who thus emerges is an impressive and appealing figure, combining the excitement of the sea with the majesty of a queen at home in that element and able to control it. She has put on her most elegant attire to attend the birth of Athena, and her realm is deeply stirred by the event. There is no cult of Amphitrite in Athens to explain her importance in Athenian art of the fifth century. Its roots are recent and historical rather than prehistoric and religious. Amphitrite, as we have said, is not so much the goddess of the sea as the personification of the sea itself. The sudden political importance of the sea in fifth-century Athens required a new iconography, and Amphitrite was the logical figure to convey it. When Kimon had the visit of Theseus to Amphitrite painted in the Theseion along with the Amazonomachy and the battle of Centaurs and Lapiths,[119] he must have meant to allude to the importance of sea victories for the greatness of Athens. As Theseus gradually came to be considered the mythical founder of the Athenian democracy,[120] and as the link between the democracy and the navy became intensified, Amphitrite will have grown in symbolic importance for the Athenians. We do not expect to find Theseus at the birth of Athena, for unlike Herakles he never became one of the Olympians, but we are reminded of him and of the democracy by the appearance of Poseidon and Amphitrite acknowledging the power of Athena. The relatively small scale which is imposed on the sea gods by their active poses serves to magnify the scale of Athena as their movement reveals her force.

The figure or group which must have balanced Amphitrite on the other side of the pediment is harder to imagine because the self-contained figure of Hera does not lead us on to it as Poseidon does to

117. *Hesperia* 21 (1952) pl. 23 a.
118. Compare also S 1494 (*Hesperia* 21 [1952] pl. 23 b), a different stylization but again richly decorative.
119. Pausanias 1.17.3.
120. Cf. Thompson, *AJA* 66 (1962) 347. If Thompson is right in seeing Theseus as the protagonist of the battle in the East frieze of the Hephaisteion, it is not surprising that Poseidon and Amphitrite are among the six divine witnesses of the struggle.

Amphitrite. Still, we feel that it should somehow serve the same purpose of receiving the impact of the event and might do so best if a like element of irrational sensibility were included. Another combination of deity and animal would best serve this purpose. Before we decide which god it should be, however, we need first to make sure of the identities of the preserved corner figures. Artemis with her stag or Dionysos with his panther would do, but Artemis has sometimes been identified in the running maiden, G, and it has become almost a *communis opinio* to see Dionysos in the powerful male figure, D, who reclines on an animal skin and faces the rising sun.

Here the balance of opinion appears to be in inverse ratio to the weight of the evidence, for the running girl looks much more like Artemis than the reclining male looks like Dionysos. Artemis is a better identification for G than either Eileithyia or Hebe because neither of these is normally shown running. Since the gods of the east pediment are not merely actors in a drama but components of a cosmos, it is essential that none of them, however startled by the event, be shaken out of his characteristic guise. The design must convey excitement through those figures to whom excitement is natural, movement by those who are commonly in motion. It is in the nature of Eileithyia to stand by; it is in the nature of Hebe to serve. Iris is the only goddess besides Artemis to whom running is natural and this cannot be Iris, for she has no wings.

Brommer [121] calls attention to two lovely late fifth century votive reliefs, one in Kassel,[122] probably from the Athenian Acropolis, and one recently found in Brauron,[123] which show a running Artemis without quiver and similar in type to G. We might add a fragment of another relief from the Acropolis which lacks the artistic merit of these but is closer to G in having the ungirt peplos with shorter overfall.[124] Brommer remarks that if the two seated goddesses E and F were Demeter and Kore the running figure might be Hekate, since she is also like the figure on the New York krater with the rising of Persephone, and since the Homeric hymn to Demeter attests the close relationship of Hekate to the two goddesses.[125] It may well be that the economy of symbolism imposed by the needs of the pedimental composition prevented direct representation of Hekate and Eileithyia as separate persons, so that we are meant to

121. *Skulpturen* 153–154.
122. Bieber, *Skulpturen und Bronzen in Cassel* no. 74, pl. 32.
123. *Ergon* (1958) 33, fig. 35.
124. Walter, *Die Reliefs im kleinen Akropolismuseum* (Vienna 1923) 63, no. 110.
125. *Skulpturen* 153.

regard them as included in the person of Artemis, with whom both
are identified in Athenian literature of the fifth century.[126]

Brommer did not face this question because he does not believe
that the two goddesses are Demeter and Kore, but in this he stands
almost alone among modern scholars. He raises three main difficulties to the accepted identification.[127] First, the rectangular chests,
κιβωτοί, on which the goddesses sit do not appear in any known
representations of Demeter and Kore. Demeter always sits on a cylindrical κίστη. Second, we never find both goddesses seated. Either
both are standing or Demeter sits and Kore stands. Third, Kore
never appears in vase-paintings of the birth of Athena and ought not
to be present in Olympos because she is an underworld goddess.

To the first objection we might reply that though we do not have
the Eleusianian goddesses represented elsewhere with κιβωτοί we
know from Pausanias that Polygnotos painted Kleoboia in the boat
of Charon holding a κιβωτός on her lap "such as they make for
Demeter." [128] To the second one could retort that at Lykosoura
Demeter and Despoina were seated side by side and Demeter rested
her hand (or arm) on Despoina.[129] Neither of these replies completely demolishes the objection, for in each case the parallel comes
from outside Attica, but they at least weaken Brommer's case. So far
as the third point is concerned, Brommer himself says of his alternative, the Horai, that though they do not appear in vase-paintings of
the birth of Athena, the pediment, with far more figures than any
such vase-painting contained, could easily have had figures not present on the vases. The same could apply to Kore. The objection that
Kore does not belong to Olympos would be valid only if we knew
that the scene was defined as Olympos. But this is by no means agreed
on.[130]

We cannot say that either of the Eleusinian goddesses never sits,

126. Cf. Kraus, *Hekate* 25, 86.
127. *Skulpturen* 150–153.
128. Pausanias 10.28.3.
129. Dickins, *BSA* 13 (1906–07) 365–368; 17 (1910–11) 81, figs. 1–2.
130. Brommer admits that Buschor's concept of the *Weltenberg* would
permit the presence of Kore, but he does not really believe in the *Weltenberg* and he does not admit the possibility of any less definitely localized
framework. Yet the very fact that the same flanking figures, Sun and Moon,
are used for the birth of Aphrodite from the sea (base of the Zeus at
Olympia, Pausanias 5.11.8) and the birth of Athena from the head of Zeus
suggests that these events did not take place in a locally defined landscape
like the chariot race in the East Pediment at Olympia. Buschor himself, by
using quotation marks around "Olympos" and "Eleusis" (*Phidias der
Mensch* 99), suggests that the *Weltenberg* is more a metaphor than a
spatially conceived entity.

for Persephone sits on her throne as queen of Hades and probably also as a child in her mother's lap.[131] The scheme of the seated Demeter and the standing Persephone in Eleusinian scenes must signify the *return* of Persephone, the mother seated at home in Eleusis and receiving her daughter back from the underworld. We would not expect this scheme at the birth of Athena. Both goddesses might stand together, as they so often do,[132] were it not that their place in the pediment requires them to sit.

Brommer has made the useful observation that when the group E–F is seen from the angle from which it was meant to be looked at, E does not appear more broad and matronly than F.[133] This preferred view also gives more prominence to the kolpos of the peplos of F and so helps to emphasize the difference in dress between the two figures. F wears the heavier peplos with kolpos and overfall. E wears the thin chiton with an overfall that is not long enough to cover the girdle in back. According to the usual iconography, therefore, F should be Demeter and E should be Kore. The dresses of the two figures have been assimilated to some extent, just as their poses have been assimilated by showing them both seated. Kore wears her chiton fastened only on the shoulders, without buttoned sleeves, and Demeter has draped her himation around her instead of letting it hang symmetrically down her back. This enhances the compositional unity of the group without depriving the two figures of their recognizable identities. The coiffures will doubtless have offered the first difference to strike the observer, and the upper parts of the two dresses, with the soft, rounded and clinging neckline of Kore's chiton and the harsher angular V of Demeter's peplos will have made the distinction clear.

It is right that Demeter as the Olympian goddess should be nearer to the center of the pediment than Kore and should receive the news of the birth directly, but it is also right that she not be deprived of her daughter's company in this birth scene where the relationship of child to parent is the dominant personal note.

The two Eleusinian goddesses are appropriately dressed, then, and appropriately placed in the pediment, even if we have no parallel in

131. [See Harrison, "U and Her Neighbors in the West Pediment of the Parthenon," *op. cit.*]
132. E.g. the relief of the bridge-building decree of 421/0, Mylonas, *Eleusis and the Eleusinian Mysteries* (Princeton 1961) fig. 69; Lippold, *Handbuch der Archäologie* III¹, *Die Plastik* pl. 73, 3; fragment of a relief on the Acropolis, *ArchEph* (1893 pl. 8; Casson, no. 1348; relief in Munich from Rhamnous, *ArchEph* (1893) suppl. pl. 38; statuette pair from Mycenae, Mylonas, *AJA* 66 (1962) 303–304, pl. 80.
133. *Skulpturen* 150, pl. 35.

art for their sitting on chests. It would be a great mistake to say that
the chests prove who they are, for the way of this art is not to
prove but to persuade. If a figure contains enough familiar elements
to be recognized for what it is, the artist is then free to add something that elaborates or extends its meaning. In Attic Greek it is sufficient to use the dual of the word "goddess" in order to designate
the Eleusinian goddesses. Two female figures clearly conceived as a
pair and dressed in the fashion usual in this period for Demeter and
Kore announce their identity without needing further attributes. The
chests are then allusive rather than indicative, their meaning multiple,
not single. The closed containers suggest the *cista* [a box or chest for
sacred objects] with its mystic contents though they do not represent it. Their form is that of a piece of household furniture on which
it appears natural for women to sit. If we look for other representations of persons seated on such chests, we find them in indoor scenes
on vases showing women or heroines with Eros, Aphrodite, Dionysos and the other deities who belong to weddings. In their common-
est use they are clothes-chests, and they may easily be understood to
stand for the dowry of the bride.[134] The one on which Helen sits as

134. In the case of the Parthenon figures the suggestion of clothes-chests
is reinforced by the fact that folded garments instead of cushions are laid
on top of them. Schunck, *Jdl* 73 (1958) 34, notes 44 and 45, gives a list of 19
representations on Attic and South Italian vases which depict persons sitting
on chests. All are women, he says, except for one satyr. He takes the list to
support Jeppesen's remark that the chest is used simply to indicate the
gynaeconitis. Diligent searching could no doubt expand the number of examples, for the world of wedding symbolism to which they belong is very
widely represented in late 5th and 4th century vase-painting. A survey of
the examples listed is sufficient, however, to show that it is this wedding
symbolism rather than the *gynaeconitis* per se that is common to all of
them. Neither Ariadne as the bride of Dionysos (Kerch Pelike, Leningrad
B 2232, Schefold, *Untersuchungen zu den Kertscher Vasen* pl. 8, 2) nor a
Hesperid as bride of Herakles (Apulian krater in Naples, Heydemann,
Vasensammlungen in Neapel 584ff, no. 3255; Reinach, *Répertoire des Vases
Peints* I 236) is to be thought of as indoors. Margarete Bieber has convincingly connected the Kerch vases on which Eros and Dionysos both
appear with the role which Dionysos played in Athenian wedding ceremonies (*Hesperia*, Supplement 8, 31–38). On the skyphos in New York
(Bieber, *op. cit.* pl. 4, 3; Richter and Hall no. 170, pl. 165; Schefold,
Kertscher Vasen pl. 9) we see not only the chest but also the processional
basket. Here too, then, as in the case of the Eleusinian Mysteries, the rectangular chest is not per se the ritual container, but by association it may
well have come to carry some of the notion of the hidden sources of fertility. This may be why a Faliscan vase shows Dionysos himself sitting on a
chest (Beazley, *Etruscan Vase-Painting* 111; Amsterdam 479, *CVA*, IV B, pl.
2, 3 [Pays Bas pl. 88]). Thus in the one case where a satyr sits on one it
hardly seems necessary for Schunck to advance the explanation that it is a
"Satyr von weibischen Formen" (*op. cit.* 34 n. 48).

she prepares to go away with Paris [135] contains a stolen dowry, but it is a dowry nonetheless. Used here in a broader context the chests symbolize all stored possessions, all preserved resources, in a word, Ploutos. Firmly seated on their chests, the goddesses announce that wealth is in their keeping. Ploutos is born out of the earth in the realm of the agricultural deities, but by the works of Athena the meaning of wealth is extended to include a far wider range of material goods, the things that are made by men as well as the things that grow.

It was because he is next to Demeter and Kore that the nude reclining male figure D was first named Bacchus, Iakchos, and then Dionysos.[136] If we had the figure alone outside the context of the pediment no one would think first of calling him Dionysos. The pose, leaning on the left elbow, is that of one who reclines to eat or drink, and a well-known relief from the Peiraeus shows Dionysos reclining like this on a banqueting couch, but the attitude is not peculiar to him—being borrowed from the familiar scheme of the hero reliefs.[137] It is also true that Dionysos, like Apollo, sometimes has short hair in this period, but short hair is not characteristic of him. Carpenter has said, too, that it is doubtful whether one would find Dionysos represented nude so early as the 430's.[138] As a matter of fact we do find him on vases not so long after this time, reclining like D on his mantle instead of having it wrapped around him. But again it is a variation, and if we notice the context of these appearances we will see that it is generally out-of-doors among his satyrs and maenads. When he dines in the presence of the other gods or even of human actors, he assumes a more formal guise.[139] The powerfully muscled body of D is so splendidly effective that it must have been meant to be significant. And this powerful physique is not characteristic of Dionysos.

I have left the animal skin until last because it is, after all, the last

135. Hydria in Berlin, 3768 (Schefold, *Kertscher Vasen* pl. 3 b; Ghali-Kahil, *Les Enlèvements et la retour d'Hélène* pl. 15, 3–4; krater in Berlin, F.3182, *ibid.* pl. 29, 3; Von Lücken, *Greek Vase-Painting* (The Hague 1921) pl. 25.

136. See the chronological table of interpretations in Michaelis, *Der Parthenon* 165. The interpretation of E–F as Demeter and Kore preceded that of D as Dionysos, and it was not until 1861 that Lloyd proposed a different identification for E–F while retaining D as Dionysos.

137. Svoronos, *Das Athener Nationalmuseum* pl. 82.

138. *AJA* 66 (1962) 268.

139. See, in addition to the Piraeus relief supra n. 137, Metzger, *Les Représentations dans la céramique attique du 4ème siècle* pls. 13–15 (nude Dionysos with thiasos) and pls. 16, 21 (half-draped, banqueting in company).

thing one notices about the figure. It could be a panther skin or it could be that of a lion. If our recognition of the person depended on which kind of cat it was, the artist would have shown the head, but he expects us to know, by the time we see the big feline paws stick-ing out from under the folded mantle.

There is just one dweller in Olympos for whom the banqueting pose, the heroic nudity, the short hair and the powerful physique are all truly characteristic and that is Herakles. He alone comes nude into the presence of Zeus and the other gods. The nudity of the athlete, the fighter, the laborer is his, and it is the true mark of his identity, the badge of his career. Archaic art, which saw things in moments of successive narration, had Herakles put on a mantle to banquet after his labors,[140] just as he put on a chiton between fights. The classical image of the nude banqueting Herakles embodies the image of the labors along with the immortal repose that they have won.[141]

Herakles turns his back on the Eleusinian goddesses to greet the rising sun, but that does not mean that he has no relation to them. Not only does he share with Persephone the experience of having descended to the Underworld and returned. He was himself initiated into the Eleusinian Mysteries,[142] and the Lesser Mysteries in Agrai were said to have been instituted for his sake.[143] Being a mortal who

140. E.g. the banqueting Herakles of the Andokides amphora. For ar-chaic images of the repose of Herakles, see Metzger, *op. cit.* (supra n. 139) 218–219.

141. He seems to have worn sandals as a further token of rest from his labors. A hole in the left ankle of D was interpreted by Michaelis as an at-tachment for the thyrsos of Dionysos, but others see it much more reason-ably as a fastening for the straps or laces of metal sandals. See Brommer, *Skulpturen* 8. Herakles' club was presumably of bronze, with its lower end resting on the cornice and its upper end in the left hand. Sauer (*AthMitt* 16 [1891] 68 and *AntDenk* I, text to pl. 58 B) mentions green patina that has washed in under the plinth of the figure onto the three setting-tables. This might be partly from the sandals and partly from the club.

142. Mylonas, *Eleusis and the Eleusinian Mysteries* 240.

143. This part of the tradition is less uniform than the fact of Herakles' initiation. Apollodoros, 2.5.12, says that Herakles was initiated by Eumolpos, who first purified him. The purification might involve the Lesser Mysteries, but they are not mentioned. Xenophon, *Hellenika* 6.3.6, says that Triptole-mos initiated Herakles. The institution of the Lesser Mysteries for Herakles is mentioned by Diodoros, 4.14, and a scholion to Aristophanes, *Ploutos* 1013, as well as by Stephanos of Byzantion s.v. "Αγρα καὶ "Αγραι. A Hel-lenistic votive relief found in the bed of the Ilissos has been interpreted by Möbius as the initiation of Herakles into the Lesser Mysteries (Athens N.M. 1778, Skias, *ArchEph* [1894] pl. 7; Möbius, *AthMitt* 60–61 [1935–36] 247ff, pl. 90; Hausmann, *Griechische Weihreliefs* [Berlin 1960] 80 and fig. 47). Two famous Roman reliefs, the Lovatelli Urn and the Torre Nova Sarcophagus, show the purification of Herakles but apparently without

has attained immortality, he is the representative of the human race in the assembly of the gods. What is more natural than that he should sit next to the goddesses who promise a blessed afterlife to mortals?

Just as Brommer has said that Kore as an Underworld goddess has no right to be with the Olympians at the birth of Athena, so he declares that Herakles as a hero would be out of place in the Olympos of the divine birth.[144] The fact that Herakles does actually appear on two archaic vases representing the birth of Athena he explains away by saying that the archaic artist has contaminated the scene with the Introduction of Herakles into Olympos.[145] But we have a more reliable index for this question than either archaic paintings or modern notions of divine etiquette. We do not have to wonder what Pheidias would have done because we have an example of what he actually did. Pausanias names for us most of the gods who were shown in the birth of Aphrodite on the base of the statue of Zeus at Olympia, and Herakles is there together with Athena.[146]

It is Athena, the goddess of work, who made Herakles able to perform his labors. As such she is the wellspring of his immortality. In the archaic vase-paintings it is normally she who introduces him into Olympos. If the archaic artist was really confused when he inserted Herakles into the birth scene, his confusion at least sprang from a valid conviction that Athena and Herakles belong together. The classical artist who expresses in the cosmos of attendant divinities the fullest meaning of the goddess who is being born can have had no motive to omit Herakles, for in him we see the fulfillment of Athena's promise to humankind.

As the day is the time for work, the man who labors faces the rising sun. Herakles greeting Helios as he comes up out of the ocean is not a new invention of Pheidias, for we have it already on black-figured lekythoi of the first half of the fifth century.[147] But there it is a moment on his travels. Here it becomes the illumination of his

---

specific reference to Agrai (Mylonas, *Eleusis* 205–208, figs. 83–84). For representations of the initiation of Herakles on 4th century Attic vases, see Metzger, *op. cit.* (supra n. 139) 237–238.

144. *Skulpturen* 149.
145. *RGZM* 8 (1961) 74. The vases: Amphora, Group E, British Museum B 147; *CVA* pl. 24; Beazley, *Attic Black-Figure Vase-Painters* (hereafter *ABV*) 135, no. 44; *Marburger Winckelmann-Programm* 1960, pl. 5, and Florence 3804, Cook, *Zeus* III, fig. 477, Gerhard, *Auserlesene Vasen-Bilder* I, pl. 5, 2. It probably means something that in both these examples Herakles and Ares are grouped together.
146. Pausanias 5.11.3.
147. Haspels, *Attic Black-Figured Lekythoi* 120–123. She lists five examples. I owe this reference to Otto Brendel, who was also the first to persuade me that the Parthenon figure represents Herakles.

essential nature. To look to the day is as natural to him as for Aphrodite to look to the night.

Helios, the god who comes up with his chariot horses out of the waves, is the only one of the preserved figures from the east pediment about whose identity there can be no mistake. That his female counterpart whose spent horses sink down on the other side must be either Night or the Moon seems equally certain, but the choice between the two is not easy to make. In either case day and night together form the framework of this universe, and the rising of the light above the darkness sets the stage for a mood of exultation. The sheer beauty of the magnificent horses' heads, not less impressive in the sinking than in the rising team, makes us see the two together as a cosmic framework before we think of them in terms of contrast. The separate personalities of the charioteers, however much the lost heads may have emphasized them, will not have prevailed over this sense of community. Light does not banish darkness from the world, for neither can exist without the other.

Aphrodite is not central to the birth of Athena, though without her Athena could never have been born. She reclines facing the waning of the night, neither active nor exhausted, a rich, compelling presence whose beauty is its power. There are so many images of Aphrodite in the late fifth century art of Athens that correspond in dress and attitude to the reclining M that each year's harvest of archaeological discoveries does something to erase the question-mark that has clung to this identification.[148] If we accept the principle that has seemed apparent in all the existing figures we have examined so far, that pose and dress are the main vehicles of the identity of the figures, with attributes playing a secondary role, we are almost forced to accept M as Aphrodite. Within the bounds of Periklean art it would be simply impossible to imagine another figure more appropriate to Aphrodite in these respects than the one we have before us.

The figure, L, in whose lap she reclines is not so closely characterized. She must take her identity from that of Aphrodite. We have found Hera next to Hephaistos and Demeter next to Kore and that is enough to suggest that the person on whose knees Aphrodite rests is her own mother, Dione, especially since the Iliad has given us just such a picture of mother and daughter.[149]

148. For the reclining Aphrodite see especially Langlotz, *Aphrodite in den Gärten* (Sitzb. Heidel. Ak. d. Wiss., Phil.-Hist. Kl., 1953/4, 2). The same draping is transferred to a standing figure in the Aphrodite Doria-Pamfili, from which the Aphrodite in the Agora (supra n. 35) is descended.

149. 5.370-371: ἡ δ᾽ ἐν γούνασι πῖπτε Διώνης δι᾽ ᾽Αφροδίτη, μητρὸς ἐῆς ["But fair Aphrodite flung herself upon the knees of her mother Dione," trans. A. T. Murray].

The other seated figure, K, whose head was preserved in Carrey's time though it is missing now, did not look toward the group of Aphrodite and her mother but toward the center of the pediment. She is the compositional counterpart of the seated Demeter, so we expect next to her a counterpart of the running Artemis. Various scholars have believed that this should be a running Hermes.[150] That would answer our requirements that the pose be characteristic of the person as well as satisfy the demands of the composition. That Hermes should be near Aphrodite is very natural,[151] and we have only to ask what goddess it is that can logically come between them. Pausanias seems to give us the answer when he says that on the Olympia base Hestia came next to Hermes and after her came Eros receiving Aphrodite as she rose from the sea.[152] Hestia is one of the Twelve Gods and it is right that she be present. She appears next to Hermes on the altar of the Twelve Gods from Ostia.[153] Unfortunately she is so infrequently represented in art that we cannot say exactly what clothes she ought to wear. Chiton and himation seem to be usual, though her head is sometimes veiled and sometimes not. We can at least say that the dress of K is more suitable for Hestia than it is for Leto, who normally wears a peplos in this period.

The one thing that is fundamental to the nature of Hestia is that she be seated. On the altar from Ostia she is the only one of the Twelve Gods besides Zeus who is sitting down. There she sits on a kind of round altar with moldings above and below. An actual hearth would make a seat too low to accord with the dignity of this goddess, which seems to be her most valued possession.[154] It is too bad that the object on which K sits is not well enough preserved for us to be sure of its shape. It is generally said that K is sitting, like L and M, on a "rocky seat," but there does not seem to be any surface left that preserves the characteristic bumpy stylization of rocks such as we find on the seats of L–M and of west U. A smoother form, suggesting some kind of built clay or stone platform, would seem more appropriate to the household goddess than the irregular shape of the natural rock.

There is a kind of inherent correspondence between Demeter and Hestia that makes them suitable counterparts in the composition, and the same is true of Artemis and Hermes in their common function

150. See Carpenter, *Hesperia* 2 (1933) 18; Buschor, *ArchEph* (1937) 455; *Phidias der Mensch* 36.
151. Cf. *Agora* XI, p. 138.
152. 5.11.8.
153. *Annuario* n.s. 1–2 (1939–40) pls. 3–4.
154. Cf. Homeric Hymn V, 29–30.

as Propylaioi, a title which Artemis gains from her identification
with Hekate.[155] The close association between Hermes and Hestia
is not based simply, as Becatti has suggested, on delight in the contrast between the sedentary goddess of the fixed abode and the cease-
lessly mobile messenger of the gods.[156] Their functions were more
closely related. Hermes protects the entrance door of every house
as Hestia guards its hearth. Especially to the Athenians of the fifth
century this protective aspect of Hermes, embodied in the Attic
herm [an image, common in Greece, in the form of a stone pillar
surmounted by a head of Hermes], was deeply familiar and strongly
felt.[157] If news of the birth of Athena comes from the outside world
to the hearths of men, it must come via Hermes. We cannot help
feeling that these running figures really are bearers of tidings as well
as gods whose nature is to run. The side of Artemis that includes
Hekate is strengthened thereby, for it was Hekate who first brought
Demeter news of her daughter.[158]

When all these relationships are so satisfactory, it seems only
reasonable to proceed on the assumption that the corner figures have
been correctly identified. Nothing seems more natural, once G is
accepted as Artemis, than to believe with Buschor that next to her
came a seated, lyre-playing Apollo and a standing figure of Leto.[159]
Apollo playing his lyre is a frequent figure in vase-paintings of the
birth of Athena and his normal place is behind the throne of Zeus,
that is, in the left-hand side of the picture. Leto is identified by an
inscription in one of the vase-paintings and may possibly be present
in others.[160] The tendency that we have already observed to show
mothers with their children would lead us to expect her, especially
since she so often forms a triad with her children in votive reliefs.[161]

155. Pausanias 1.38.6 mentions a temple of Artemis Propylaia at Eleusis.
The present temple is of Roman date, but the identification of Artemis with
Hekate goes back to the 5th century. See supra n. 126.
156. *Annuario* 1-2 (1939-40) 112.
157. See *Agora* XI, 108-122.
158. Homeric Hymn II, 52-58.
159. *ArchEph* (1037) 456; *Phidias der Mensch* 99: "den sitzenden Leier-
spieler Apollon, die stehende Leto darf man hier, von der gleichen Hand
gemeisselt, vermuten" ["one may suppose that the seated Apollo playing
the lyre and the standing Leto were carved by the same hand"].
160. Cook, *Zeus* III, fig. 491; *ABV* p. 96, 13; Brommer, *RGZM* 8
(1961) 76.
161. Athens, N.M. 1380, Svoronos *Das Athener Nationalmuseum*, pl. 49;
N.M. 1389, Süsserott, *Griechische Plastik des 4. Jahrhunderts vor Christus*
(Frankfurt am Main 1938) pl. 13, 4, Svoronos, *op. cit.* pl. 54; N.M. 1400,
ibid. pl. 60; N.M. 1892, *ibid.* pl. 95; relief in Dresden from Miletos, Hausmann, *Griechische Weihreliefs* fig. 34; relief in Museo Barracco, *Enciclo-
pedia dell' arte antica* IV, p. 503, fig. 590.

The floor in blocks 8 and 9 would accommodate two such figures very well [text fig. 60]. Carpenter had given the greater part of these two blocks to a single figure, his profile seated Fate, [162] but since Brommer has shown that the Artemis was placed diagonally and overlapped very little into the block to the north of her [163] [text fig. 56], the already wide gap between her and Carpenter's figure would become intolerable. Also, a profile seated figure extending from block 8 into block 9 would have to press its legs closer to the tympanon than the rest of its body,[164] and that would be out of harmony with the placement of all the figures we have looked at so far. We must ask, then, how a seated figure would fit into block 8. The slanting line near the front of the block that is easy to see in Balanos' and Brommer's photographs as well as in Carpenter's drawing suggests that the front edge of the plinth came very close to the edge of the cornice in the north part of the block. The dowel hole in the edge of the cutting for G is too far outside the boundary of the plinth of G to belong to that statue. It must have belonged to the one in block 8. Probably it marks the edge of the statue or nearly so, for the floor is heavily patinated beyond this point.

Actually, there is nothing about the floor-marks to prove that this was a seated rather than a standing statue, but a seated figure would give more variety to the composition and would focus attention on Apollo as the central member of the triad. Buschor assumed a seated Apollo, and we find Apollo seated between Artemis and Leto on the early fourth-century votive relief dedicated by the son of Bakchios.[165] The scale would present a problem, for the seated figure would neecssarily be considerably larger than its neighbor to the south. The break in scale from the charioteer G in the West Pediment to the figure north of her is analogous to what would have happened here. But there the charioteer is divine and the next figure human, which makes the break permissible. Apollo could reasonably be somewhat larger than his sister, but the scale should not be so discrepant that he appeared to belong to another order of beings.

It may be that we have the evidence for how this problem was

162. Carpenter, *Hesperia* 2 (1933) 25–28. See especially the detailed drawing of the floor-marks on blocks 8 and 9, p. 26, fig. 5.

163. Brommer, *AthMitt* 73 (1958) 107–109, Beil. 76; *Skulpturen* 12–13.

164. The edge of a bedding, the patination in front of this bedding and a pry-hole in front of the patinated area all show that the south end of block 9 was uncovered for a space of 30–35 cm. from the front edge of the cornice. This is clearest in Carpenter's drawing, *Hesperia* 2 (1933) 26, fig. 5, but it is clear also in Balanos, pl. 110 and Sauer, *AntDenk* I, pl. 58 B.

165. N.M. 1389. See supra n. 161. A seated Apollo between standing figures is also to be found on the votive relief of Xenokrateia, Athens N.M. 2756, Svoronos pl. 181.

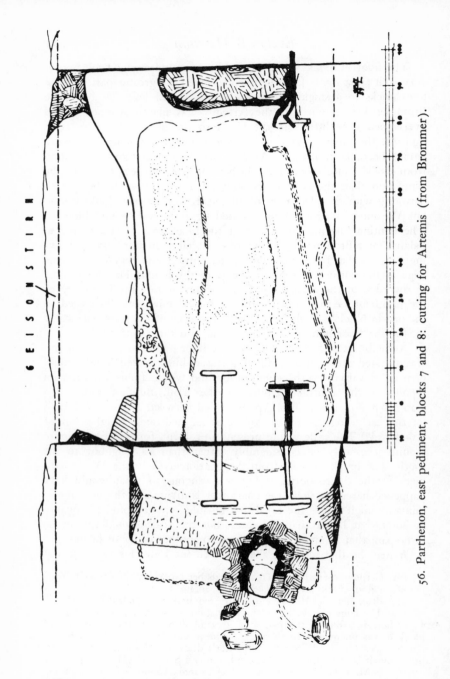

GEISONSTIRN

56. Parthenon, east pediment, blocks 7 and 8: cutting for Artemis (from Brommer).

solved. The fact that the plinth of G was sunk into the pediment floor could well be explained by the desire to give Artemis as large a scale as possible in her position. A substantial plinth was needed in order to give enough stability to the running pose, but by sinking it into the floor one could reserve all the clear height for the figure. This is a more likely explanation than that the statue unexpectedly proved too tall for its place.[166] The excessive length and breadth of the cutting indicate that it was prepared ahead of time, before the exact placement of the statue became known. If this is so, one might imagine that the discrepancy in scale between the brother and sister would be further reduced by giving the seated Apollo an unusually high plinth.

In fact there is one fragment that has been attributed to the Parthenon in recent years which shows such a high plinth [text figs. 57–59]. I had myself doubted whether this piece could belong to the pediments, but the more closely one examines it the more genuinely suitable it appears in every way for this place in the composition. If we accept it as belonging to the pediments at all, this is the one place where it can go, and at the moment I am strongly inclined to accept it. It is Acropolis 6713, a severely weathered fragment that preserves part of the lower legs and plinth of a large seated figure wearing chiton and himation. Both feet are missing and were attached separately. The plinth beneath the right foot is 0.24 m. high and the left foot is set 0.05 m. higher.[167] The left shin slants outward so that the knees will have been farther apart than the feet. On the proper right side, which is desperately weathered and battered, one can make out a straight line that seems to be the underside of a chair or stool.

The fragment was identified by Wegner as belonging to the Parthenon and assigned by him to the female charioteer G of the West Pediment.[168] Since it does not correspond in either pose or dress to Carrey's drawing of this figure, Berger [169] and Brommer [170] rightly rejected this attribution and suggested a place somewhere in the East

---

166. Carpenter assumed, *Hesperia* 2 (1933) 25, that the statue "could not be moved sufficiently far toward the left because of interference between the head and the raking cornice. . . . To remedy the error in height, the statue was rolled away and a bed to a depth of 0.05 m. scooped out of the pediment floor."

167. In the present setting in the Acropolis Museum the plinth is unfortunately sunk into the base, so that its full height is no longer visible.

168. *Festschrift Schweitzer* (Stuttgart 1954) 185–191.

169. *Parthenon-Ostgiebel* 52–53.

170. *Skulpturen* 97–98, no. 8, with list of scholars' opinions. Add Jeppesen, *ActaA* 34 (1963) 72. His estimate of the height is impossibly small.

57. Fragment of Apollo (?). Athens, Acropolis Museum.

58. Fragment of Apollo (?). Athens, Acropolis Museum.

59. Fragment of Apollo (?). Athens, Acropolis Museum.

Pediment.[171] Brommer cautiously refrained from suggesting what the place should be. Berger argued unconvincingly that the piece ought to be seen, not from three-quarters right, as others had advocated and as he himself showed it in one of his variant reconstructions, but from three-quarters left. His final decision was to give it to Hestia (whom he did not see in K), but he admitted himself in the text that the proportions seemed small for the position in block 16 where he had set her.[172] The drawing in his plate I clearly shows this, since the legs are obviously too small for the figure in which they are incorporated.

The height of the original statue can be calculated approximately by comparison with the Apollo on the Mantinea base at about 2.02 m.[173] That would fit snugly into block 8, where the cornice height runs from 2.03 m. to 2.28 m. It would fit with more headroom in block 9 but there is not footroom for it there because the patination shows that the front of the block was uncovered. The other side of the pediment is excluded because the figure would be facing the wrong way or, as in Berger's reconstruction, would present the wrong side to the audience. So it seems impossible that the piece was further elevated by a "Zwischenstück" some 10 cm. thick inserted between the already thick plinth and the floor. Wegner [174] postulated such a piece because there is a cutting like a small dowel hole in the underside of the plinth of Acropolis 6713. This small cutting, 0.025 m. square and 0.05 m. deep, is not near the edge of the plinth and can only have been used for a dowel if there was a pour-channel in the surface on which it rested. Since there are no such pour-channels anywhere in the floors of the Parthenon pediments, we must assume one of four things: (a) Acropolis 6713 does not belong

171. An attribution to the West Pediment seems excluded by the fact that the figure does not correspond with any shown by Carrey, and the one missing figure, U*, had not enough headroom to incorporate the fragment with its high plinth. The piece was lying in front of the west end of the temple before 1900 (Brommer, *loc. cit.* supra n. 170) but there is no record of where it was excavated. The extremely weathered condition makes it seem probable that it was once buried and then excavated and left lying out in the open. Excavated marble weathers much faster than that which has never been buried.

172. *Parthenon-Ostgiebel* 56.

173. The underside of the knee (i.e. the top of the seat) is 0.60 m. above the plinth. The proportion of this length to the total height in seated figures varies considerably, but a survey of typical Attic grave and votive reliefs shows that the total height is generally under rather than over three times this length. If it is more than three, the lower legs look disproportionately short. 1.80 m. + 0.25 = 2.05 m. might therefore count as a reasonable maximum height for the figure.

174. *Festschrift Schweitzer* 189–190.

to the Parthenon pediments, (b) there was an additional member between the plinth and the floor, (c) the cutting is not a dowel-hole, or (d) the cutting belongs to a reuse of the stone. I formerly preferred (a),[175] but as I have become persuaded of the Parthenonian character of the fragment, I feel that we can only choose between (c) and (d). There is no structural logic in inserting a thin plaque of marble under such a heavy piece and doweling the two together with an unusually small dowel. The slightness of this dowel suggests the possibility of some kind of preliminary fastening in the workshop. Otherwise, the hole might come from some kind of reuse.

If the problem of the "dowel-hole" is thus dismissed, there seems to be no real obstacle to taking Acropolis 6713 as part of our Apollo. The lyre-playing Apollo still appears with the linen chiton under the himation in vase-painting of this period,[176] and something stiff and heavy about the form of the preserved leg that was vaguely disturbing so long as the statue was considered to be female becomes right and proper once we recognize it as male.

Buschor suggested reasonably that we would expect to find Apollo and Leto carved by the same master as the running Artemis G.[177] If we examine Acropolis 6713 with a sympathetic eye that restores as clear ridges what the weathering has reduced to feeble intimations of lines, especially in the nearly obliterated folds over the right shin, we see that not only does the fragment have much in common with G but the lines of the two figures, if they were placed side by side, would complement each other in a most satisfactory way. The long related lines that radiate from behind the right knee and curve down over the shin to rise again in the direction of the left knee would echo the long curves in the skirt of the running maiden, and the forked folds, one above the other, between the legs of Apollo find their response in a pair of forked folds in the overfall of Artemis. "Modelling lines" and "motion lines," to borrow Carpenter's phraseology,[178] have been combined into an intelligible unity.

If we look at the fragment simply from the point of view of choosing the angle from which it looks best, we realize that the intended aspect was probably more profile than we see in the angle views published by Wegner and Brommer [text fig. 58]. (Brommer's

175. *AJA* 60 (1956) 303f.
176. E.g. the Apollo on the kalyx-krater by the Peleus Painter from Spina, Alfieri and Arias, *Spina* (Munich 1958) pls. 90–92; *ARV*² 1038, no. 1, and the Apollo on the volute krater by Polion in New York, Richter and Hall, no. 154, *ARV*² 1171, no. 2.
177. Supra n. 159.
178. *Greek Sculpture* (Chicago 1960) 124–151.

is better lighted and seen from a little higher up, but the angle of revolution is about the same in the two.) A comparison with one of the seated Athenas from the Nike Parapet is instructive.[179] Broad triangular surfaces in the folds between the legs that one sees when one views the slab edge on melt into luminous edges backed by shadow in the intended profile view. The vertical chiton folds on our fragment are also helpful. Berger remarked quite truly that the spacing of the folds between the feet is excessively wide when one sees them head on [180] [text fig. 59]. That of the folds on the outside of the right ankle is narrower. One has to revolve the piece until the disparity is lost.

It is clear that the "Artemis Master," as Buschor would call him, thinks as a relief sculptor even though he follows the general design of the pediment in placing his figures diagonally. This relief-like quality in Acropolis 6713 is the strongest argument for its belonging to a pedimental figure rather than to a freestanding monument.

What we have observed about the optimum angle of view for Acropolis 6713 accords very well with what we see on the pediment floor [181] [text fig. 60]. The outside trace of the plinth runs at an angle of about 10° to the front edge of the cornice and the plinth was clearly wider than it was deep. A nearly profile seated figure with feet close together is just what is called for. The outer edge of the plinth seems to be a straight line and this suggests that the platform on which the seat rested as well as the seat itself had some kind of squared form, i.e. was not an irregular mass of rock. The seat itself could be any sort of rectangular *diphros* [seat]. What of the platform? Berger correctly remarked that a plinth so high in proportion to its statue must have been significant iconographically as well as structurally, but his restoration as Hestia was not a very happy solution.

It may be that Wegner, the student of Greek music, has suggested the right answer even though he himself rejected it. In interpreting the fragment as part of a charioteer, he said that the figure was not mounting a bema [platform], as for example the auletes on the Euphronios krater in Paris.[182] We have a number of pictures of cithara-players standing on such a bema. I do not know any of a seated cithara-player on a bema, but it does not seem at all unreasonable that the seated player should also be elevated above his audience.

179. Carpenter, *Sculpture of the Nike Temple Parapet* pls. 19 and 21, 3.
180. *Parthenon-Ostgiebel* 55.
181. See Carpenter, Balanos and Sauer, *loc. cit.* (supra n. 164).
182. *Festschrift Schweitzer* 186.

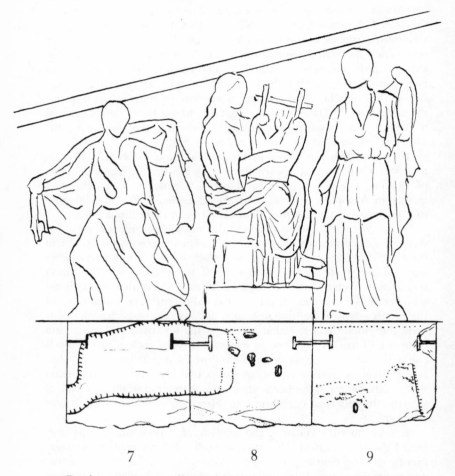

7   8   9

60. Parthenon, east pediment, blocks 7–9: Artemis, Apollo, Leto. Floor after Carpenter. Scale approx. 1:40.

Apollo and Orpheus when they give concerts in the wilderness seem to sit on unusually high rocks.[183] The high straight-sided plinth of our statue will have suggested rather than depicted the musician's platform. The little step under the left foot would have to represent

183. Apollo: Mantinea base; Orpheus: column-krater by the Orpheus Painter in Berlin, Pfuhl fig. 554, *ARV*[2] 1103, no. 1.

some kind of low footstool or prop on which Apollo set his left foot but not his right.[184] Its form was probably unobtrusive. Both feet may well have projected beyond the surface on which they rested, so that their being made separately was a genuine economy in the vertically grained marble block. The extent of the platform will have had to be restricted, not only because of the great weight it would have added to the statue but because the floor space was limited. The plinth of G extended only about 10 cm. into block 8 and there is nothing to prevent our thinking that Apollo's plinth in its final position somewhat overlapped the preliminary cutting for G, especially since there is no marked change of color on the floor outside the cutting to suggest the south edge of the plinth. It is clear, however, that the plinth did not extend over into block 9, even though some part of the figure may have overhung it. The patination in the front part of block 9, like that in the back part of 8, indicates an uncovered area. There will have been, therefore, not more than about 0.95 m. available for the longest side of the plinth, even if it formed, as both the floor-markings and the position of the feet on our fragments suggest it did, a somewhat acute angle at the right front corner. If we make a rough calculation of the probable depth of the seated figure on the basis of a human model in a comparable pose, it appears that it would be a little over 96 cm. including the feet. This does not allow for any projection of the seat and plinth behind the back of the hips of the figure, but a little such projection is usual. The reason for the separately attached overhanging feet is therefore apparent. As in the Apollo of the Mantinea base, the detachment of the feet from the ground will have called attention to the elevated place of the citharist. That Apollo is shown in a setting reminiscent of the Odeion and the contest rather than of Parnassos or Helikon is probably again a way of showing the influence of Athena, to whom nothing wild belongs. To see a specific reference to the Panathenaia might be farfetched, but as an overtone it would be rich in implications.[185]

184. A relief in the Athens National Museum that depicts Asklepios (N.M. 1388, Svoronos pl. 53) shows a quite similar relative position of the feet. A direct influence from our pedimental figure would be by no means impossible. It might explain the curious treatment in the relief of the vertical folds behind the left foot of Asklepios, which must logically belong to Hygieia's dress but look as if they belong to him. For another example of a seated *musician* with the left foot higher than the right cf. the kylix from Spina connected with the Fauvel Painter, Alfieri and Arias, *Spina* pl. 113; *ARV²* 1286.

185. J. A. Davison, *JHS* 78 (1958) 33–41, suggests that Perikles reinstituted the contests for performers on the cithara and aulos in the Panathenaia about 450 and at the same time put the Odeion into shape.

We can see now why the seated Apollo required a dowel in the left rear corner. Not being one of the solidly seated frontal figures on a low broad seat but rather a high-perched relief-like statue in profile that was much less deep than wide and less than half as wide as it was high, its proportions more resembled those of a standing or striding figure. Wegner's fragment fits the requirements of the space, subject-matter, and style so peculiarly well that its attribution seems virtually certain.

Leto is harder to visualize, and if fragments of her exist they will be harder to identify. She is not a strongly characterized person, and her iconography seems to be influenced by that of Hera. Commonly she wears the peplos, most often with kolpos and overfall but sometimes girded over a long overfall. Her head is sometimes covered, sometimes not. Usually she stands quietly. Occasionally she sits. If we look at the floor in block 9, we find it easy to imagine that here she was a more or less frontally standing figure, placed back against the tympanon like the running figure F in the West Pediment who meditates between the charioteer and the seated groups. The trace that suggests the front edge of a plinth is the same distance, ca. 0.55–0.50 m., in front of the tympanon in each case.[186] As with west F, there are no clear marks on the floor to indicate the lateral limits of the plinth. One has the impression that it was broader than a simply standing figure would need, though not nearly so extensive as that of the running Artemis. Berger, who put Hebe here, set her in gentle motion,[187] and Sauer called for a striding figure.[188] Neither would do for Leto.

It is when we ask, as the artist must have done, how the motion of the running Artemis could be picked up in a standing figure that forms the third member of the triad, that we see what the solution must have been. The relief in Stockholm which copies figures from the base of the Nemesis at Rhamnous shows standing peplos figures whose mantles, spread out behind them, form gentle flourishes of gracefully swinging folds.[189] Our running Artemis, G, held out her mantle behind her, with the left arm raised and apparently bent, the right arm lowered and more extended. The middle figure of the

186. Cf. Sauer, *AntDenk* I, pls. 58 A (right half of block 8) and 58 B (left half of block 9).
187. *Parthenon-Ostgiebel* 45–46, pls. 11a and 11b (with more movement in a than b).
188. *AthMitt* 16 (1891) 88; *Weber-Laborde'sche Kopf* 93–96: "nicht ein eiliges, sondern ein verweilendes Schreiten" ["a stride not hurried, but lingering"].
189. Kjellberg, *Studien zu den attischen Reliefs des v. Jahrhunderts v. Chr.* (Uppsala 1926) pl. 7. Becatti, *Problemi Fidiaci* fig. 20.

Stockholm relief likewise held up the mantle with the bent left arm, and her right arm was lowered and extended. If our Leto had such a mantle held in a somewhat similar fashion, the gestures of her arms could have echoed those of Artemis with the same sort of subtle response and variation that we find in the running Artemis and standing Leto of the beautiful homeless metope in the Villa Albani formerly attributed to Rhamnous.[190] Probably our Leto also, like these two figures, should have had the weight on the right leg, so that the curved folds swinging out to the left foot would have been in harmony with the swinging folds of Artemis' skirt and the dipping lines of Apollo's himation. The left foot would then have been set back somewhat, as on the standing Demeter in Eleusis which is like a translation of the Nemesis figure into the round. All this fits the traces on the pediment floor.[191] We see on the Eleusis statue how the plinth is extended to the side to give support to the hanging mantle, which would account for the extra breadth of Leto's plinth.[192] Possibly the back of the mantle was cut flat to rest against the tympanon like that of G and so helped stabilize the statue without any need for doweling. Later Attic statues such as the Eleusis Demeter and the Aphrodite of Fréjus which show a curious combination of three-dimensional stance and flat back may owe more than we have realized to such pedimental figures. If all this is so, the Leto of the Parthenon like the Artemis will have stood near the head of a beautiful company of late fifth century figures. Buschor was surely right to lament her loss.

The scale of Leto could have been the same as that of Apollo, in the normal proportion of female to male.[193] On the opposite side of

190. Langlotz, *Scritti in onore di B. Nogara* 225, pl. 21; Dinsmoor, *Hesperia* 30 (1961) 199–203, pl. 32 d; S. Karouzou, *AthMitt* 77 (1962) 182, Beil, 50, 1. Mme Karouzou ignores rather than contradicts Dinsmoor's demonstration that the metope is too small to have belonged to the temple at Rhamnous. Meanwhile, Dinsmoor's measurements of the relief have been independently confirmed by others (B. Schlörb, *Untersuchungen zur Bildhauergeneration nach Phidias* [Waldsassen/Bayern 1964] 58 n. 39). The Artemis of the metope is similar in dress and movement to our Artemis of the Parthenon, and once again direct influence seems possible. It is hard to agree with the opinion of Miss Schlörb (*loc. cit.*) that the style of the relief might be South Italian.

191. Brunn-Bruckmann 536. Schefold, *Festschrift R. Boehringer* 564, figs. 28 and 29.

192. The bedding line is farthest forward near the south edge of block 9 where the right foot would have been. The inset right foot of the Demeter is interesting as one of the few 5th century parallels for the inset feet of the Parthenon Apollo.

193. The cornice height will have been around 2.34 m. where the head of the statue should have come. If the figure, not counting plinth, was 2.20

the pediment, in the place symmetrical to that of Apollo, i.e. in block 18,[194] there is an irregular bedding which Carpenter reads as the outline of a rocky seat.[195] This is indeed what it resembles, and that leads us to look for another profile seated figure. Carpenter suggested that the advanced left foot of the statue was made separately and rested on the front part of the cornice in block 17. This seems perfectly possible and would be aesthetically satisfactory. Carpenter took this figure for a seated Apollo, and used his cithara to fill the space above the outstretched leg [text fig. 38]. But we have found Apollo on the other side, and such an inanimate space-filler seems rather inadequate for the richly plastic composition that we have been discovering. It is much easier to assume, as Sauer, Furtwängler, Cook and Berger [196] have done, that there was a separate statue in the north part of block 17. Placed close to the tympanon, such a figure would permit the extended leg of the seated person to overlap it, and it would be symmetrical to our Leto of the other side.

Carpenter objects that if there had been another statue there would have been another pry-hole and perhaps another dowel, but we have seen a larger statue set in block 11 without any dowel or pry-hole. The statues which rested on iron bars *had* to be set without prying, and the same method could presumably have been used for statues that did not rest on bars.[197]

Carpenter also says, "a statue occupying only the right half of 17 and the small part of 18 to the left of the pry-hole would be only 0.60 m. wide even if it touched both its neighbors, while the cornice height here ranges from 2.26 to 2.42 m. and these are practically impossible proportions for a statue to assume." If we turn again to the Erechtheion caryatids, however, we find that such proportions would not be impossible for a frontally standing female figure in a quiet pose. Even if one allows less than Carpenter's 20 cm. allowance (10

---

m. high, and if we assume 7.4 head-heights in the standing figure, the head will have measured 0.297 m. (up to 0.31 m. if the proportions were stockier, 7:1, which is still possible for the Parthenon). Apollo's head-height should be one-half or at most a little more than one-half the measurable distance from ground to top of seat (0.61 m.), so 0.305 m. or a little more.

194. The most detailed record of blocks 17–18 is given by Carpenter, *Hesperia* 2 (1933) 19, fig. 2, but this should be supplemented by Sauer, *AntDenk* I, pl. 58 B, Balanos pl. 113 and Brommer, *Skulpturen* pl. 16, 1 and 2.

195. *Hesperia* 2 (1933) 21.

196. See supra n. 72.

197. Prying was doubtless most needed when the head of a statue came higher than the drip of the cornice in front of it, so that it had to be eased into position from the side.

cm. for plinth and 10 cm. for headroom, which is a bit too generous by usual Parthenon standards), taking a height of, say, 2.20 m. (2.34 m. cornice height minus 0.08 m. for plinth and 0.06 m. for headroom) we find that the maximum plinth width of 0.60 m. goes into it 3.6 times. The caryatids from top of plinth to bottom of bead and reel (this would be about where the crown of the head would come) measure ca. 2.10 m. Their widths at the lower edge of the kolpos on the side measure from 0.544 to 0.539 m., and this is in each case more than the width of the bottom of the skirt. But 0.544 m. goes 3.8 times into 2.10 m., so that our figure need not be quite so narrow as the caryatids.

Also the plinth can have been wider at the back. Sauer records the slanting edge of a bedding close to the north edge of the big bedding in the south part of the block, and though Carpenter does not show it, it seems to be visible in Brommer's photograph. There is no clear mark of the front line of the plinth unless we take it to have extended all the way to the front edge of the cornice, where Sauer again marks a bedding line. In this case, it will have narrowed toward the front to leave uncovered the patinated area in the front north corner of the block.[198] That seems like an unwieldy shape, however, and it is probably better to take this line as Carpenter does for the separately made plinth of the advanced left foot of the statue in block 18. It doubtless seemed well to load block 17 as lightly as possible, since the large plinth of the group carried by the iron bar in block 16 extended a good way into it. Making the leg in a separate piece would save weight as well as being economical of marble. A seated figure with one foot extended would be quite wasteful if carved from a single block.

Who should these two figures be? The seated person was apparently not raised on a high plinth like the Apollo and therefore should be larger in scale than his neighbors. Carpenter has argued for a lightly draped male figure. These specifications fit particularly well the one missing god who traditionally faces Athena in the vase-paintings depicting her birth.[199] This is Ares, with whom she shared a cult as Athena Areia.[200] The associations of Ares with the Areopagus

198. Cf. Carpenter, *Hesperia* 2 (1933) 20.
199. Brommer, *RGZM* 8 (1961) pls. 24–27, 30, 31, 35.2. On the amphora in Richmond, Virginia, where Athena is frontal, Ares is to the right of the picture.
200. Pausanias saw an altar of Athena Areia on the Areopagus (1.28.5) which was said to have been founded by Orestes after his acquittal. In the Temple of Ares in the Athenian Agora Pausanias mentions two statues of Aphrodite and one of Athena. This temple was moved in Roman times, and the evidence suggests that it was moved from outside the city, from

make it natural that he be seated on a rock. The reference may be not only in a general way to the rocky hill itself but specifically to the unwrought stones on which accused and accuser sat in trials on the Areopagus.[201] Ares himself was tried there for the murder of Poseidon's son, Halirrhothios.

Generally speaking, there are two female figures with whom Ares might be paired, his consort Aphrodite and his sister Hebe. Aphrodite is here ruled out, because we have identified her in the reclining M who faces away from Athena, but this need not surprise us. The gigantomachy of the Altar of Zeus at Pergamon places Ares and Ahprodite back to back at the northeast corner, with Ares facing Athena and Aphrodite facing the gods of the night.[202] This, like so much else in the great frieze, may well be influenced by the Parthenon pediment.

The connection of Hebe with Ares is tenuous so far as myth and cult are concerned but gains force with the increasingly abstract treatment of all these divinities as personifications of areas of human life.[203] Ares and Hebe are brother and sister in Hesiod,[204] and in the Iliad Hebe bathes her brother after he has been wounded.[205] But the cult connections of Hebe are with Hera and with Herakles rather than with Ares.[206] Yet Ares and Hebe are linked in meaning. It is the youth of the country that goes to war, and older men need the strength of youth when they have to fight. So Iolaos in the *Herakleidai* of Euripides prays Hebe to restore his youth for one day so that he can win the war.[207] On this basis P. N. Boulter has

---

Acharnai according to a plausible suggestion of H. A. Thompson (*AJA* 66 [1962] 200). If it was from Acharnai, Athena Areia will have been the original *paredros* [companion] of Ares, and the two statues of Aphrodite will have been added later, perhaps only in Roman times.

201. Pausanias 1.28.5.

202. *Altertümer von Pergamon* III, 2, Beil. 2–3; Evamaria Schmidt, *Der grosse Altar zu Pergamon* (Leipzig 1961) Beil. I.

203. Of all the principal Olympian gods, Ares is the one who is most like a personification (cf. Nilsson, *Geschichte der griechischen Religion* I² 518–519).

204. *Theogony*, 921: ἣ δ' ῞Ηβην καὶ ῎Αρηα καὶ Εἰλείθυιαν ἔτικτε ["(Hera) brought forth Hebe, Ares, and Eilithyia," trans. Hugh G. Evelyn-White].

205. *Iliad* 5.904–5:
ὣς ἄρα καρπαλίμως ἰήσατο θοῦρον ῎Αρηα.
τὸν δ' ῞Ηβη λοῦσεν, χαρίεντα δὲ εἵματα ἔσσεν.
["Even so swiftly (Paeëon) healed furious Ares. And Hebe bathed him and clad him in beautiful raiment," trans. A. T. Murray.]

206. Hebe was worshipped with Hera in the Argive Heraion and she had an altar in Athens in the Herakleion at Kynosarges (Judeich, *Topographie von Athen*² 423).

207. *Herakleidai* 851 ff.

tentatively identified as Hebe the akroterion from the fifth century
temple of Ares,[208] which was moved into the Agora of Athens in
the Roman period, but which was perhaps originally built at Acharnai. In the fourth century we find inscriptions at Acharnai at-
testing to a cult of Ares and Athena Areia.[209] Athena Areia
was worshipped at Plataiai (where Pheidias made her cult statue),
and this cult, described as instituted after Marathon, may have been
the source of the one at Acharnai.[210] The priest of Ares and Athena
Areia at Acharnai in the fourth century had the oath of the Athenian
ephebes carved together with the so-called Oath of Plataiai on a
stele in the sanctuary. The *ephebeia* did not yet exist as an institution
in the time of the Parthenon, but one has only to look at the young
cavalrymen of the Panathenaic frieze to see how far youth was
identified with the strength of the city.

It is possible that Ares and Hebe are represented in a class of
Attic votive reliefs that have been variously interpreted in the past. A
woman pours out wine for a warrior into a libation bowl. The fact
that the reliefs are votive is made clear by the presence of worshippers
on a smaller scale. The warrior is in hoplite armor with cuirass and
shield. Sometimes there is an altar. The woman is dressed either as a
young girl or as a bride, both types that are proper to Hebe, though
they are shared with other goddesses, especially Hygieia.

Three of these belong closely together, and it may be that a careful search would reveal more.[211] All are Attic in style and seem to
belong to the first half of the fourth century. One is in the Louvre,
one in Venice and one in Palermo. All have been known for a long
time. The one in Venice has traditionally been called Ares and Aphrodite and is still so named in the guide book. Furtwängler[212] and
Deneken,[213] however, objected to this, preferring to regard the
warrior as a hero. Furtwängler did not name the woman. Deneken
called her the wife of the hero. This does not work, however, for the

208. *Hesperia* 22 (1953) 141–147.
209. L. Robert, *Études épigraphiques et philologiques* (Paris 1938) 292–
316; G. Daux, *Orlandos Festschrift* (1965) 78–90, pls. I–IV.
210. Kirsten, *RE* 20 (1950) 2326, s.v. Plataiai.
211. 1. Paris, Louvre, *Catalogue sommaire des marbres antiques* (Paris
1922) 45, no. 742. From Greece via the Nointel Collection.
2. Venice, Tamaro, *Il Museo Archeologico del Palazzo Reale di Venezia*
(Rome 1930) 30, no. 7. Grimani Collection.
3. Palermo, Arndt-Amelung, *Einzelaufnahmen* no. 562. From Athens.
All three reliefs are mentioned by Deneken in Roscher's *Lexikon*, s.v.
Heros, col. 2562 as hero reliefs.
212. *Sammlung Sabouroff* I, *Skulpturen*, Einleitung 39, n. 11; *AthMitt*
8 (1883) 370.
213. *Loc. cit.* (supra n. 211).

Palermo relief, in which she wears the open peplos of a young girl with the right leg visible to the knee. No wife would be so dressed. On this relief a small Nike flies toward the warrior. The worshippers are a man and a young boy.

The identification of the warrior as Ares is made more likely by the relief on the decree from Acharnai which provides for building the altar of Ares and Athena Areia.[214] Athena is crowning a frontally standing warrior in hoplite armor who is as tall as she is. The content of the decree calls for Ares, and the size of the warrior proves that he is a god.[215]

The fact that the worshippers in these votive reliefs are always male may be important, though one would like to have more than three examples in order to be sure. The usual hero reliefs have worshippers of both sexes.[216] A connection with the preparation of Athenian boys for citizenship and military service seems not unlikely. Men and boys also appear on votive reliefs to Herakles and Theseus, which likewise show the style of the early fourth century.[217]

Hermes, who comes next to Ares in the pediment, is the special patron of the gymnasium and becomes the special patron of ephebes. The combination Hebe-Ares-Hermes [text fig. 61], though not a cult triad like Leto-Apollo-Artemis, would still have a definite meaning for the Athenians as representing the flower of Athenian youth trained for the defense of their country. If Poseidon and Amphitrite attest to the greatness of Athenian sea power, Hebe, Ares and Hermes personify the strength, especially the defensive strength, of the land forces. As such they rightly come between the sea (Amphitrite) and the hearth (Hestia). So we have on the side of Athena in the pediment a panorama of the military greatness of Athens.

In the opposite wing, where the key figure is Hephaistos, we seem to have rather the products of Athens, spiritual as well as material.

214. Robert, op. cit. supra n. 209, pl. 1; G. Daux, Orlandos Festschrift (1965) 87–90.

215. When Athena crowns a human individual or representative of a Tribe he is shown smaller than she. See Walter, Reliefs im kleinen Akropolismuseum nos. 38, 55.

216. Cf. the relief to the Hero Aleximachos from Tanagra in Berlin, Blümel, Katalog III, K 112, where the whole family appears. This is a good example of the kind of libation scene that suggested that our reliefs represented a hero.

217. Süsserott, Griechische Plastik des 4. Jahrh. B.C. pl. 14, 2 and 3, pl. 16, 4; Venice, Tamaro, op. cit. (supra n. 211) p. 13, no. 11, ill. p. 53.

There is one figure still missing in our reconstruction and there is just one major deity who commonly appears in vase-paintings of the birth of Athena and is still not represented.[218] This is Dionysos, whose chief festival was second only to the Panathenaia and whose gifts were of prime importance for the life of Attica. The Oath of the Ephebes calls to witness, besides the gods of war and the borders of the state, πυροί, κριθαί, ἄμπελοι, ἐλάαι, συκαῖ [wheat, barley, grape vines, olive trees, fig trees].[219] The πυροί and κριθαί belong to De-meter, the ἐλάαι to Athena. Ἄμπελοι and συκαῖ are gifts of Dionysos.

To place Dionysos here accords better with the vase-paintings, in which he is one of the more frequently occurring figures, than would a position on the outskirts of the scene. The symmetry with Amphi-trite is repeated on the great altar at Pergamon,[220] and once again it is possible to suspect Parthenon influence. The nearness to Apollo emphasizes the musical and poetic gifts of both gods as well as the traditional opposition between them. Dionysos recalls the Theater as Apollo recalls the Odeion.

The juxtaposition with Hera [text fig. 62] may seem surprising, but we have it again on the Polion krater in New York mentioned above.[221] There Hera makes a gesture of astonishment which would also be appropriate to the Hera of the Parthenon. Of course, there is a good mythological connection between Dionysos and Hera, which the nearness of Hephaistos readily calls to mind. It was Dionysos who brought back Hephaistos to free Hera from the magic throne, and this was his entrée to Olympos.[222] But as we have seen so many divinities in this assembly treated as personifications, we are tempted to look for some relation of meaning also between these two. Hera, who has no Athenian cult to speak of, is par excellence the goddess of marriage. And Dionysos, the bridegroom of the principal sacred marriage of Athens, with the wife of the Archon Basileus,[223] plays an ever more important role in Athenian wedding ceremonies.

There is no direct clue such as we had with Ares to suggest the form in which Dionysos appeared. The outlines on the pediment

218. Brommer, *RGZM* 8 (1961) 76 n. 10.
219. Robert, *op. cit.* (supra n. 209) 303.
220. See supra n. 202.
221. N. 176.
222. This, too, was depicted by Polion on a volute-krater from Spina, Alfieri and Arias, *Spina* pls. 110–111. Instead of showing the procession he depicts Hera, Dionysos and Hephaistos in Olympos prior to the moment of freeing Hera.
223. Deubner, *Attische Feste* 100–102; Bieber, *Hesperia*, Supplement 8, 31–38.

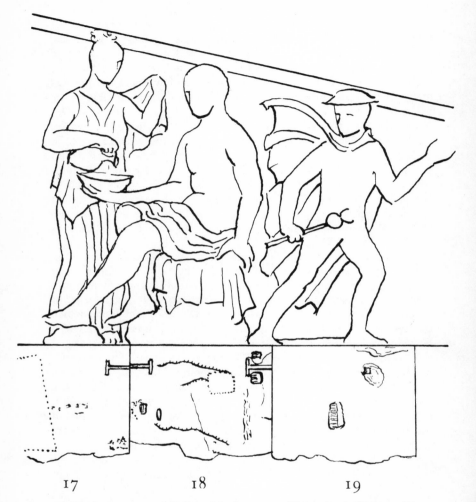

61. Parthenon, east pediment, blocks 17–19: Hebe, Ares, Hermes. Floor after Carpenter. Scale approx. 1:40.

floor suggest a broad, straight-edged plinth similar to that on which we have placed Amphitrite.[224] They do not *disprove* Carpenter's

224. The left-hand edge, in block 9, is clearly marked in all the drawings and photographs. The right-hand edge is not clear but must have run close to the left edge of the bedding for Hera in block 11. On the extent of Hera's plinth, see supra [pp. 249–252].

62. Parthenon, east pediment, blocks 10–11: Dionysos and Hera. Floor after Carpenter. Scale approx. 1:40.

assumption of a pair of standing statues dividing their weight between the two bars, since cornice block 10, over which the heaviest weight should come to rest on the diagonal iron bar, is almost entirely broken away. Nevertheless the analogies with the outlines in blocks 16–17 and with the bar-cuttings of the West Pediment argue strongly for a single broad plinth. This, as well as the demands of symmetry,

HELIOS   HERAKLES   KORE DEMETER ARTEMIS   APOLLO   LETO   DIONYSOS   HERA HEPHAISTOS ZEUS

63. Parthenon, east pediment. Reconstruction
by Harrison, with names of divinities.

suggests that Dionysos was not alone but was accompanied by his
panther as we find him in the metope below.

Absolute symmetry would demand that Dionysos *ride* the panther, but we have no example of the riding Dionysos so early as this,
and such a group would not fit the available space nor the disposition
of the iron bar. There was room for the forelegs of Amphitrite's
sea-horse to overlap the diagonally placed figure of Poseidon, but the
massively columnar statue of Hera came so near the front of the
cornice as to permit no overlapping. Also a riding Dionysos would
destroy the impression of a partnership with Hera. A striding Dionysos with his panther running beside him, as we find him in vase-
paintings of the late fifth century,[225] would form a group with its
greatest weight nearer the north end and would lead up in a sweep-
ing motion to the vertical of Hera. If he held a thyrsus before him
in his left hand, this would balance the trident of Poseidon on the
other side of the pediment.

It is hard to decide on the age, coiffure and dress of Dionysos,
for this is a period when many types are possible. In the frieze he
seems to have been beardless and to have had short hair. He is dressed,
like all the other male gods watching the procession, in a draped
himation without chiton. In the metope he has either a short chiton
and himation or the himation only. Praschniker has restored him after
the later fashion beardless with long hair, short chiton, pantherskin
and boots.[226] This is possible, though by no means certain from the
surviving traces. The Dionysos on the Kerch pelike in Leningrad that
imitates the central scene in the West Pediment is so dressed, but

225. E.g. the pelike in the Louvre, Devambez, *Greek Painting* pl. 125.
226. *Parthenonstudien* 148–151, 192, fig. 119.

ATHENA   POSEIDON   AMPHITRITE   HEBE   ARES   HERMES   HESTIA DIONE APHRODITE   SELENE

Aphrodite and Hera appear there in fourth-century types that can have had little or nothing to do with the Parthenon.[227] A bearded Dionysos in a long chiton is the normal type in vase-paintings of the late fifth century that represent the return of Hephaistos.[228] Such a Dionysos might best suit the associations implied by his placement in the pediment. If we have accepted a beardless Hephaistos when he is bearded in the frieze, we could do the same in reverse for Dionysos. It must be confessed, however, that there is no real evidence either way.

All the places are filled, then, and the total company is this: Helios, Herakles, Kore, Demeter, Artemis, Apollo, Leto, Dionysos, Hera, Hephaistos, Zeus, Athena, Poseidon, Amphitrite, Hebe, Ares, Hermes, Hestia, Dione, Aphrodite, Selene, twenty-one in all [text fig. 63]. As we have seen, a variety of essential and significant relationships of these divinities to one another and to Athena herself determined their positions in the triangle. No space was wasted, and background areas as such had relatively little importance in the composition, since the deeply plastic figures will have overlapped one another from almost every point of view. As in a thickly massed relief the movements of bodies and limbs and the lines of drapery will have worked together to keep the figures rhythmically united from one end to the other of the broad and complicated scene. This almost continuous massing of the bodies will have given, as we see also in Carrey's drawing of the West Pediment, a special prominence to the

227. Pfuhl, *Malerei und Zeichnung* fig. 604; *Comptes-rendus de la Commission impériale archéologique* (1872) pl. 1; Schefold, *Untersuchungen zu den Kertscher Vasen* no. 161, pp. 132f.

228. E.g. the Kleophon Painter, volute-krater in Spina, Alfieri and Arias, *Spina* pl. 83; *ARV*[2] 1141, no. 1. This vase shows clear influence from the Parthenon frieze in the picture on the other side, a procession to Apollo. The subject of the Return of Hephaistos is very popular with late 5th-century Attic vase-painters. See the mythological index to *ARV*[2].

heads, which alone will have stood out against the background. With their rich hair and splendid diadems they will have been like the brilliant points of a gorgeous stephane worn by the temple itself.

Also as in the West Pediment, where we have Carrey's drawing for witness, there were numerous and considerable alterations of scale from one figure to the next. But the persons seem to have been so juxtaposed that hardly any change of scale between *adjacent* figures was without motivation in the character or the person portrayed. If we tabulate these changes, we see that there was nearly always one reason, sometimes more than one, entirely apart from the demands of pedimental space.

Figures	*Changes of Scale*	*Reason*
Helios-Herakles	decrease	god to hero
Herakles-Kore	slight decrease	male to female
Kore-Demeter	same scale	
Demeter-Artemis	decrease	grown woman to young girl
Artemis-Apollo	increase	female to male
Apollo-Leto	slight decrease	male to female
Leto-Dionysos	increase	female to male
Dionysos-Hera	increase	simple divinity to queen of the gods
Hera-Hephaistos	increase	female to male, goddess not related to Athena to god who is Partner of Athena
Hephaistos-Zeus	increase	god to supreme god
Zeus-Athena	decrease	male to female, father to daughter, supreme god to goddess
Athena-Poseidon	decrease	principal deity of the temple to secondary deity
Poseidon-Amphitrite	decrease	male to female
Amphitrite-Hebe	decrease	grown woman to young girl
Hebe-Ares	large increase	young girl to tall man
Ares-Hermes	decrease	tall man to man of ordinary size
Hermes-Hestia	increase?	?
Hestia-Dione-Aphrodite	same scale	
Aphrodite-Selene	nearly same scale	

By the nature of the event that is celebrated, Athena and Zeus are together and Hera and Zeus are separated. This determines the pattern of personal relationships for the rest of the figures. Altogether four mothers are grouped with their children: Demeter with Kore, Leto with Apollo and Artemis, Hera with Hephaistos and Dione with Aphrodite. If we add Zeus and Athena, eleven out of the twenty-one figures are shown in the relationship of parent and child. This partly explains why the gods are so much outnumbered by the goddesses, but that is also a feature of Greek religion in general. Husbands and wives are not together except where, as Poseidon and Amphitrite, they preside over the same realm.

None of the Twelve Gods is missing and none of the gods certainly portrayed in vase-paintings of the Birth of Athena is absent except for the Eileithyiai. Their absence results directly from the fact that the meaning of the event rather than the action involved in it is portrayed. They preside over the *process* of birth and in the Parthenon Athena is already born. The birth-goddess as a helper of mankind should not be absent, however, and we have suggested that she is included in the person of Artemis. Herakles appears in vase-paintings as well as in the pediment.

A winged figure on a hydria in the Cabinet des Médailles might be either Iris or Nike,[229] and it is just possible that the goddess next to Ares in the pediment is Nike instead of Hebe, but this vase also has a figure that might be Hebe. Deities that have not so far been identified on any vase-paintings of the Birth of Athena are Kore, Hestia and Dione. Hestia is one of the Twelve Gods, and Kore and Dione belong to parent and child groups.

Much is conjectural in our restoration and no drawing can hope to come close enough to the original to permit one to judge it on aesthetic grounds. Still it is necessary to try to draw each figure because anyone accustomed to the more airy recent restorations is likely to question whether so many figures can really be fitted in. Yet surely if we did not have the surviving corner statues, no one would have dared to imagine them so thickly massed as Carrey actually saw them. They are even more closely grouped than the corner figures of the West Pediment.

Buschor went so far as to say at one time that the crowded look of Schwerzek's and Furtwängler's reconstructions warns us not to insert more than twelve figures between Demeter and Hestia, so this also would support the division of the center between Zeus and

229. Brommer, *RGZM* 8 (1961) 78.

Athena.[230] But a few years later he assumed twelve *lost* figures, the same number that we have postulated, and placed Zeus in the center, flanked by Hephaistos and Athena.[231]

It is this central position of Zeus, fully confirmed by all the technical evidence that survives, that is the real key to the whole conception of the pediment. Zeus is already a supreme being, already partaking of the new idea of religion that later ages found in the Pheidian Zeus of Olympia. Athena is above all else the patron goddess of Athens, or as Herington has put it, "Athena *is* Athens; the best that Athens stands for." [232] She is that Athens which we hear described in the Funeral Oration of Perikles. The special relationship of Athena to Zeus expresses the preeminence of Athens not only in wealth and power but in all the higher forms of human achievement. The gods assembled to receive the birth represent in their persons these several areas of man's activity. They are shown in recognizably characteristic guise but often with some modification of attributes or companionship that makes clear how they are affected by the gifts of Athena, the accomplishments of Athens. In their summing up of the life and functions of the *polis* they are more like the gods we find in Plato than those we know from Homer.[233] The mythological relationships of the Olympian gods to one another as we meet them in poetry are not the formative principle of the representation. But neither is poetry rejected as Plato would reject it.[234] The main theme, after all, is a poetic myth, and the memories of other myths are found, like overtones, all through the composition.

Herakles greeting the rising sun evokes the memory of his labors and his journeys. Artemis–Hekate running with news to Demeter recalls the loss and finding of Persephone. Hera immobile between Dionysos and Hephaistos brings to mind the return of Hephaistos to Olympos and the triumphant disorderly entrance of Dionysos. Poseidon yielding to the force of Athena directly echoes the myth of the West Pediment, while Amphitrite makes us think of Theseus and his visit to the bottom of the sea. Ares attended by Hebe reminds us of his wounding in the *Iliad;* his sitting on a rocky seat goes back to his trial on the Areopagus. Aphrodite in the lap of her mother is again reminiscent of the *Iliad,* and of the heroines whom she caressed as Dione caresses her. Richly fleshed and clothed

230. *ArchEph* (1937) 455.
231. *Phidias der Mensch* 36.
232. C. J. Herington, *Athena Parthenos and Athena Polias* (Manchester 1955) 56.
233. E.g. *Laws* 11.920 D–E, 921 C; *Critias,* 109 B–C; *Protagoras* 321 C–D.
234. E.g. *Republic* 2.377–378.

with their mythical personalities all these gods and goddesses have a color and an emotional force which purely allegorical figures could never have attained. To a people whose minds and eyes were feasted year by year with the best of Attic tragedy, these associations will have been much richer and more complex than they can be to us.

Neither does this new vision of the gods deny their old religious roots. Modern scholarship, dazzled by the lofty spectacle of an Olympos become worldwide, has sometimes felt impelled to protect the nobility of this conception by divorcing it as much as possible from the Acropolis itself.[235] What, compared with the *Weltenberg*, is this lowly home of owl and snake, this prehistoric female-dominated rock? But the temple spoke in many voices to many men and turned its back on none, least of all on the "citizens of the least educated classes," [236] who made up a substantial proportion of Periklean Athenians. If we stand on the Acropolis and greet the gods assembled here between the rising sun and the setting moon, with the brightness of the southern side to our left and the shade of the north to our right, the wedges of the gable point like arrows to the places where these deities have their oldest cults in Athens. With the exception of the heraldic central group all the gods of the southern half of the pediment have Athenian sanctuaries to the south of the Acropolis, those of the northern half to the north of the Parthenon, on the Acropolis and beyond [237] [text fig. 64].

Looking toward Herakles we look toward the Ilissos and toward the Herakleion in Kynosarges.[238] This was not the only sanctuary of Herakles in Athens, but with its gymnasium and its sanctuary of the Eponymous Hero Antiochos, the son of Herakles,[239] it was the one most like a real heroon, the place where the Athenian people will have felt most directly in contact with the hero. It was here that the Athenian Herakleia appear to have been celebrated.[240] Nearby

235. Cf. Berger, *Parthenon-Ostgiebel* 40: "Die anwesende Göttergesellschaft lässt sich nämlich nicht einfach (wie hartnäckig immer wieder geglaubt und versucht wird) als eine Versammlung der auf oder um die Akropolis Kult besitzenden Gottheiten oder der sog. Hauptgötter des attischen Landes verstehen" ["The present company of gods can be understood not simply (as was stubbornly believed and attempted) as an assembly of deities having cults on or about the Acropolis, or the so-called principal gods of Attica"].
236. Herington, *Athena Parthenos and Athena Polias* 51.
237. See especially the plans in Travlos, 'Η πολεοδομικὴ 'Εξέλιξις τῶν 'Αθηνῶν (Athens 1960) pls. 3–5.
238. On the location see Travlos, *op. cit.* (supra n. 237) 91–92, pl. 4. For general information Judeich, *Topographie*[2] 422–424.
239. See Karouzos, *Deltion* (1923) 98–99; Harrison, *Agora* XI, 118, n. 80.
240. Deubner, *Attische Feste* 226.

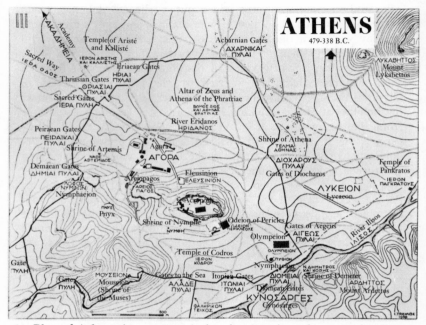

64. Plan of Athens (459–338 B.C.) showing location of sanctuaries. From Travlos.

upstream, though its place is not certainly fixed, was the Metroon in Agrai, the sanctuary of Demeter and Kore where the lesser Mysteries took place,[241] and also nearby was the Temple of Artemis Agrotera,[242] to whom 500 goats were sacrificed yearly in fulfillment of a vow made at Marathon.[243] The so-called Temple on the Ilissos, which is roughly contemporary with the Parthenon,[244] should belong to one of these two sanctuaries, though it is disputed which one.

The Pythion, across the Ilissos from Agrai, is evidently regarded by Thucydides as the oldest sanctuary of Apollo in Athens.[245] The earliest and most sacred precinct of Dionysos was generally agreed to be the Dionysion en Limnais, but there is less agreement about

241. Judeich, *Topographie*[2] 420–421.
242. *Ibid.* 416.
243. Aristotle, *Ath.Pol.* 58.1; Xenophon, *Anabasis* 3.2, 12; Plutarch, *De Herodoti Malignitate* 861 F.
244. Dinsmoor, *Architecture of Ancient Greece* 185; I. M. Shear, *Hesperia* 32 (1963) 388–399.
245. 2.15.4. Judeich, *Topographie*[2], 386–387.

its location. A position south of the Acropolis seems to have the strongest claim.[246] In any case the Dionysion en Limnais is included by Thucydides along with the Pythion in those sanctuaries which lay more or less to the south. It was here that the ceremonies preliminary to the sacred marriage of the wife of the Basileus took place.[247] Hera had no temple of her own in Athens until the time of Hadrian.[248] Such cult as she may have had will have been together with Zeus in the Olympieion. But as Hera Teleia she presided over every Athenian marriage,[249] and the formidable deposit of wedding vases of the archaic and classical periods found in the Sanctuary of the Nymph south of the Acropolis suggests that this was an important spot for the ritual of weddings.[250]

Only with Hephaistos, whose place to the left of Zeus is dictated by his symbolic partnership with Athena, is the chain of local associations really broken. But we pick it up again with Poseidon. On the north side of the Acropolis, soon to be enclosed in the area of the Erechtheion, were the tokens of his contest with Athena, the salt sea and the trident marks in the rock, and Pausanias says that there was an altar of Poseidon in the Erechtheion on which sacrifices were also made to Erechtheus.[251] Amphitrite has no *cult* here, but if, as we have suggested, she *is* the sea, there is a special sense to her being in this place. As, in the West Pediment, it does not seem absurd for her to arrive at the place of the contest accompanied by the creatures of the sea, because everyone knew that as a result of this contest the sea was actually present on the Acropolis,[252] so here her presence at the Birth of Athena as if she were still in her own element is logical both for the cosmic and for the local picture.

The Amazons were supposed to have sacrificed to Ares on the Areopagus when they besieged Athens in the reign of Theseus,[253] and Pausanias saw an altar of Athena Areia on the hill.[254] It is doubtful whether Ares had any *temple* in Athens at the time the

246. Travlos, *op. cit.* (supra n. 237) 22–23, favors a position near the Theater. Hooker, *JHS* 80 (1960) 112–117 argues for a location near the Ilissos.

247. Deubner, *Attische Feste* 100f.

248. Judeich, *Topographie*² 100.

249. Aristophanes, *Thesmophoriazousai* 973–975.

250. *Ergon* (1957) 5–12.

251. Pausanias 1.26.6.

252. There is an implication of a connection with the real sea in the story that when the south wind was blowing one could hear the noise of waves.

253. Aeschylus, *Eumenides* 689–690.

254. Pausanias 1.28.5.

Parthenon was built.[255] Hermes and Hestia did not have temples. Properly speaking, they belonged to every door and hearth. But for each there was one location of special importance for the civic life of Athens, the Herms at the northwest corner of the Agora [256] and the state hearth in the Prytaneion on the north slope of the Acropolis.[257] Together with the Herms was Hermes Agoraios, and there was also a sacred hearth in the Bouleuterion.[258] The mobile and the stable elements in the process of government are effectively summed up in the two figures of Hermes and Hestia, and the buildings in which the government of Athens was carried on were all to the north of the Acropolis.

Since we do not know the exact location of the Prytaneion in Athens we cannot say whether it was near to the sanctuary of Aphrodite and Eros on the north slope of the Acropolis, but it may well have been so, for Pausanias mentions it immediately after the sanctuary of Aglauros.[259] The north slope sanctuary of Aphrodite was evidently the one to which the Arrephoroi descended from the Acropolis by an underground passage, bringing one burden of mysterious objects and taking back another. The apparently ancient character of the ritual and the fact that the passage dates back to Mycenaean times suggest that this is in fact the oldest Athenian sanctuary of Aphrodite, though no ancient author tells us so.[260] There were two other sanctuaries which were certainly more pretentious than this, the Temple of Aphrodite Ourania near the northwest corner of the Agora and the sanctuary of Aphrodite in the Gardens near the Ilissos. There was also a sanctuary of Aphrodite Pandemos somewhere near the west entrance of the Acropolis which Pausanias says was founded by Theseus. But the antiquity of the cult on the north slope and its direct connection with Athena Polias made it natural for the artist of our pediment to visualize this Aphrodite first of all. Her figure, reclining on a couch of shelving rock, suggests even by its contours the slope of the sacred terrain. Lying in her mother's lap she spans the whole range of conceptions of the goddess of love, from the primitive to the Homeric. The most earthbound of all the gods portrayed, the embodiment of generation itself, she is the fitting

255. See supra n. 200.
256. See Harrison, *Agora* XI, 108–117.
257. Wycherley, *Agora* III, pp. 166–174, especially nos. 544, 553, 562, 569, 570.
258. Wycherley, *Agora* III, p. 128 and nos. 389, 391, 397, 398.
259. 1.18.2.
260. See especially Broneer, *Hesperia* 1 (1932) 49–55; 4 (1935) 125–132; 8 (1939) 428–429.

pendant to Herakles, the Olympian who began as a mortal and fathered generations of mortal men.

So the sacred landscape assumes the shape of the actual landscape, yet loses neither the grandeur of a cosmic spectacle nor the abstract clarity of a cosmos explained. As the rock of the Acropolis forms the base for the temple, so these local associations form the basis for all the wider meanings included in the Pheidian vision of the Birth of Athena. At this brief moment of splendor when Athena was born on the Parthenon, it was no disparagement to the goddess to say to all the world that Athena was Athens.

PHILIPP FEHL
[Gods and Men in the Parthenon Frieze —
1961] *

In the following selection, Philipp Fehl discusses the interpretation of the various groups of gods and human figures at the head of the Panathenaic procession on the east frieze of the Parthenon. Because the original essay was not primarily intended to deal with the problem of interpretation of the east frieze, Professor Fehl very kindly provides us with a foreword of his own to the excerpts which were selected for this volume. In this selection, our attention is focused on the complex spatial problem of the east frieze, without an understanding of which, according to Fehl, the entire frieze is unintelligible. The original essay was published under the title "The Rocks on the Parthenon Frieze," and was a study of the representation of landscape elements in the frieze. With the approval of the author, some of the longer footnotes in the original, which provide a review of earlier opinion on the interpretation of the frieze, were elevated into the text. As here presented, the parts reprinted include pages 8 to 10 and 13 to 19 of the original essay. The premise for the development of the argument concerning the spatial relationship between the gods and the officiates in the frieze, a detailed description of the rocks represented under the feet of the seated gods (pages 10 to 13 of the original), is here omitted. Philipp Fehl is professor of art history at the Urbana campus of the University of Illinois.

Foreword

The pages that appear below are two sections of a larger essay that I published many years ago under the unlikely title "The Rocks

* From Philipp Fehl, "The Rocks on the Parthenon Frieze," *Journal of the Warburg and Courtauld Institutes*, XXIV (1961), pp. 1–44. Excerpts reprinted by permission of the editors.

on the Parthenon Frieze." I chose this title because previously, students of the frieze had not particularly (if at all) noted these rocks which, if I am right, in certain places suggest elements of two landscapes: the one through which the procession winds its way to the Acropolis, and the one in which the Olympian gods are seated. My purpose, however, was far from counting rocks. The frieze so happily shows the joining of the worlds of gods and men, when the gods are propitious and men are good and pleasing in their sight, that we may turn to it, as I suppose did the ancients, to find a nostalgic solace in the music of its serenity and well-adjusted peace. We naturally sense this attunement of the two worlds when we walk along the frieze and are touched by the beauty and the relaxed, confident piety of the participants in the procession. When, however, we come to stand before the gods we may—or, perhaps, *should*—wonder about what moved the artist to show the gods to us in two groups that are isolated from each other, each group being flanked by men who are turned away from the gods, while the gods appear not to pay attention to the human beings. The question is, I think, important because it moves us to try to see more precisely what the artist wanted and was able to tell us about the nature of the gods and the ways in which they participate in the life on earth. I plead in my paper that the seeming estrangement or cold separation of the two worlds in just the places where the figures of gods and men are physically most proximate to each other is, as it were, an optical illusion of the modern viewer who tends to look at the work in the terms of the solid placement of its component forms on the relief plane. If, instead, he will look at the picture before him as the artist's attempt to represent nature within the obvious limitations set by the medium in which he tells his story, the work may come to life for him quite differently. One day, as I stood, not so much thinking as musing, in front of the marvelous group of Eros and Aphrodite on the east frieze (text figs. 65 and 66) [1] the left index finger of Aphrodite wriggled a little and I saw suddenly that it was pointing downward and into a far distance. "Don't you see," the goddess seemed to smile at me, "that we are seated on Mount Olympus and look down upon the world of men?" It was easy, after that, to see that there were rocks under the feet of the gods which, in the shorthand formula for mountains to which we are quite accustomed in paintings

---

1. The group is now mutilated but can be reconstructed with the help of fragments and a cast from the so-called Fauvel mold, which was taken in 1787 when the unit was still entire. For details see Arthur H. Smith, *The Sculptures of the Parthenon* (London, 1910), p. 54, and notes 28 and 29 of the original essay.

on Greek vases, quite appropriately indicate the heights of Mount Olympus. It was this discovery that led me to look for other representations of rocks on the frieze and to attempt to see to what extent they, too, may be indications of the landscape in which the actions depicted on the frieze take place. I then wrote my paper, as it were, from the outside in and also included a number of other observations on the variety of ways in which the artists of the Parthenon related their sculptures to the suggestion of a real locale and so anchored them in time and place.

I should like to stress, however, that it is not necessary to identify the rocks on the east frieze in order to place the gods on Mount Olympus. A Greek viewer, I am persuaded, immediately upon seeing their images, placed the gods on Mount Olympus because he knew that that was where they, under the circumstances, belonged. It is necessary only for us who cannot afford to take anything for granted in the study of a work of art so important but also so removed from us in time as the Parthenon to look at the rocks, which can be no more than an accident of the purpose of the whole, with a keen and detailed attention. We should not, however, in the pursuit of such work, forget that we became engaged in it because we hoped it would help us see better the purpose of the artist's tale and the beauty and majesty of the likenesses he shows us as he develops it.

[The East Frieze]

There is depicted on the frieze of the Parthenon not only the Panathenaic procession, but also a stretch of land. The representation of the landscape continues uninterrupted, just like that of the procession itself. Neither the procession nor the landscape are shown in their total extension; both are given in abbreviated forms which stress characteristic aspects of significant units. These follow each other in a connection which is so subtle that an impression of the whole is given. Depending on the circumstances created by the action and the occasional presence of suitably shaped rocks, the ground plane may represent a part either of the Outer Kerameikos, where the procession was assembled, or the slope of the hill of the Acropolis, or its plateau.

It is sometimes suggested that the subject of the frieze is not the Panathenaic procession itself, but a sequence of separate, significant events selected from the programme of the entire festival and arranged in the manner of a procession. The chief argument for this view is, perhaps, the absence of the ship of Athena, on which the peplos was displayed. If, however, we consider that the spectator is introduced to the procession while slowly overtaking it, and that the ship with the peplos was at the very head of the procession, we have a situation in which the spectator does not reach the head of the procession until he is in front of the Parthenon. There, of course, the peplos is in evidence (the ship, if indeed a ship was used at all as early as the 5th century, was not taken up to the Acropolis; Pausanias, I, 29, 1). * * * It is sometimes said that the horses in the procession did not go up to the Acropolis owing to the difficulty of the terrain. Note, however, Aristophanes, "Clouds," II, 69–70: "The babe caressing fondly, she would say, 'When wilt thou be a man and drive to town thy chariot purple rob'd, like Megacles?' " The Scholiast remarks, and has generally been given credence, that "to town" here means "to the Acropolis." [2]

Our intuitive understanding that the figures on the frieze move over a given terrain (and not in an "ideal space" as is often maintained) [3] has probably something to do with the illusion of their movement which we have when we walk beside the frieze. [4] We do not ever see the procession as if at any given moment it held its pose and stayed thus forever, so that we could inspect it. [5] The fiction of the piece appears to me rather to be that, within certain obvious limits, the procession is shown as a contemporary might have seen it when he got up early in the morning to watch its formation and then to let it go by him, as he himself walked up to the Acropolis. Such a man would first see the preparations of the horsemen in the Outer Kerameikos, would then enter the city gates, be overtaken by the horsemen, and occasionally halting at different points on the sacred way to the Acropolis, see different elements of the procession at different periods of its advance. When he arrived in front of the

2. W. G. Rutherford, "Scholia Aristophanica" (London, 1896) 133.

3. Cf. especially A. Michaelis, "Der Parthenon," 1871, p. 221.

4. Similar, perhaps, is the "anomaly" of Myron's 'Discobolos'. It is a favourite subject of academic instruction to show that the statue is not the image of a discus thrower frozen stiff at a given moment of his action. It is probably also not an image of the "idea" of a youth throwing a discus—or, at least, not directly. We see a succession of characteristic movements, from the very beginning of his turn to the moment of his throw, so that the eye, as it looks at him, moves with him and sees all of these gestures in their quick development. Hence, perhaps, the illusion of life.

5. An example of this kind of frieze is the charming sequence of engravings of the funerary cortege of the Duke of Wellington, which is displayed in full length at Apsley House. A more serious example is probably the length reliefs of the Ara Pacis in Rome. The question of the difference in the representation of motion on Greek and Roman reliefs is considered by P. H. von Blanckenhagen in "Narration in Hellenistic and Roman Art," *AJA* LXI (1957) 78–83.

Parthenon it would be high noon, or perhaps even later. He is just in time to witness the arrival of the victims. The head of the procession (on the east frieze) has already taken its stand in the front of the east façade. The scenes, in other words, follow each other like those on a Chinese scroll on which is represented the journey of a group of pilgrims in a continuing landscape. It would seem quite natural to see the pilgrims reappearing at measured intervals because the time it takes to unwind the scroll represents in some proportion the time it takes the pilgrims to proceed on their journey. In the contemplation of the frieze the source of "animation" is the locomotion of the spectator.[6] His trip was really a double one, his actual walk along the Parthenon, and his fancied journey along the entire road taken by the procession. This illusion may well have been enhanced by the fact that he himself had climbed the hill of the Acropolis only a short while before he arrived to see the marble procession doing the same. A spectator's feeling for the unity of time and place is not really disturbed by the continuous presence in his view of those parts of the procession, which, properly speaking, have passed out of time, because the expanse of the frieze is so great that his eyes can at no time encompass more than a fraction of it. The fancy of the Athenian spectator was further protected by the much criticized effect of the colonnade in front of the frieze which allowed him to see no more than segments of the frieze at any given moment.

In the east frieze, a series of rocks are disposed in a loosely symmetrical manner, and all are distinguished by the fact that they are touched by the sandals of the gods, or, in the case of Aphrodite, by the hem of her garment. Under the feet of Hermes their slope as-

6. Consider Homer's description of the shield of Achilles, "Iliad," XVIII. As the shield is moved, so the action depicted on it is shown to be in progress. The landscape is clearly continuous, cf. esp. 573 ff. (Pope's translation):

> Here herds of oxen march, erect and bold
> Rear high their horns, and seem to low in gold,
> And speed to meadows on whose sounding shores
> A rapid torrent through the rushes roars.
> Four golden herdsmen as their guardians stand,
> And nine dour dogs complete the rustic band.
> Two lions rushing from the woods appear'd,
> And seized a bull, the master of the herd;
> He roar'd . . . in vain the dogs, the men withstood;
> They tore his flesh, and drank his sable blood.
> The dogs (oft cheered in vain) desert the prey,
> Dread the grim terrors, and at distance bay.

65. Parthenon, east frieze. Eros and Aphrodite. London, British Museum.

cends. Under the feet of Zeus this ascent continues in a modified form, somewhat approaching the horizontal. The rocks on the right half of the frieze present a similar image, but in a mirror-like reversal. I should like to suggest that the rocks, in their entirety, when the frieze was in its place on the temple wall, suggested the presence of a mountain, on the top of which the gods are seated. Zeus and Hera sit at the very summit, or rather to one side of it. Athena and Hephaistos occupy the corresponding position of distinction at the

66. Parthenon, east frieze. Eros and Aphrodite, restored by J. E. Platt (RCA). London, British Museum.

other side. Hermes [fig. 36] and Aphrodite [text figs. 65–66], who are most immediately concerned with human affairs, sit where the mountain slopes off. In spite of the mutilations they have suffered, it seems clear that both are looking into the far distance. Aphrodite, in terms of tactile facts, is pointing her finger at the small of the back of the man directly in front of her, a man vastly too old to be the natural object of her concern. In fiction, however (the more likely residence of the truth of even so tactile an art as relief sculpture),

Aphrodite would seem to be pointing out to Eros someone who is very far away. The inclination of her index finger and, even more tellingly, the direction of the languid gaze of Eros indicate that the object of their interest is down below, as well as far away.

An interesting similarity exists between the group of Aphrodite and Eros and Raphael's fresco 'Venus pointing out Psyche to Cupid' [7] in the Villa Farnesina in Rome. The original of this type is clearly the Aphrodite on the Parthenon frieze. The possibility exists that Raphael may have used a drawing taken from the Parthenon frieze as a model for his Venus. According to Vasari, Raphael sent to Athens to have drawings, which have not survived, made of the antiquities there.

The only mountain upon which an assembly of the gods might take place is, of course, Mount Olympus. The possibility that the rocks in the east frieze might represent the hill of the Acropolis must be excluded, because all the human participants in the action of the east frieze are located on top of this hill, and the image of the mountain is evidently raised above the level on which they stand.

If we accept this interpretation, several incongruities which have often been remarked upon [8] find a natural explanation. The gods are no longer invisibly present on the Acropolis itself and bored with the proceedings (it looks as if they had turned their back upon the scene in the very centre of the frieze), nor do they have to be accommodated in a vacuous ideal space. They are above the scene and at home.[9] The subjects of the frieze would now appear to be related to the other works of sculpture decorating the east façade. The pediment shows the great event of the birth of Athena, the figures of Zeus and Athena being disposed on the pediment as they are on

7. Arnold von Salis suspected an antique precedent for the group and published a fragment of a small Hellenistic relief in clay as a possible example of the type: "Antike and Renaissance" (Zurich, 1947), p. 199 and pl. 59a. Cf. also a bronze mirror cover in the Louvre, 'Aphrodite and Eros', second half of the 4th century, where Aphrodite is shown leaning against a huge rock; reproduction in J. D. Beazley and Bernard Ashmole, *Greek Sculpture and Painting to the End of the Hellenistic Period* (Cambridge, 1932), fig. 141.

8. Especially angry objections will be found in Thomas Davidson, "The Parthenon Frieze and Other Essays," London, 1882; and Anton von Premerstein, "Der Parthenonfries und die Werkstatt des Parthenaischen Peplos," *JOAI*, XV, 1912, p. 1 ff.

9. "So saying, the goddess, flashing-eyed Athene, departed to Olympus, where, they say, is the abode of the gods that stands fast forever. Neither is it shaken by winds nor ever wet with rain, nor does snow fall upon it, but the air is outspread clear and cloudless, and over it hovers a radiant whiteness. Therein the blessed gods are glad all their days, and thither went the flashing-eyed one, when she had spoken all her wont to the maiden." ("Odyssey", VI, 40 ff.)

the frieze. The locale of the action is presumably Mount Olympus. On the metopes, the gods are shown in their awful majesty, fighting the giants who are storming Olympus, and on the frieze we may see them serenely beautiful, in the quiet possession of the sacred mountain, presiding over the affairs of men. We may, perhaps, even feel that the entire sequence of struggles depicted on the metopes— which comes to its climax on the east façade—is thus connected with the subject of the frieze and brought to its fitting conclusion.[10]

I see the disposition of the figures on the east frieze as follows:

The priestess of Athena (in the very centre of the frieze) and the two figures on either side of her, form a self-contained unit which is placed directly above the entrance of the Parthenon [fig. 42]. They perform their presumably ritual functions (which are patently ignored by everyone else represented on the frieze) with an air of graceful ease, without reference to the huge figures of the gods or to the human beings in the procession. They are inside the Parthenon (I think we should imagine the doors to be open), or perhaps in the "pronaos".

The effect of the suggestion of an extension of the realm of action into depth at the very centre of the frieze accentuates the natural importance of this most idyllic scene and makes it, so to speak, the keystone which holds the entire frieze together. The gods are not to be read as separated into two groups by the scene inside the temple. They are the most important figures on the frieze and occupy its true centre, Mount Olympus, on a level which is above the tactile expanse of the frieze. This manner of representing. the idea of a mountain on a frieze is not too different from the one employed in the representation of the ascent of the Acropolis on the long friezes. The whole scheme would thus be brought to a fitting climax on the east, the climax of the Olympian gods on their mountain.

It will, perhaps, be in order to question again the traditional identification of the self-contained groups of four men on either side of the gods with the mythical heroes of Athens.[11] It was arrived at chiefly because the need was felt to establish a connecting link be-

10. The gods on Mount Olympus could also be seen on the base of the statue of *Athena Parthenos* (The Creation of Pandora), on the inside of the shield of Athena and on the peplos itself (a *gigantomachia* [battle of the gods and giants] in either instance).

11. This view was put forward by K. Weissman, "Zur Erklaerung des Ostfrieses des Parthenon", *Hermes*, XLI (1906) 618 ff., and A. S. Arvanitopullos, "Phylen-Heroen am Parthenon-fries", *AM*, XXXI (1906) 38 ff. It has generally found favour, cf. e.g. L. Ziehen, in *RE* (1949) "Panathenaia", col. 463/4. For an opposed opinion cf. F. Studniczka, "Neues über den Parthenon", *NJbb*, XV (1912), 251.

tween the "ideal" realm of the gods and that of men, but no particular
evidence exists which would establish their super-human identity. It
is, I think, more likely that they are high-ranking dignitaries who
(although some are old) are still quite alive, and that they stand
somewhat aside from the procession proper, perhaps on the steps of
the Parthenon. They, like all other human beings on the frieze, seem
to be waiting for the next phase in the development of the procession, perhaps for the arrival of the sacrificial animals which we have
seen approaching round the corner.

Next to the group of dignitaries comes a herald [fig. 34] giving a
signal with his right hand to the maidens on the other side of the
frieze [fig. 35], or perhaps to his two colleagues in front of them who
are talking to each other and have not yet noticed his gesture. I find
it a pleasant relief that it is not necessary to think of the gods as in-
corporeal beings whose presence somehow does not interfere with
the ready exchange of a communication which would pass directly
through them. Omitting the deities, the frieze is evidently made up
of participants in the procession. They are drawing up in a new formation, probably in the open space to the east of the Parthenon.[12]

I am well aware that a certain flavour of absurdity adheres to
my attempt to show that figures which can be plainly seen to be disposed at some distance from the geometric centre of the frieze are
really in the artistic or true centre of the image, and that the ground
plane, which looks so obviously horizontal, may be so variable in its
character. I think, however, that this may be the result of an attempt
to express in words what the eye, without interference of language,
may comprehend readily when it is guided by a certain expectation of
what is natural in the representation of an assembly of the gods and
of the Panathenaic procession on a frieze.

We may deduce from a number of paintings of related subjects on
vases that a representation of the story of the Parthenon frieze as it is
here told would have shown the gods on a level separated from and
above that of the mortals. A suitable example is provided by a painting on a krater in the Museo Nazionale in Naples which shows
Dareios and his counsellors plotting the destruction of Greece, while
above them, the outcome of the action which they are still contemplating is being determined by the gods.[13] This is, of course, the

12. Cf. especially Heinrich Brunn, "Bildwerke des Parthenon," *Sitzungs-
berichte der k. bayrischen Akademie der Wissenschaften, Philosophische-
philologische Classe* (1874) 43–44.
13. For a detailed discussion of this painting cf. Roger Hinks, *Myth and
Allegory*, London, 1939, pp. 64–67. See also F. M. Cornford, *Thucydides
Mythistoricus*, London, 1907, pp. 195 f., and Heinrich Brunn, *Kleine
Schriften*, vol. III, pp. 60 ff.

most natural form of representing such a thing. Pheidias, who had to accommodate the story to the narrow confines of a decorative frieze, could not use it. He therefore collapsed the two scenes of his image into one, and presented the gods and the human beings on one stage. A naïve spectator will anticipate the obvious limitations of the medium in which an image is shown him: he will find a statue lifelike and not observe (precisely because he knows better) that it is not soft to the touch or that it cannot move. Similarly, he will not expect the gods to be on a stage above the stage if, as in a frieze, there is room only for the lower stage. The eye will see what really matters; that is, the spectator will interpret the stage properties for what they signify, and not for what they are. So long as he knows as a matter of course that the gods assemble on Mount Olympus and not in an ideal space or on the Acropolis, he will see them where they belong.

The idea of representing the assembly of the gods in a frieze in this way was, for that matter, not new at the time of Pheidias. It has never been in doubt that on the frieze of the Siphnian treasury at Delphi we can deduce from the action of the gods that its locale must be Mount Olympus. We can see the different gods engaged in argument concerning the fate of Troy, according to Homer,[14] represented on the same ground plane on which, directly next to the gods, we see the battle of Troy itself. New, however, is the Pheidian approach to the problem. The artist of the relief at Delphi quite naturally stressed the difference between the appearance of gods and men. The spectator is immediately struck with the extraordinary size of the gods. Since they are shown together in a block-like unit, it is quite clear that they exist in a separate world, and there is no need for rocks or other devices to show that they do not exist on the same ground. On the Parthenon frieze, the gods are still roughly twice the size of the human figures, but they look natural, and there is a subtle connection between the realms of gods and men that somehow has the appearance of an inherent necessity. This connection between the two realms is established by means of a landscape element employed as a kind of stage device. It would seem that the challenge of the exigencies of frieze sculpture provided the artist with the opportunity to weave the images of the gods into the fabric of the frieze with such cunning that we feel, as we see the gods on Mount Olympus, that they can also be at any place, at any time, and therefore, perhaps, with us now.

14. The recently corrected reading of the inscriptions of the frieze (E. Mastrokostas, in *AM*, LXXI (1956) 74 f.) makes it quite certain that the fallen warrior is Sarpedon, and that the scene represents the battle fought over his body (*Iliad*, II). Immediately before and after this, Homer shows us the assembly of the gods.

DORIC ORDER

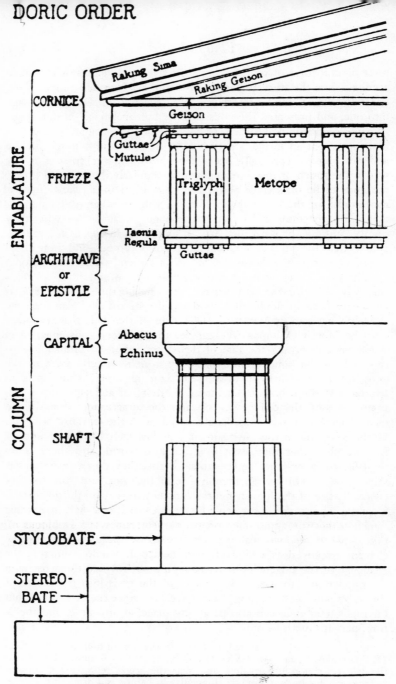

Raking Sima

Raking Geison

CORNICE

Geison

Guttae
Mutule

ENTABLATURE

FRIEZE

Triglyph   Metope

Taenia
Regula

Guttae

ARCHITRAVE
or
EPISTYLE

CAPITAL

Abacus

Echinus

COLUMN

SHAFT

STYLOBATE

STEREO-
BATE

67. Diagram of Doric order. Harry Dixon.

GLOSSARY OF MYTHOLOGICAL AND ARCHITECTURAL TERMS

(Words appearing in SMALL CAPS in the definitions are themselves defined in the glossary.)

Abacus: the uppermost part of a CAPITAL, usually a flat, rectangular slab. (See text fig. 67.)

Acanthus: a plant, the leaves of which were copied in Greek decoration, particularly in CORINTHIAN and COMPOSITE CAPITALS.

Acropolis (Greek, "upper town"): the Greek name for the citadel or stronghold of a town. (See text fig. 3.)

Acroteria: roof ornaments in the form of figures or of carved relief plaques placed at the apex and ends of a PEDIMENT.

Agora: an open space, often a market place, in a Greek city. (See text fig. 1.)

Anathyrosis: a method of fitting stones closely together by putting a fine polish on the surfaces to be joined, and recessing parts of the joining surfaces so as to reduce the area of contact.

Ancones: 1) brackets or console forms on either side of a doorway, used to support the CORNICE; 2) projections left on blocks of stone (such as the DRUMS of a COLUMN) to assist in lifting them into position.

Antae: the prolongation of the side walls of a building to form a PORCH.

Antefixes: upright ornaments used along the edge of a roof to conceal the joints between the rows of tile.

Anthemion: an ornament, common in Greek and Roman architecture, based on the honeysuckle and/or palmette.

Apse: a semicircular termination of a building or a recess in a wall.

Architrave: the lowest part of the ENTABLATURE; the blocks which are supported by the COLUMNS and carry the weight of the roof. (See text fig. 67.)

Arris: the sharp edge formed by adjoining FLUTES in a DORIC COLUMN.

Ashlar: masonry of squared blocks.

Astragal: a small convex molding often of the BEAD AND REEL type.

Asymptote (literally, not falling together): in mathematics, a straight line approached by a given curve as one of the variables in the equation of the curve approaches infinity.

Athena Nike: Athena Victory.

Athena Parthenos: Athena as a virgin goddess; also, the statue by PHEIDIAS in the Parthenon. The term *parthenon* refers to the room in Greek houses that was set aside for the use of a maiden before she was married.

Athena Promachos: Athena Champion, first in battle, or Protectress.

Attic: 1) (n.) the story above the CORNICE of a classical façade; 2) (adj.) of or pertaining to Attica (Athens).

Base: the lowest or supporting member of a COLUMN, ANTA, or wall.

Bead and reel: a convex molding in which bead forms, singularly or in groups, alternate with disc forms.

Bema: a platform, especially that part of a temple that faces the altar.

Boss: an ornamental knob or projection.

Brace: a diagonal iron or wooden strut sometimes applied inside masonry joints (in addition to dowels) to prevent the joints from separating because of earthquakes or ground settling.

Capital: the uppermost part of a COLUMN. (See text fig. 67.)

Caryatids: sculptured figures used as COLUMNS (as on the south porch of the ERECHTHEUM.)

Cella: the enclosed principal chamber or sanctuary of a temple; also known as the NAOS. (See text fig. 1.)

Centaur: a creature combining the head, arms, and torso of a man and the body of a horse. In Greek mythology, centaurs represent man's barbarism and animal instincts. The best-known centaur myth is the fight between the centaurs and the LAPITHS. The centaurs, invited to the wedding of the Lapith king Pirithous, became drunk and attempted to rape the bride and her attendants. This myth is represented in the south METOPES of the Parthenon.

Chryselephantine: a process in which the wooden core of a statue is overlaid with gold and ivory, the nude parts of the figure being covered in ivory and the drapery cast in gold. The Pheidian statues of ATHENA PARTHENOS at Athens and of the *Olympian Zeus* were both colossal chryselephantine statues.

Colonnade: a series of COLUMNS, usually spanned by an ARCHITRAVE.

Columns: vertical, circular, weight-carrying architectural members, consisting of BASE (omitted in the DORIC ORDER), SHAFT (made up of sections called DRUMS), and CAPITAL. (See text fig. 67.)

Composite: a late Roman order that combines both IONIC and CO-RINTHIAN elements.

Corinthian: most ornate of the Greek architectural ORDERS and characterized by the CAPITAL in the shape of an inverted bell enveloped by ACANTHUS leaves.

Cornice: the top, projecting section of an ENTABLATURE. (See text fig. 67.)

Crepidoma: the stepped BASE of a Greek temple, comprising the STYLOBATE, the STEREOBATE, and their masonry foundations.

Crepis: see CREPIDOMA.

Cyma recta: a double-curved molding, concave above and convex below.

Cyma reversa: a double-curved molding, convex above and concave below.

Demeter: Greek goddess of agriculture, some of whose attributes are ears of corn and a torch.

Dione: consort of Zeus, mother of Aphrodite, and the subject of cult worship in Athens in the late fifth century B.C.

Diphros: low chair with a leather seat, four legs, and no back or arm rest, which could be folded up and carried.

Doric order: the architectural ORDER that evolved in the Dorian or western regions of Greece, especially in Attica and the Peloponnesus. (See text fig. 67.)

Drum: one of the cylindrical sections of a COLUMN SHAFT.

Eaves: the overhanging edge of a sloping roof.

Echinus: the convex molding or cushion immediately below the ABACUS of a DORIC CAPITAL. (See text fig. 67.)

Empollion: a plug of wood set into the DRUM of a COLUMN to hold a pin used for centering and connecting the drums.

Engaged column: a COLUMN attached to or partly sunk into a wall.

Entablature: the superstructure carried by COLUMNS and usually divided into three zones: ARCHITRAVE, FRIEZE, and CORNICE. (See text fig. 67.)

Entasis: the slight convex curve given to the profile of a COLUMN.

Epistyle: the Greek term for ARCHITRAVE.

Erechtheum: the most ancient temple of Athena on the ACROPOLIS at Athens. The Periclean Erechtheum, begun in 421 B.C. and finished in 407 B.C., housed a number of ancient cults and sacred objects, among which were the olive tree of Athena Polias, the golden lamp made by Callimachus, and the salt well, the mark of Poseidon's trident. There was also an altar of Poseidon and Erechtheus.

Fascia: 1) a horizontal band mostly used in combination with moldings in an ENTABLATURE; 2) specifically, the three superimposed bands of the IONIC EPISTYLE.

Fluting: shallow, concave grooves running down the length of a SHAFT or other surface.

Frieze: a painted or sculptured band running horizontally along a wall or ENTABLATURE. In the DORIC ORDER, the frieze is divided into TRIGLYPHS and METOPES. (See text fig. 67.)

Geison: the Greek term for CORNICE.

Guttae: small, droplike projections carved below the REGULAE beneath the TRIGLYPHS. (See text fig. 67.)

Header: a cross member in a series of beams; in masonry, a brick or stone with its end toward the front surface.

Hexastyle: a Greek temple having six COLUMNS across the front.

Hippocampus: a sea horse or a legendary sea monster with the head and forequarters of a horse and the tail of a dolphin or fish.

In antis: signifying a form or structure in which the side walls are extended to provide a PORCH enclosed at the sides. COLUMNS *in antis* are set between the ends of the extending walls, or ANTAE, as in the entrance to a Mycenaean MEGARON or the PRONAOS of the temple of Zeus at Olympia. The Parthenon does away with the antae, its PORCH COLONNADES standing free of the NAOS walls.

Ionic order: an architectural ORDER evolved in Asia Minor. It is particularly characterized by the scroll or VOLUTE used as part of its CAPITAL.

Jamb: the side of a window or doorway against which the sash or door abuts.

Lapiths: a Thessalian people. (See CENTAUR.)

Lintel: a horizontal beam or stone placed over an opening.

Marble (always a pure, white limestone unless otherwise specified): a stone usually in one of two main varieties: the close-grained PENTELIC from Athens; and the coarse-grained, translucent Parian, Naxian, etc., from the Aegean islands. Less frequent were the pure white, soft marble found near Sunium and the blue-clouded marbles of Hymettus and Deliana.

Meander: the decorative, geometric Greek fret or key pattern.

Megaron: the principal hall in a Mycenaean palace.

Metope (Greek, "between the holes"): the panels between the TRIGLYPHS of a DORIC FRIEZE. (See text fig. 67.)

Mutule: a flat block on the underside of a DORIC CORNICE.

Naos (or *neos*): see CELLA.

Narthex: an entrance vestibule or space.

Nave: the central aisle of a temple or church.

Necking: a narrow molding around the bottom of a CAPITAL.

Octastyle: a Greek temple having eight columns across the front, rear, or both.

Odeum (or *odeon*): an ancient Greek roofed theater.

Opisthodome: a PORCH in the rear of a Greek temple, sometimes enclosed with bronze grilles. (See text fig. 1.)

Orders: architectural schemes for development of COLUMN, CAPITAL, and ENTABLATURE in Grecian and other classical building. The most important orders are the DORIC, IONIC, and CORINTHIAN.

Ovolo: a wide convex molding.

Parthenon: see ATHENA PARTHENOS.

Pediment: the triangular openings at the ends of a building with a peaked roof. In temple architecture, it usually receives sculptural decorations.

Pentelic marble: marble that comes from Mount Pentelicus, in southeastern Greece.

Peripteral: a building that is surrounded by a COLONNADE or PERISTYLE.

Peristyle: 1) a row of covered COLUMNS that surrounds a building; 2) an inner court lined with a COLONNADE.

Peukina: (n.) pine wood planks; (adj.) made of pine.

Pheidias: the Athenian sculptor who was overseer of the reconstruction of the Acropolis of Athens under Pericles.

Plinth: the projecting BASE of a COLUMN or pedestal.

Porch: the covered entrance to a building.

Pronaos: the PORCH of a Greek or Roman temple, situated in front of the NAOS or CELLA, and enclosed by a row of COLUMNS in front. (See text fig. 1.)

Propylaea: the entrance gate-building to a temple enclosure or other precinct.

Propylon: singular form of PROPYLAEA, used for a less elaborate or smaller gate building.

Raking (adj.): sloping; inclining from a perpendicular direction.

Regulae: short blocks in a DORIC ENTABLATURE beneath the TRIGLYPHS, their lower surfaces decorated by GUTTAE. (See text fig. 67.)

Scotia: a concave molding.

Shaft: the main body of a COLUMN, between the BASE and the CAPITAL. (See text fig. 67.)

Sima: the Greek term for the crowning element of the CORNICE.

Socle: a foundation block, higher than a PLINTH, sometimes continuously carried along or around the building to form the lowest course of blocks in the walls.

Soffit: the underside of a LINTEL, arch, or other spanning member.

Stereobate: the temple substructure below the STYLOBATE. (See text fig. 67.)

Stoa: a roofed portico with a COLONNADE in front and a wall at the back.

Stretcher: a unit of masonry placed with its length parallel to the face of the wall.

Strombate: that part of the CREPIDOMA that supports the flooring.

Stylobate: the top step of the substructure that supports the COLUMNS and walls of a PERISTYLE structure and forms the floor of the peripteron halls. (See text fig. 67.)

Taenia: a band crowning the ARCHITRAVE of a DORIC ENTABLATURE. (See text fig. 67.)

Techniatae: skilled workmen or craftsmen.

Tholos: a Greek circular building.

Thyrsus: a staff surmounted by a pine cone or a bunch of grapes or berries, carried by Dionysus and his followers.

Toichobate: that part of the CREPIDOMA that supports the walls.

Triglyph: a block with vertical grooves, separating the METOPES in a DORIC FRIEZE.

Tympanum (or *tympanon*): a triangular wall forming the back wall of the PEDIMENT, enclosed by the RAKING CORNICE of the PEDIMENT and the horizontal cornice of the ENTABLATURE underneath.

Volute: a spiral scroll on an IONIC CAPITAL.

SELECTED BIBLIOGRAPHY

Additional bibliography on special topics will be found in the footnotes to the Introductory Essay and to the various selections in
the anthology.

General Works

Balanos, Nicolas. *Les Monuments de l'Acropole: Relèvement et conservation.* Paris, 1938.

Berve, Helmut, and Gottfried Gruben. *Greek Temples, Theaters and
Shrines.* New York, 1963.

Beulé, Charles Ernest. *L'Acropole d'Athènes.* Paris, 1853–54.

Boutmy, Emile G. *Le Parthénon et le génie grec.* Paris, 1897.

Collignon, Léon Maxime. *Le Parthénon: L'Histoire, l'architecture et
la sculpture.* 2nd ed. Paris, 1925.

Dinsmoor, William Bell. *The Architecture of Ancient Greece: An
Account of Its Historic Development.* 3rd ed. London, 1950.

D'Ooge, Martin Luther. *The Acropolis of Athens.* London, 1908.

Hege, Walter, and Gerhardt Rodenwaldt. *Die Akropolis.* Berlin, 1930.

Hooker, G. T. W., ed. *Parthenos and Parthenon.* Oxford, 1963. (This
is a collection of essays on the Parthenon published as a
supplement to vol. X of the periodical *Greece and Rome.*)

Laborde, Léon de. *Athèns aux XVᵉ, XVIᵉ, et XVIIᵉ siècles.* Paris, 1848.

Marquand, Allan. *Greek Architecture.* New York, 1909.

Martienssen, R. D. *The Idea of Space in Greek Architecture, with
Special Reference to the Doric Temple and Its Setting.*
Johannesburg, 1956.

Michaelis, Adolfe. *Der Parthenon.* Leipzig, 1871.

Norre, A. D. "Studies in the History of the Parthenon." Diss. Univ.
of California. Los Angeles, 1966.

Omont, Henri A. S. *Athènes au XVIIᵉ siècle: Dessins des sculptures
du Parthénon attribuées à J. Carrey.* Paris, 1896.

Penrose, Francis C. *An Investigation of the Principles of Athenian Architecture.* London and New York, 1888; rpt. College Park, Md., 1971.

Pollitt, J. J. *Art and Experience in Classical Greece.* Cambridge, England, 1972.

Praschniker, C. *Parthenonstudien.* Augsburg and Vienna, 1928.

Richter, Gisela M. *Handbook of Greek Art.* London and New York, 1969.

Scranton, Robert L. "Interior Design of Greek Temples." *AJA,* L (1946), pp. 39–51.

—— *Greek Architecture.* The Great Ages of World Architecture Series. New York, 1965.

Scully, Vincent. *The Earth, the Temple and the Gods: Greek Sacred Architecture.* New Haven, 1962.

Stuart, James, and Nicholas Revett. *The Antiquities of Athens and Other Monuments of Greece.* London, 1762–1815; rpt., 3 vols., New York, 1968.

Works on the Architecture of the Parthenon and Related Archeological Problems

Carpenter, Rhys. *The Architects of the Parthenon.* Baltimore, 1970.

Cooley, A. S. "Athena Polias on the Acropolis of Athens." *AJA,* III (1899), pp. 345–408.

Dinsmoor, William Bell. "The Date of the Older Parthenon." *AJA,* XXXVIII (1934), pp. 408–448.

—— "The Hekatompedon on the Athenian Acropolis." *AJA,* LI (1947), pp. 109–151.

—— "Attic Building Accounts I, the Parthenon." *AJA,* XVII (1913), pp. 53–80.

Dörpfeld, Wilhelm. "Untersuchungen am Parthenon." *AM,* VI (1881), pp. 283–302.

—— "Der Altere Parthenon." *AM,* XVII (1892), pp. 158–189.

Elderkin, George. *Problems in Periclean Buildings.* Princeton, 1912; rpt. College Park, Md., 1971.

Hill, B. H. "The Older Parthenon." *AJA,* XVI (1912), pp. 535–558.

Koch, M. "La Courbure du stylobate du Parthénon." *AnnArch,* XXXIV (1963), p. 231.

Mavrikios, A. "Aesthetic Analysis Concerning the Curvature of the Parthenon." *AJA,* LXIX (1965), pp. 264–268.

—— *Sculpture in Architecture: The Sculpture of the Parthenon.* Athens, 1960.

Noack, F. "Raumgestaltung des Parthenon." *Eleusis.* Berlin and Leipzig, 1927, pp. 167–175.

Orlandos, Anastasios K. "Roof Tiles of the Parthenon." *Hesperia,*
Supplement VIII. Princeton, 1949, pp. 259–267.

Praschniker, C. "Die Akroterien des Parthenon." *JOAI,* XIII (1910),
pp. 5–39.

Stevens, G. P. "Concerning the Curvature of the Steps of the
Parthenon." *AJA,* XXXVIII (1934), pp. 533–542.

—— *The Setting of the Periclean Parthenon. Hesperia,* Supplement
III. Princeton, 1940.

—— "Concerning the Impressivenes of the Parthenon." *AJA,* LXVI
(1962), pp. 337–338.

Weickert, Carl. "*Erga Perikleus:* Studien zur Kunstgeschichte des 5.
Jahrhunderts, II." *Abhandlungen der deutschen Akademie der
Wissenschaften zu Berlin.* Philosophisch-historische Klasse.
Berlin, 1950.

Sculptures of the Parthenon: General

Adams, S. *The Technique of Greek Sculpture in the Archaic and
Classical Periods.* London, 1967.

Ashmole, Bernard. *An Historical Guide to the Sculptures of the
Parthenon.* London, 1961.

Brilliant, Richard. *Arts of the Ancient Greeks.* New York, 1973, pp.
180–214.

Brunn, Heinrich. *Die Bildwerke des Parthenon.* Munich, 1874.

Carpenter, Rhys. *Greek Sculpture: A Critical Review.* Chicago, 1971.
(See especially ch. VI, "Temple Pediments: Classic Drapery,"
pp. 109–151.)

Corbett, Percy Edward. *The Sculpture of the Parthenon.* Harmonds-
worth, Middlesex, 1959.

Devambez, Pierre. *L'Art au siècle de Périclès.* Lausanne, 1955.

Gialouris, Nikolaos, and F. L. Kenett. *Classical Greece: The Elgin
Marbles of the Parthenon.* Greenwich, Conn., 1960.

Haynes, D. E. L. *An Historical Guide to the Sculptures of the
Parthenon.* London, 1962.

Murray, Alexander, Stuart. *The Sculptures of the Parthenon.* London,
1903.

Smith, Arthur H. *The Sculptures of the Parthenon.* London, 1910.

Thimme, Dieter, and Theodore R. Bowie. *The Carrey Drawings of
the Parthenon Sculptures.* Bloomington, Ind., 1971.

The Pheidias Problem

Becatti, Giovanni. *Problemi Fidiaci*. Milano and Firenze, 1951.
Blümel, Carl. *Phidiasische Reliefs und Parthenonfries*. Deutsche
    Akademie der Wissenschaften Sektion für Altertumwissen-
    schaft, Schriften X. Berlin, 1957.
Buschor, Ernst. *Phidias der Mensch*. Munich, 1948.
Johansen, Peter. *Phidias and the Parthenon Sculptures*, trans. J. Ander-
    son. Copenhagen, 1925.
Langlotz, Ernst. *Phidiasprobleme*. Frankfurt am Main, 1948.
—— *Phidias und der Parthenonfries*. Stuttgart, 1965.
Laurenzi, Luciano. "Umanità di Fidia." *Studia Archaeologica*, III
    (1961), pp. 1–22.
Lechat, Henri. *Phidias et la sculpture grecque au Ve siècle*. Paris,
    1906.
Petersen, Eugen. *Die Kunst des Phidias am Parthenon und zu Olympia*.
    Berlin, 1873.
Poulsen, Vagn H. *Fidias*. Stockholm, 1949.
Schrader, Hans. *Phidias*. Frankfurt am Main, 1924.
Schweitzer, Bernhard. "Prolegomena zur Kunst des Parthenon-
    Meisters, I." *JdI*, LIII (1938), pp. 1–81.
—— "Zur Kunst des Parthenon-Meisters, II: Der Entwurf und der
    Parthenon-Meister." *JdI*, LIV (1939), pp. 1–96.
—— "Pheidias, der Parthenonmeister." *JdI*, LV (1940), pp. 170–241.

The Pediments

Brommer, Frank. *Die Skulpturen der Parthenon-Giebel*. 2 vols. Mainz
    am Rhein, 1963.
—— "Zu den Parthenongiebeln: I." *AM*, LXIX–LXX (1954–55),
    pp. 49–66.
—— "Zu den Parthenongiebeln: II." *AM*, LXXI (1956), pp. 30–50.
—— "Zu den Parthenongiebeln: III." *AM*, LXXI (1956), pp. 232–244.
—— "Zu den Parthenongiebeln: IV." *AM*, LXXIII (1958), pp. 103–
    116.
Carpenter, Rhys. "New Material for the West Pediment of the
    Parthenon." *Hesperia*, I (1932), pp. 1 ff.
—— "The Lost Statues of the East Pediment of the Parthenon."
    Hesperia, II (1933), pp. 1–88.
Harrison, Evelyn B. "A New Parthenon Fragment from the Athenian
    Agora." *Hesperia*, XXIV (1955), pp. 85–87.

—— "Athena and Athens in the East Pediment of the Parthenon." *AJA*, LXXI (1967), pp. 27–58.

—— "U and Her Neighbors in the West Pediment of the Parthenon." *Essays in the History of Art: Presented to Rudolf Wittkower*, ed. Douglas Fraser et al. London and New York, 1969, pp. 1 ff.

Rumpf, Andreas. "Die Datierung der Parthenon-Giebel." *Jdl*, XL (1925), pp. 29–38.

Sauer, Bruno, *Der Weber-Laborde'sche Kopf und die Giebelgruppen des Parthenon*. Geissen, 1903.

Schuchhardt, Walter Herwig. "Die Eleusinischen Kopien nach Parthenonsculpturen." *Festschrift Kurt Bauch*. Munich, 1957, pp. 21–28.

The Metopes and Frieze

Brommer, Frank. *Die Metopen des Parthenon: Katalog und Untersuchung*. 2 vols. Mainz am Rhein, 1967.

—— "Ein Bruchstuck vom Sudfries des Parthenon." *AA* (1967), pp. 196–198.

Buschor, Ernst. *Der Parthenonfries*. Munich, 1961.

Ebersole, William S. "Metopes of the West End of the Parthenon." *AJA*, III (1899), pp. 409–432.

Eckstein, P. "Die Südmetopen der Parthenon und die Carreyschen Zeichnungen." *Jdl*, LXVIII (1953), pp. 79–97.

Elderkin, George Wicker. "The Seated Deities of the Parthenon Frieze." *AJA*, XL (1936), pp. 92–99.

Fehl, Philipp. "The Rocks on the Parthenon Frieze." *JWC*, XXIV (1961), pp. 1–44.

Haynes, D. E. L. *The Parthenon Frieze*. London, 1959.

Holloway, R. Ross. "The Archaic Akropolis and the Parthenon Frieze." *Art Bulletin*, XLVIII (1966), pp. 223–226.

Kardara, Chrysoula. "Glaukopis, the Archaic Naos and the Theme of the Parthenon Frieze." *ArchEph 1961* (1964), pp. 61–159 (in Greek).

Rodenwaldt, Gerhardt. "Kopfe von den Südmetopen des Parthenon." *Abhandlungen der deutschen Akademie der Wissenschaften zu Berlin*. Philosophisch-historische Klasse. Berlin, 1948.

Schuchhardt, W. H. "Die Entstehung des Parthenon Frieses." *Jdl*, XLV (1930), pp. 218–280.

Stillwell, Richard. "The Panathenaic Frieze: Optical Relations." *Hesperia*, XXXVIII (1969), pp. 231–241.

The Elgin Controversy

Hamilton, William R. *Memorandum on the Subject of the Earl of Elgin's Pursuits in Greece*. London, 1815.

Nisbet, Mary, Countess of Elgin. *The Letters of Mary Nisbet of Dirleton, Countess of Elgin*, arr. by Lieutenant-Colonel Nisbet Hamilton Grant. London, 1926.

Report from the Select Committee of the House of Commons on the Earl of Elgin's Collections of Sculptured Marbles. London, 1816.

Rothenberg, Jacob. *"Descensus ad Terram:* The Acquisition and Reception of the Elgin Marbles." Ph.D. diss. Columbia University, 1967.

St. Clair, William. *Lord Elgin and the Marbles*. New York, 1967.

Smith, Arthur H. "Lord Elgin and His Collection." *JHS*, XXXVI (1916).